A SHORT HISTORY OF ASIA

A Short History of Asia

Stone Age to 2000 AD

Colin Mason

St. Martin's Press
New York

A SHORT HISTORY OF ASIA
Copyright © 2000 by Colin Mason

St. Martin's Press, Scholarly and Reference Division,
175 Fifth Avenue, New York, N.Y. 10010

First published in the United States of America in 2000

Printed in Hong Kong

ISBN: 0–312–23059–1
ISBN: 0–312–23060–5

Library of Congress Cataloging-in-Publication Data

Mason, Colin, 1926–
A short history of Asia : stone age to 2000 AD / Colin Mason.
   p. cm.
Includes bibliographical references and index.
ISBN 0–312–23059–1 (cloth) – ISBN 0–312–23060–5 (pbk.)
1. Asia–History. I. Title.

DS33.M29 2000
950–dc21   99–056873

'History is a mirror for the future.'
— **Jiang Zemin**

Contents

1 Introduction   1

PART I   Before Imperialism

2 The First Indian Civilisations: Harappa and
   the Aryan Invasion   11
3 The Development of Indian Culture: Hinduism
   and Buddhism   17
4 Early South-East Asia: The Ships from India   29
5 China: The Eternal Nation   42
6 Early Japan and the T'ang Dynasty in China   58
7 The Awakening of Europe and the Challenge
   of Islam   70
8 China: The Sung, Mongol and Ming Dynasties   76
9 China: The Years of Decline   87
10 The Three Makers of Japan and the Tokugawa
   Period   99

PART II   The White Man's Burden

11 The Dominators and the Dominated   113
12 South-East Asia: The European and Chinese
   Incursions, and Later History of the Mainland
   States   121
13 The Malay World: Majapahit and Malacca   134
14 Indonesia: The Last Independent Kingdoms and
   the Extension of Dutch Rule   141
15 India under Two Masters: The Grand Moguls and
   the East India Company   150
16 Gandhi's India: The Struggle for Liberty   163

PART III The Modern Nations

17 The South Asian Nations: India, Pakistan and
Bangladesh 175
18 China: Two Revolutions 188
19 Modern China: The Communist State 195
20 Indonesia: Sukarno and After 209
21 Malaya: Malaysia, Singapore and Brunei 225
22 Japan: The Iron Triangle 236
23 Thailand: Land of the Free 247
24 The Philippines: Trouble in Paradise 254
25 Korea: Divided Nation 265
26 Vietnam, Laos and Cambodia 278
27 Burma: Rule by the Gun 288
28 Asia Today – and Tomorrow 296

Suggested Further Reading 306

Index 310

I
. . . .
Introduction

Western attitudes towards Asia are frequently bedevilled by inaccurate perceptions, even at the most fundamental levels. Many Westerners still hold views coloured by the opinions of the colonial period, with assumptions of white supremacy, and vague, shocking concepts like the well at Cawnpore and 'the black hole of Calcutta.' Others visualise a picture of 'Asian tigers', vast communities almost magically transforming themselves into clones of Western consumerist societies, or equally mysteriously, visited by economic catastrophe. These Asian people sometimes say and do things which seem not to make sense. This, like anything else not understood, prompts uneasiness.

Most inappropriate of all is to visualise 'Asia' as a homogeneous unit, when in fact it is a term of convenience embracing widely-varying peoples and cultures. But it is also necessary to recognise a certain commonality of problems, of social and economic attitudes which is increasingly coming to overlay that variety. Many of these 'Third World' problems – underdevelopment, extreme poverty, ugly and unhealthy urbanisation, difficulties of government, internal civil war, over-population among them, can be traced back to the colonial era.

Hence a proper understanding of the Asian region demands some knowledge of its cultures and history, including a realistic assessment of the colonial phase. There is a certain urgency about this because of the growing importance of the Asian nations in the world economy and political balance of power. For instance, China may well become one of the world's largest economies early in the third millennium. China will probably lead a loose zonal union of developing nations in Asia which were former colonies of European, Japanese and American imperialists into enhanced power and world status, in spite of – and possibly because of – the region's economic downturn of 1997. Pan-Asian economic co-operation must increase, if only because of perceived responsibility of the Western economic system for the Asian crisis. For this reason and for others this zonal group is already beginning to see itself as an entity with common interests – and this need do nothing to diminish its variety and the individuality of its component peoples.

The Asian nations have shouldered their way into virtually every area of modern technology, they typically have an active and able middle-class, at least four have nuclear weapons or the means to make them, and they influence regions outside Asia, like Africa and the Middle East. The products of their industry now feature prominently in the lives of almost every Westerner.

This new power bloc must increasingly affect, and even challenge, the rest of the world. A reported statement of the then Chinese Premier, Li Peng, in August, 1997 is relevant. It attacked 'the Western world order', supported a call from Indonesia for a review of the UN Human Rights Charter to place less stress on individual rights, and promised Chinese support to an east Asian economic union.

China's growth has been due substantially to a remarkable reversion to private enterprise in recent decades. That transition has been driven by powerful motivations, themselves rooted millennia-deep in the traditions of the past: Hard work, familial connections, respect for learning, a distancing between business and government, a passion for money and material success, acceptance of authoritarian government are among them. These are all elements of a Chinese ethic that can be traced back thousands of years, and which made China through most of her history the world's largest, wealthiest and most literate society. Always evident, this ethic was suppressed by a rigid authoritarianism during the first decades of the Communist mainland state, although it prospered in Hong Kong, Taiwan and Singapore.

These 'Asian values' are not exclusively Chinese. They are shared by other Asian peoples. Again, it is ridiculous to regard 'Asia' as a monolith ethnically or culturally, but it is equally important to recognise these common qualities, and that there is an Asian point of view – perhaps more accurately Asian points of view – which the Asian nations themselves see as different from Western ones. The fact that educated Asian people often wear Western clothing, speak English, use the same technologies, can easily lead to the assumption that they are becoming 'westernised'. This surface appearance is misleading. The Japanese, Indian, or Thai in his office at his computer, wearing a Western business suit, speaking English, will be a very different man at home in the evening, in his religious observances, when he contemplates marriage, in his relationship with his family, in his view of the world.

China's move towards world supremacy – and that without doubt is her intention – is unlikely to be military, although military strength will be there to back it. It will be economic and social, and its front-line forces will be the influential network of Chinese businessmen and women in most Asian countries, and Chinese multi-national corporations, substantially based on Hong Kong and Shanghai. This is not to forecast the development of a vast Chinese territorial empire in Asia. The world's other powers would be unlikely to permit such a thing, in the first place. In the second place, China has had opportunities for that before, as far back as the fifteenth century, and rejected them. Her traditional attitude has been to maintain a loose authority among states peripheral to China – not unlike the relationship the United States has in the Americas. These general statements are intended to introduce two important and basic ideas: The first, that the Asian region, occupied by more than half of all humans, is rapidly becoming an economic and social zone of great significance, unable to be ignored by the rest of the planet; the second, that, whatever the outward appearance, this development is powerfully influenced by Asia's traditions, and Asia's past – its history.

In the year 1407, 2000 Chinese scholars compiled an encyclopedia of the thought and writing of their nation's past. When completed it occupied over 11 thousand volumes, and so was too large to print. Any single volume of reasonable proportions that seeks to encompass the history of the Asian nations requires ruthless selection, and special care in priority of material. This has led to the omission of many interesting and important facts from this book, and the inclusion of more general statements than the writer would have liked.

The reader needs to know the basis on which selection has been made. The first objective has been to follow broad trends – constants as it were – especially where these still have effect today. A common quality of Asian societies is the importance of the past, of tradition. Why is it that the Tamil Tigers pursue their rebellion against the central government in Sri Lanka with such dedication and ferocity? Why was it seen by modern Indonesians as natural that their first president ceremonially contacted the earth with his bare feet, exposed himself to electrical storms, hugged trees? Why has Western democracy generally not succeeded in the Asian nations? Why might Indonesian schoolchildren reasonably think their nation has a historic right to all of New Guinea, parts of the Philippines, possibly even some of northern Australia? The answers to these questions and many others emerge from a knowledge of Asian history, especially that before the colonial era.

Links to the past become all the more important because the new nations of Asia look back beyond the colonial era to their own often legendary and shadowy past for a sense of national identity. And sometimes they identify what was probably not real, exaggerate something quite minor, in theories which have more to do with present-day political ideology than history.

A second priority is to sketch the enormous variety of cultures and peoples in Asia, and to give due credit to the achievements and greatness of its societies, which are by no means properly understood or appreciated. It is, for instance, extraordinary that many Western children are still taught that Johann Gutenberg invented printing with movable type in Germany around 1450 when movable type had been developed in China 400 years earlier; and that European mariners 'discovered' Asia.

Most people would know that fireworks and the wheelbarrow were first used in China, but it comes as news to them that the eleventh century Sung society used credit banking and cheques, and could inoculate against smallpox, and that there were Indian cities with mass-produced standard housing and efficient urban sewerage systems as early as 2500 BC. Too often Asian histories by Europeans have been unduly preoccupied with the activities of European colonisers. This book tries, among other things, to redress that balance.

Asia's past is often obscure, with much of the story of its great civilisations buried beneath the ruins of later and inferior cultures. During this past, such records as existed were not informed by any precise sense of history. In most cases the earliest written records, and many later ones, have little historic value because they did not attempt to set down reliable fact, but to flatter the aristocracy and justify the actions of kings. In other cases no written record exists, because there was no writing. Of the enigmatic Harappa civilisation of north India, records of a kind exist, but cannot be deciphered.

The present nations of south and south-east Asia substantially follow the boundaries of convenience and expediency set by the colonising powers. Here again, the past can hint at future possibilities. In time, shared problems, shared faiths and languages crossing borders are almost certain to alter national boundaries. This process has begun in India, where state boundaries have been greatly changed since independence. Civil war and regional conflict on a major scale have resulted from boundaries at odds with the traditions in Sri Lanka, Vietnam, Korea, Burma, and the Philippines.

Transplanted Western concepts of nationhood and government, which grew in Europe with painful slowness and have
had varied fortunes, have generally not prospered in Asia. It
is not an Asian tradition that individual freedoms should extend as far as national politics. Typically the rule of the past
has been authoritarian and individuals have been obliged to
conform to it. Around this central authority, usually one man
arrayed not only with the honours but the disadvantages of
near-divinity, has been grouped an aristocracy whose duties,
rights and obligations have also been rigidly defined by tradition. Terminology may have changed, but to a considerable
extent this situation continues today.

The perceptive reader will notice another constant, common to virtually all Asian history – a pattern of economic and
social elites exploiting the majority of the people ruthlessly
and with often self-defeating avarice, using the backing of
armed force. This less than admirable tradition can readily be
observed in many of the Asian nations today, and has much
to do with their problems.

Asia contains the mightiest mountains on the planet, a series
of ranges, rocky escarpments and bleak uplands, from which
rise the Himalayas. Among this wild and lightly-peopled mountain country the big rivers find their source in the perpetual
snow and glaciers. As they flow south, east and west, these
rivers broaden, meander, and slow down into great, turbid,
discoloured streams. Some of them, like the Mekong and the
Ganges, reach the sea in the midst of delta regions characterised by miles of backwaters, with low marshy swamps and
almost impenetrable mangroves. Above these swamps are flat,
fertile plains which are regularly flooded and enriched by fresh
deposits of alluvial silt. These plains have been for thousands
of years the regions best suited for growing food-crops. They
have become both the centres of successive civilisations and
a temptation for less well-endowed marauders from outside.

As one proceeds north from India, progressively higher mountain ranges block the way, giving the few possible roads, like the Khyber Pass, great strategic and political importance. Once across Afghanistan, Kashmir, Nepal and the southern valleys of Tibet, civilisation peters out into a region of desolate, high plateaux, swept perpetually by snow-laden winds. These plateaux, the Pamirs and northern Tibet, give place in the east to the shifting sands and dun-coloured parched soils of Sinkiang (Xinjiang) in China.

Thence, across Mongolia through the loose dunes of the Gobi, the terrain changes to the fertile loess soils of northwest China and the grasslands of Manchuria. This is east Asia, a second major concentration of population and culture. Once again, in China it is the fertile river valleys that make up the heartland. The valley of the Yangtse River downstream from its celebrated gorges is the most fertile and populous.

The high, arid deserts of central Asia, with their cold, thin air and perpetual requirement of constant struggle to maintain a bare existence, have bred a group of toughened races who, for thousands of years, invaded and conquered the plains below. Good horsemen, bred from childhood to the saddle and the sword, they were typical nomads, who moved constantly from one grassy valley to the next, living in felt tents, driving their herds with them. The names of these nomad people and their leaders ring through history, the very epitome of battle and conquest – the Huns, the Vandals, the Mongols, Timur, Genghis Khan.

To the south the picture is different. Tropical Asia consists of two big promontories and thousands of islands. India projects nearly a thousand miles into the ocean that bears her name. On the other side of the Bay of Bengal is another peninsula nearly as large, shared by the mainland south-east Asian states: Burma, Thailand, Malaysia, and the three Indo-Chinese nations, Vietnam, Cambodia and Laos.

Finally, in a great arc, swinging from west to east and then northwards, lie an almost continuous chain of islands. Some, like Kalimantan (Borneo) and Sumatra, are among the major

islands of the world, but the rest range down to tiny specks
of land with only enough soil to support a few palm trees a
foot or so above the heave of the sea. One of the smaller of
these islands, linked to the Malaysian mainland by a causeway, contains a dynamic mostly Chinese city-state, Singapore.
Three thousand more, running across 3000 miles of equatorial
sea to the south of Malaysia, make up Indonesia, the world's
fourth most populous nation. To the north, across the atoll-
studded Sulu Sea, the archipelago merges with the islands of
the Philippines. Less than 200 miles north from the principal
Filipino island of Luzon is the southern promotory of Taiwan;
once again to the north the Ryukyus lead to Japan.

The traveller has passed from the tropics to the temperate
zone, then through the Japanese islands to the northernmost,
Hokkaido, into a region of ice, snow and fiery volcanoes. The
craggy and inhospitable Kuriles lead to the last peninsula,
Kamchatka, pointing out into the Pacific, south-west from the
Arctic Circle.

Part I
Before Imperialism

2

The First Indian Civilisations: Harappa and the Aryan Invasion

The Asia of remote prehistory was very different from the teeming continent and islands of today. Its population was tiny and dispersed, living mostly on the seacoasts and the plains of the big rivers, each small group of humanity separated from the others by virgin forest, full of wild animals. Families stayed together, developed into clans for mutual protection. Life was precarious, death came early and was often sudden and violent.

The most recent glacials of the quaternary ice-age had major effects on the development and distribution of humans. Rigorous conditions caused by the extension of the ice shifted the areas of population. People, still in insignificant numbers, were forced towards the central belt of the planet, or were trapped behind barriers of ice, to adapt as best they could to the centuries of bitter cold.

These glacials lowered the level of the seas as much as 300 feet, so that much of what was water became dry land. Australia was linked through Indonesia, except for two straits, to the Asian mainland. People could cross landbridges over much of what is now sea, and there is abundant evidence they did so. Many of the racial patterns of the region were set then. In the inter-glacial periods the reverse was true; the sea flooded deeply into the mainland, and submerged islands. An east Asian mountain range became the islands of Japan.

The remains of what might be considered a human creature have been found in Java, dating back, on some estimates, as much as a million years. Similar remains, found in the Western Hills outside Beijing, show evidence of the use of fire and of bone tools, indicating a later, more advanced society. Even so, to modern eyes these creatures would seem ape-like. Skulls recovered show them to have have had low, slanting brows and small though developing brains. They are classed as 'hominids' mainly because they stood upright and showed signs of significant development of the frontal lobe of the brain. This human evolution in Asia was not very different from that elsewhere in the world. Eventually, what seem to have been early *homo sapiens* appears – cave-dwellers, able to use fire, to domesticate animals, first the dog, then the horse, goat and cow, and to make tools from flints and other hard stone.

Differing racial types began to emerge. It is believed the Mongolian type, that of the Chinese and other east Asian peoples, had its origins on the northern steppes of Siberia. One theory considers the distinctive features of these people are due to the effects of the extreme cold on their ancestors, trapped for many generations in Siberia during the last glacial age. It is claimed that under these extreme conditions humans evolved protective features – the flat brow to protect the sinuses, deep-set eyes and high cheekbones.

However, Asia had a developed society, the largest and most sophisticated in the world of its time, as early as 2500BC, contemporaneous with the earliest dynasties in Egypt and the first Mesopotamian kingdoms. This society is called Harappa from the name of one of its major cities, although there was also a second and similar city, Mohenjo Daro. Over almost 1000 miles along the Indus River are the remains of many other towns and villages with common characteristics, indicating a considerable society for that time. The location of this culture on the banks of a big river is no accident, since the earliest cities were generally so situated. In most regions the soil became exhausted quickly from cropping and people had to move on to new fields. Only on the river plains, where annual floods deposited rich, new layers of silt on the land, were they able to stay long in one place. The city civilisations of Mesopotamia depended in this way on the Tigris and Euphrates Rivers, and those of Egypt on the Nile.

The ruins of Mohenjo Daro are in Sind, in what is now hot, forbidding desert. Those of Harappa are 350 miles northeast in the Punjab. However, distinctive Harappan artifacts have been found over an area larger than present-day Pakistan, indicating that at its height its society was considerably larger than either Egypt or the Sumerian empire at that time. The Harappa civilisation had a flair for standardisation unusual in the ancient world. Its kiln-baked mud bricks were of uniform size everywhere and this has made it possible to identify Harappa remains with relative ease. Cotton and wool clothing were in use, and there is evidence of trade with Mesopotamia, ornaments made from imported materials – seashells, turquoise and lapis lazuli. The two main cities were strikingly similar. They must have presented a curiously-modern appearance, although a drab one. The buildings were plain and in the same style, the layout of streets and lanes was geometrical. The houses had bathrooms and closed drainage, with plumbing outlets leading to main drains in the streets outside. Some of the tiled bathroom floors still show signs of polish from the repeated contact of the bare feet of their users. The largest buildings seem to have been public ones – in Mohenjo Daro a granary and a large pool, probably designed more for ritual washing than for bathing.

The cities had internal fortifications but not outside surrounding walls, which seems to suggest a small privileged class in control of the mass of the people rather than a need for protection against an outside invader. There is other evidence to support this. The ruins include long, monotonous rows of small, barrack-like structures which were probably workers' tenements, contrasting with other, larger, presumably upper-class, dwellings.

These latter show an almost fanatical desire for privacy and seclusion, with thick upper storey, windowless walls facing the streets, concealed doorways of quite small dimensions and steep, narrow stairs. It is likely that here was a highly-regimented and efficient dictatorship controlled by an elite. It could well have been an aristocracy of priests.

It was once thought that the Harappa civilisation emerged fully-fledged about 2500BC, existed for 1000 years, and was then destroyed just as mysteriously. However, later archaeology indicates a continuous agrarian society from perhaps 7000 years ago which was probably the authentic beginning of Indian civilisation. Excavations at the Mehrgarh site indicate a farming society that grew wheat and barley and had domesticated sheep and goats and the typical Indian hump-backed cow. There is evidence of a considerable pottery manufacture, using the potter's wheel by 3500BC.

Although the Harappa cities are presumed to have developed from this earlier society, they had distinctive and unusual features that still pose unanswered questions. Harappa had a written language, found on some 2000 soapstone seals recovered in Sind, but this has not been deciphered. The Harappa showed considerable artistry in small objects. Among the ruins small figures in soapstone, alabaster and marble have been found depicting people, often in a sophisticated and lively style. There was a well-developed, distinctive system of weights and measures. Copper and bronze were used for weapons, tools and ornaments.

The nature of the religion is unclear, but there are some indications of a connection with gods of the later, Hindu, period. This is interesting because it is traditional Indian belief that a lightskinned people who much later invaded India from the north-west were the first to evolve an ordered civilisation there. The early Indian epics assert that when these invaders came they found only a simple village culture in north India. This was indeed the commonly-held historical view until the Harappa ruins were investigated from 1922 onwards.

This second influx of people began to enter India from about

1500BC – relatively soon after the postulated demise of Harappa, which seems to have been sudden. Some theories postulate a disaster, possibly major flooding caused by the destruction of irrigation dams by earthquake. Whatever the reason, Harappa was so far into decline that the survivors seem to have offered little resistance to the newcomers.

These later arrivals had leaders who called themselves *aryas*, which means noble. The modern name of Persia, Iran, is significantly derived from it, and so is the term Aryan applied to the language group to which these people belonged. This language group is now more commonly called Indo-European because of close links between the north Indian written language, Sanskrit, and some early European languages, including Greek, Celtic and High German. Hence a single ethnic group has been postulated, which spilled over into Europe as well as the north Indian plain.

At one stage, notably in Nazi Germany, it was romanticised into ideas of a super-race with almost divine rights to ascendancy over other humans, and a duty to maintain its genetic purity. However, India's new settlers appear to have been a simple people, much less sophisticated than the Harappa, herdsmen and hunters who worshipped deities that were manifestations of the elemental forces of nature. Their art was unspectacular and their architecture, in particular, suffers in comparison with Harappa. Since they used only wood, none of their buildings survive, but accounts in the Sanskrit classic, the *Rigveda*, describe small hut-like houses, grouped together inside earth and wooden palisades.

The *Rigveda* makes it quite clear than the newcomers disliked and despised the people they found already in north India. While there was, no doubt, more intermarriage with the existing population than the classics admit, the invaders seem to have been much concerned with their racial purity. They were a light-skinned people, and placed much store on colour. It was regarded as good to be light-skinned and shameful to be dark – a prejudice still strong in India, and elsewhere, today. When my family lived in a north-east Thai market town people

asked if they might simply touch my children, who were fair-
haired with blue eyes, to bring good fortune.

By the eighth century BC the former nomads had spread
eastward across north India to the banks of the Ganges River.
By 600BC they were using iron and planting rice, strengthen-
ing their agricultural society and expanding southwards from
the Ganges plain. A major point of interest about them was
the gradual accumulation of a vast mass of religious stric-
tures, legends and epics which were committed to memory
and carried on by word of mouth, and which are now a basis
of several major religions, and especially of Hinduism.

The extent to which these reflect the times in which they
originated is doubtful. They must have been added to and
modified extensively over the period – perhaps 1000 years –
before they were written down. Out of the obscurity of this
early period one can still make some deductions. The nomadic
herdsmen who had come in from the north learned to be farmers
and town-dwellers. There was probably a merging, both racial and cultural, between the newcomers and the remnants of
the Harappa. There can be no question of an Indian 'nation'
at this time. But there did evolve on the north Indian plain a
group of states who fought each other ceaselessly in a struggle for land and power, but who nevertheless shared a common
cultural heritage.

3

The Development of Indian Culture: Hinduism and Buddhism

One of the major aspects of the culture that evolved during this Aryan expansion was a class system of such vigour that it still exists today, although it is now infinitely more complex. This culture and religion – for it is both – came to be known as Hinduism.

Ancient India had four major castes. The highest, the priest-teachers, or *brahmins*, soon came to hold authority, even over nobles, by virtue of the roles they assumed as interpreters of religion. The old gods changed, and worship became more complex. Rituals and formality clouded what must once have been fundamentally a simple faith.

The second important class were the *kshatriyas*, the soldier-nobles, whose duty it was to fight for the state. Some historians believe that the many successful invasions of India, often by quite small armies, were effective because it was believed that only *kshatriyas* could or should fight back – in contrast with Korea, for instance, where peasant and even slave guerilla forces attacked invaders from Manchuria and Japan ferociously.

A third Indian caste of less importance were the *vaishyas*, the merchants. These three main classes, of lighter skin colour, had important privileges. They were described as 'twice-born' for, during late childhood, they were initiated into the rites of their high position. This was regarded as a mystic second birth.

The fourth main class, the *shudras*, lived on the fringes of society. They were a servant class, forbidden to read, or even hear, the sacred scriptures.

Even in the centuries before the Christian era, there existed a fifth caste, corresponding to the present 'untouchables'. Most of these were the dark-skinned descendants of slaves and aborigines and were restricted to filthy and menial tasks. Once born into their class, death was the only escape from it. Generation after generation were compelled to carry out lowly and unpleasant work, nor could they marry outside their caste. That they correspond to the suggested 'working class' of the Harappa cities is an intriguing possibility.

At the very bottom of the social heap are the *chandals*, the caste who carry out the actual work of cremations – cremation over a wood fire is the usual way of disposing of the bodies of adult Indians. Children's bodies are simply placed in rivers. The *chandals* use long iron rods to stir the ashes and remains, and to smash the skull and other larger bones so they will be totally consumed – this might take seven or eight hours. Although they no longer have to shout or ring bells to announce their presence, to avoid the ritual contamination of any other Indian, they are effectively cut off from the rest of society. Higher caste persons would be contaminated even if the shadow of a *chandal* should fall on them. There are caste divisions even among the 'untouchables'. In ascending order on the social scale are leatherworkers, lavatory cleaners and sweepers, laundrymen.

This set pattern of privilege inevitably resulted in discrimination, oppression and harsh laws. The mass of the people, living in villages similar to those of today, were heavily taxed to support their masters. A complex legal code provided sweeping discriminatory provisions covering virtually every aspect of life for the lower orders. Often taxation reached such ruinous levels as to leave the peasants destitute, and even minor weather fluctuations resulted in major famines. The death penalty was imposed for a multitude of offences. B.H. Farmer, in his *Introduction to South Asia* gives the opinion that idealised

concepts of Indian traditional village life by European writers –
including Karl Marx – are flawed because the village councils,
considered democratic and egalitarian, were in fact fettered
by the caste system. The point is worth noting because this
idea of an idyllic village life was an important part of the
rhetoric of Indian nationalists in the 20th century – Gandhi in
particular, promoted it.

However, social inequality and art often flourish together,
and such was the case in ancient India. This era produced the
great Indian epics – the *Mahabharata* and the *Ramayana*. These
writings stress the basic lesson that everyone must maintain
his or her due place in society, that 'it is better to do one's
own duty badly than another's well' – thus guaranteeing the
privileged position of the twiceborn.

The *Mahabharata*, which is a collection of poems rather
than a single story, is largely based on the fortunes of two
rival ruling familes, but its major significance is its statement
of the duty of the religious, law-abiding man.

The other great epic is the story of Rama, a legendary prince
who, although he is the legal heir, accepts banishment for twelve
years. While in exile his wife Sita is kidnapped by the devil
king of Ceylon, Ravana. Rama, going to her rescue, enlists
the aid of the monkey king who provides an army of mon-
keys to tear up rocks, earth and trees to build a bridge between
the Indian mainland and Ceylon. Rama crosses the causeway,
kills Ravana, and rescues his wife.

These epics must not be thought of as antiques without any
present or future significance, for they play a much greater
part in the lives of ordinary people in at least six Asian countries than equivalent epics do among westerners. Few people
in most of mainland south-east Asia and in many parts of
Indonesia, as well as the Indian continent itself, would fail to
hear stories from these epics almost as soon as they could
talk. Ceremonies and carnivals, which often involve whole
communities, annually celebrate the victory of Rama over
Ravana. Art, especially painting, sculpture and the shadow
theatre, uses themes from the epics extensively, as also do

much of literature and drama. Although Indonesia is predominantly a Moslem country, Islam is the top layer of a succession of faiths, and Arjuna, one of the heroes of the *Mahabharata*, is a widely-revered and loved figure.

The growing complexity of the Hindu religion resulted in a huge variety of schools and shades of thought. The present state of the Christian religion is comparable. Basic to all systems, however, was the feeling that life is evil, that all material things are deceptive if not downright illusory, and that man's objective is a purification of the spirit achieved by suffering a renunciation of carnal desires in a succession of lives. This belief in reincarnation became, and remains, a major theme. Perhaps its most important implication is that the present condition of an individual is not a matter of chance, but a consequence of their good or evil actions in previous lives.

The caste system is intended to regulate this process of slow advancement through a series of lives. The whole religious concept would be meaningless if individuals could be allowed to move from the station in life to which they were born, since the Hindu faith has it they were not born into that life by accident, but by virtue of a divine plan. The caste system then, is much more than a social order, it is deeply involved with the religious beliefs of the people – it has an inevitability that reinforces its acceptance by those who believe in it.

As the centuries passed castes split into sub-castes, and these again into even more and complicated categories. That remains the case in India today. I had Indian friends in Singapore, both well-educated, a doctor of medicine and a journalist, of differing castes. When this couple married they found it expedient to live outside India.

Meanwhile in the India of today, *harijans* – untouchables – continue to be sweepers, leather workers, rubbish collectors, in spite of attempts by the central government to change things. Even within the small but growing educated middle-class, caste influences basic matters such as marriage alliances.

Implementing national policies, especially on a matter so fundamental as caste, is all the more difficult because of an effective regionalism resulting from India's multiplicity of languages and dialects. The print media, radio, television generally operate in their own area, rather than as national networks. Political forces have the same constraints, thus perpetuating the strong regional influences already defined by history and tradition. India's recent political predicament, forcing frequent general elections because of a lack of a dominant unifying force, is a likely consequence. Its inability to impose reform of the caste system is another.

In the sixth century BC the son of an affluent *kshatriya* family with the clan name of Gautama became weary of the straitjacket of Hinduism, renounced his wife, home and family and became a wanderer. After six years of meditation and study he is believed to have achieved perfection in the spiritual sense and so has become known as 'the enlightened one' – the Buddha. The philosophy he has left is by no means the only heresy of this period, although it became the most pervasive and important.

Buddhism, originally an offshoot and an interpretation of 'Hindu' principles, has become immensely diverse and malleable. Even though its practice varies widely from region to region in Asia, it is basically a guide to conduct rather than a religious belief. It is largely based on tolerance, gentleness and moderation. Indeed, what it calls 'the middle way' is its essential. It seeks the abandonment of hatred, envy and anger. Its aim is the cultivation of purity and kindness.

While these sentiments are commonplace enough now, it must be recalled that Buddhism preceded Christianity by more than 500 years, and was a tremendous step forward in a world which had, until then, accepted without question the principle of an eye for an eye and a tooth for a tooth; a world in which cruelty and injustice were simply to be taken for granted. This new philosophy, born in the foothills of the Himalayas, was to become a profound influence throughout Asia.

Important things were also happening in the political sense. For almost 200 years the Punjab was a province of the great Persian empire until, in the fourth century BC, the Persian

King Darius the Third was defeated by the Macedonian soldier-adventurer Alexander the Great. Alexander's elephants pushed over the high passes of the Hindu Kush mountains and crossed the Indus River in 326BC. Alexander's death soon afterwards brought his short-lived empire to an end, but one of his generals, Seleucus Nicator, was able to take control of the Asian part, including the Indian province. Toward the end of the century Seleucus Nicator traded the Indian province for 500 elephants to a vigorous administrator of Indian birth named Chandragupta.

This man welded much of north India into a single state for the first time. There is a good deal of information available about him from the fragments remaining from the written account of the Greek Megasthenes, sent by Seleucus Nicator as his envoy to Chandragupta's capital, on the site of the present city of Patna. The dynasty founded by Chandragupta is called Mauryan and was based on a city which, Megasthenes tells us, was sprawled along nine miles of the banks of the Ganges and as much as a mile and a half inland. He regarded it as a pleasant, well-ordered place, and his account is of a people – or rather an upper class – accustomed to grace and beauty. There were large and pleasant gardens, in which jasmine, hibiscus, the water-lily and the lotus were already cultivated for their beauty and perfume; lakes and bathing pools, where the air was cooled by fountains; and contrived grottos for relaxation.

There was an organised civil service, whose officers specialised in the collection of taxes, inspection of irrigation works, road building and similar activities run and paid for by the state, almost entirely, it must be said, for its own financial benefit. This elaborate bureaucracy even had a war office with specialist sections dealing with such matters as elephants, cavalry and naval activities.

In spite of the luxury with which he was surrounded, Chandragupta's own regime was strictly ordered; we are told he was left only four and a half hours of the 24 for sleep. Administering his empire kept him fully occupied and much of his time was devoted to intrigue and receiving the reports of the elaborate network of spies he maintained. He went in constant fear of his life, regularly shifted his abode for fear of assassins, and never went out in public without an armed escort. He travelled in a gold palanquin carried by elephants, accompanied by his guards, fan, pitcher and umbrella bearers, who seem invariably to have been women. The route of his progress was marked off with ropes, and Megasthenes recorded that it was instant death for anyone who set foot inside them. The Mauryan empire reached its zenith under Chandragupta's grandson Ashoka. Ashoka was a great builder, but where his forebears had used wood, he built in stone. So for the first time since Harappa, building and sculpture were constructed that have lasted into our time. Of the numerous stone columns Ashoka set up, the capital of one, with its figures of four lions, is used as the emblem of the present government of India.

However, Ashoka is remembered mostly because instead of governing as a cruel, amoral absolute ruler he instituted quite revolutionary and remarkable reforms unique in the world of their time. Ashoka's conversion to the ways of peace are said to have resulted from an experience of the realities of war during an expedition against the neighbouring kingdom of Kalinga. In this war it is said 100 thousand people died, with as many more captives taken. Ashoka was deeply influenced by this episode of violence and loss, and by Buddhism, which spread as a result of his missionary efforts as far as Burma and Ceylon. An embassy was even sent to Egypt.

Ashoka was much given to setting up inscriptions of moral precepts. Thirty-five of these still exist in caves and on the monoliths previously mentioned. A system of law and order hitherto unparalleled is attributed to him, aimed at the protection of the sick, the unarmed and the helpless and the convenience of travellers. Staged resthouses for travellers along roads – still a feature of many Asian countries – were one of the public services he instituted. He devoted a great deal of attention to the highways, planting groves of shade trees and digging wells. He also built hospitals for the care of the sick

and infirm, who, until then, had died unless they were suc-
coured by a casual charity. There was even a corps of circuit
magistrates who travelled the kingdom resolving disputes.

At this time Buddhism developed its most significant diver-
gence from Hinduism, its rejection of the caste system (except
in Sri Lanka). Classic accounts of Ashoka's life from Buddhist
publicists presented him as a saintlike figure. Whatever the
truth of that there is little doubt he was a man of great personal
force of character, with a sense of humanitarianism rare in
his time. The Mauryan empire declined rapidly after his death.

Five centuries of obscurity, a time of many small states,
ensued, briefly illuminated by a Bactrian Greek empire in north
India under a king called Menander. Coins and statuary from
this Gandharan school show unmistakeable Mediterranean influence and have permanently influenced Buddhist art.

From the fourth to the seventh centuries much of the distinction and order of Ashoka's empire reappeared under the
Guptas. The period is notable for its Sanskrit drama, especially the plays of Kalidasa, a poet and dramatist of consequence.
Kalidasa's *Sakuntala*, based on part of the *Mahabharata*, has
been translated into many other languages and has taken its
place in world literature. So prolific and varied was this literary output there is strong evidence that it was the work of a
school of writers, possibly three people. The *Kama Sutra*, which
has remained popular around the world to this day because of
its explicit expression of erotic elements of the Hindu religion, also dates to this period.

This was the heyday of Buddhism in India, the time of the
great teaching monasteries and universities that became famed
throughout Asia. One of the great universities, Nalanda, is
said to have had 4000 students in the seventh century. Pil-
grims came from as far away as China to study in them. One
of these, Fa Hsien, who spent ten years in India in the fifth
century, has described a peaceful well-organised society with
moderate laws and taxation. Although Hinduism was again
the faith of the ruling house, the powerful and influential
Buddhist community co-existed peaceably with them.

Standards of education were high among the small lettered class and important developments in algebra and arithmetic (including the decimal system of nine numbers and the zero) occurred in India in the seventh century. These innovations, so long known as 'Arabic' in the West, seem, in fact, to have been learned by the Arabs from India. There is also evidence that the concept of the zero might have originated even farther east, perhaps in Indo-China.

Buddhism entered a decline towards the end of the era – instead there was a renewal of the influence and authority of the *brahmin* Hindu caste.

Hindu power and culture permeated only slowly to the south of India. This area of dense tropical jungle, steamy heat and dangerous wildlife such as tigers and giant snakes had little appeal to the predatory invaders from the hills. However, independent societies were evolving in the south. Two of these were located on the island of Sri Lanka (Ceylon).

Basic to an understanding of Sri Lanka is the fact that two separate migrations from the mainland occurred, the first of people who called themselves the Sinhalese – People of the Lion – in the sixth century BC, and a second, smaller one, of Indian Tamils, from about 300 years later. The Sinhalese displaced an aboriginal, hunting people called the Vedda, who have now virtually disappeared as a separate identity due to displacement and extensive intermarriage – which also had a major ethnic influence on the invaders. Recent research has indicated a migration, which must have been by sea, of southeast Asian people, well before the entry of the Sinhalese and Tamils. The Sinhalese appear to have come, not from neighbouring south India, but from the northwest, and their migration southwards coincided with the Aryan occupation of northern India. Little more is known about their origins, but they knew and worked iron, used advanced irrigation techniques to grow rice, and quite quickly developed a sophisticated urban society based on their first capital, Anuradhapura.

It was important as early as the third century BC when, according to legend, Prince Mahinda, either a brother or a son of Ashoka, visited Sri Lanka and converted its king to Buddhism. Certain sacred relics are said to have been transported to Sri Lanka, including the Buddha's alms bowl and part of his collarbone, and most celebrated of all, one of his eye-teeth. Possession of this tooth became important to establish the legitimacy of kings. Now it is kept in the pink Temple of the Tooth in Kandy, where a replica of the tooth is ceremonially carried about on elephant-back each August. This procession, the Perahera, takes place every night for two weeks.

The advent of a line of kings over the next thousand years who at times resembled Ashoka in their attitudes and achievements is an indication of the power of Buddhism to influence societies at that time. This was the era of Sri Lanka's glory, moderate well-regulated societies with their own art, notably sculpture and painting, that derives from India but has its own individuality. Taxation, set at ten per cent of production, was moderate by later standards in south Asia, although the peasants were also subject to a corvée which provided labour for the irrigation works, canals and roads. There was a strong accent on efficient agriculture and huge irrigation works, among the largest and most technically-advanced in the world. These were based on stone-walled dams and artificial lakes, which made two and sometimes three rice crops a year possible. Some of these 'tanks' still exist, irrigating thousands of acres.

Meanwhile the Tamils in the north became stronger as a result of a steady trickle of migrants from the mainland over the centuries. By the twelfth century they had evolved a separate northern state on the dry, flat Jaffna Peninsula. The Tamils have important racial and language differences from the Sinhalese. They are traditionally enterprising and energetic – qualities forced on them by centuries of farming the arid north of the island.

In the ninth century the south Indian Chola empire invaded Sri Lanka, occupying much of the north and central plains. Thousands of Tamil migrants came in at that time. However, the opportunity for major expansion came in the fourteenth century as a disastrous and extended civil war developed between rival generals and claimants for the Sinhalese throne. The Sinhalese factions recruited large numbers of Tamil mercenaries, who did not hesitate to push their own interests.

The Tamils gained control of more territory in the north, including the valuable and world-renowned pearl fishery. The decaying Sinhalese state was pushed southwards to a new capital at Kotte, near Colombo. The great irrigation works in the centre of the country were destroyed by rival armies or fell into disrepair, leaving an arid zone between the Tamil and Sinhalese kingdoms. Huge tracts of previously cultivated country reverted to dense jungle. It may have been *anopheles* mosquitoes breeding in the reservoirs and subsequent epidemics of malaria that hastened this process. Lavish pagoda-building, at huge public cost, impoverished the Sinhalese kingdom, forcing it further into decline. A new kingdom grew up at Kandy, resulting in three rival authorities controlling the island.

Such was the situation when the Portuguese arrived in Colombo in 1505, attracted by the trade in cinnamon and pepper, which were Sinhalese royal monopolies. The lack of any central authority over the island gave the Portuguese the opportunity for intrigue, and eventually conquest. They had taken over the country by the end of the century, other than the fabled kingdom of Kandy deep in the jungleclad hills of central Sri Lanka, jungles that were later to give place to tea plantations. Spirited resistance came from the Tamils of the north, who were not subdued until 1591. As elsewhere in Asia the Portuguese intermarried freely with the local people. There is a profusion of Portuguese names in Sri Lanka.

Sri Lanka was occupied by British forces during the Napoleonic Wars and became a British colony in 1802, largely on the insistence of the East India Company. The ancient kingdom of Kandy, involved in a series of rebellions, ended in 1818. Thereafter the colony faced considerable economic difficulties. When coffee was planted there the Sinhalese refused to carry out the hard and ill-paid work involved. The planters brought in Tamil labourers from India, and with them the germ of the communal problems to come. Later in the century tea and rubber proved to be more viable industries. The early twentieth century saw the establishment of state schools and a university college in 1921.

Hence, when the country was granted independence as a single state in 1948, an educated middle class existed to carry out the tasks of government. However, the largely-Sinhalese government refused citizenship to almost a million Tamils, and later attempted to impose Sinhalese as the national language. This exacerbated traditional tensions between the Tamils and the Sinhalese, leading to the bitter and protracted armed struggle that has continued until the present time. During 15 years of virtual civil war more than 50 thousand people have been killed.

Sri Lanka's main export earners, the tea, coconut and rubber plantations, which were largely British-owned, were nationalised in 1975. However, the economy has remained slow, with no substantial development of an industrial base.

The early south Indian mainland communities were based on seacoast cities and a thriving maritime trade. It seems likely that as early as 500 BC fishing boats had evolved into small ocean-going ships, engaged in trade as far afield as Burma and Malaysia. Kingdoms of consequence arose, like that of the Tamil Cholas, which dominated much of peninsular India in the eleventh century. The Chola state was relatively enlightened and advanced, with a system of village self-government, efficient revenue-raising, major irrigation works, and a distinctive Tamil literature and architecture.

This region exported pepper, diamonds, pearls, apes and peacocks. But the most consequential export was the Indian cultural influence still so evident in south-east Asia.

4

Early South-East Asia: The Ships from India

The south Indian merchant-adventurers' first journeys were probably slow passages hugging the Bay of Bengal coast, always in sight of land. Their early acquaintance with south-east Asia must have been due not so much to enterprise as the facts of geography. The art of sailing was elementary indeed, and it was not until relatively recently that one of the most important of man's inventions – how to sail efficiently into the wind – evolved.

When the first Indian argosies left the coast, they were forced to go where the wind took them. On the outward passage, between the months of June and November, that wind is the south-west monsoon, which blows with remarkable steadiness, day after day, week after week. It still propels many a sailing craft across those waters. Simply by proceeding before and slightly off the wind, a ship would naturally make her landfall on the tip of Sumatra or the Malaysian peninsula. Having arrived, the earliest Indian adventurers found it difficult to get back, since the wind persists from the south-west until the months December to May, when it blows with equal steadiness from the north-east. Hence the Indian merchant-adventurers went prepared to stay wherever they made a landfall until the monsoon changed. It was probably in this way their customs, religion and art began to spread eastward, as far as the China Sea coast of Vietnam.

It would be seriously to under-rate the south-east Asian peoples
to make the simple assumption that Indian ways were grafted
on to primitive societies. The point probably was that rulers
or would-be rulers saw advantage in a religion and culture
that would advance their own interests, and which possessed
an efficient, if Machiavellian, statecraft. The Indian merchants
and priest-missionaries were in fact providing ambitious rajahs with a blueprint for a society in which elites could control
and use the ordinary people. These, characteristically, were
wet rice farmers or fishermen – and very good ones at that, who
already had quite advanced systems of local self-government.

There is evidence of Malay shipping trading as far as China
as early as 300 BC, and engaged in the cinnamon trade by
100 BC. From this early maritime experience quite large trading vessels evolved – up to 400 tons, with two to four masts
and carvel hulls built without nails or screws. I have seen
new ships very much along these lines, using wooden dowels
to edge-fasten each plank, under construction along the Pattaya
coast of the Gulf of Thailand, as recently as 1965. Indonesian
handcrafts, like the complex creation of *batik* fabrics, are also
believed to have predated Indian influence.

Hence in the discussion which follows of 'kings' and 'states'
it is important not to over-rate the importance of their total
effect on the majority of society, or that of the 'cultural grafts',
for that matter. Since what written sources there are almost
always deal with those kings and states, it is difficult indeed
to trace the development and history of the ordinary people.
Nevertheless it is worth trying to do so.

This can be attempted through a close acquaintance with
the south-east Asian village societies as they are today, their
legends, beliefs and customs, and the evidence of archeological remains. Deduction from these is assisted by the knowledge
that these societies show all the signs of having been stable
and largely unchanging for very long periods of time, possibly thousands of years. They are also societies in which a
complex and formal pattern of personal relationships seems
to have existed for a long time. This in itself would have

tended to make the Indian cultural influence acceptable, and even welcome. The extraordinary profusion of carved scenes on the massive Javanese temple-mountain the Borobadur, created more than 1300 years ago, depict fishing, market, craft, and agricultural scenes very similar to what can be seen in real daily life today.

Prehistoric south-east Asia gives evidence of a considerable diversity of occupation by tool-using primitive societies going back at least 30 thousand years. It could be assumed that these were ancestors of indigenous Australoid peoples, the remnants of whom may be the short-statured, shy hunting peoples classed as negritos who are still found in remote jungle areas of Malaysia, Thailand and the Philippines. Others were displaced to New Guinea and Australia.

By the time of the first contacts with India, however, the islands and coastlines had long been settled by people who are Malay in type. Basically Mongoloid, they came from south-western China, through a gradual process of cultural osmosis that must have occupied many centuries.

The first Indian contacts were probably with Malay villagers close to the sea on estuaries or creeks. They made beautifully-finished and polished tools from very hard stone, were excellent navigators with some knowledge of astronomy and then, as now, sailed long, narrow and graceful sailing-craft with considerable skill. This maritime tradition is still very important. To today's Malaysian or Indonesian sailors, their craft is more a way of life than simply work – as one can see along the mudflats of coastal Singapore where the racing of light, very fast outrigger models called *jukongs* is a major Malay sport, and their construction an art.

In places such as Brunei and Palembang their way of life persists, in many respects unchanged. Many, like the Bugis, spend their entire life on their ships. People living in villages often build their houses on stilts on mudflats, so they are completely surrounded by water at high tide. Most are fishermen. Otherwise for food they depend very much on the coconut, which thrives along the beaches and on the many islands of this region. This estuary culture is found particularly in places where the soil is poor, like much of the Malaysian peninsula and Kalimantan (Borneo).

Loosely-organised principalities at the river mouths were regarded as the personal bailiwicks, and the tax revenues the personal property of the ruler and the clique supporting him. Pre-colonial Malay history is mostly a tedious and repetitive chronicle of the feuds, wars and disputes of these petty prince-lings. Often enough these principalities resulted from pirate alliances which preyed on passing merchant shipping – something that has persisted into modern times, as the looting and murder of refugees on small boats sailing out of Vietnam has testified.

Rich soils, found on plainlands, drained swamps or hillsides where water is available, have from the earliest times been devoted to the growing of 'wet' or *padi* rice. Indeed, so old is this cultivation of irrigated rice that in some parts of south-east Asia the most suitable land was devoted to it, and expanding populations seem to have been forced into hilly regions, as much as 3000 years ago.

In the mountains of northern Luzon, the main island of the Philippines, is an engineered complex of terraced ricefields and irrigation canals which is intricate in design and so large it has transformed whole mountainsides. Its construction, which took place more than 2000 years ago, must have occupied many generations. It is not know why these people, the Ifugao, decided to leave the plains and commence the staggering task of terracing the mountains. It is possible they did it to escape malaria, since the sluggish *anopheles* mosquito is seldom found higher than 2000 feet above sea-level.

But whatever the reason, the Ifugao must have been remark-ably determined and resourceful people. If these terraces were laid end to end, they would extend 12 thousand miles. First a stone wall was built and the land behind it excavated. The trench so made was lined with impervious clay so it would hold water, then levelled with sand and soil. Another such terrace was built above and below this, until entire hillsides were covered with parallel terraces like giant flights of steps, engineered to follow the contour lines.

Coupled with this skilful engineering the Ifugao showed a considerable knowledge of hydraulics. The waterfalls and torrents of the hillsides were harnessed, bamboo pipes being used to provide a water supply to the rice terraces. Forest growth was controlled on the divides to prevent flash flooding and erosion.

While these Ifugao structures are of special interest because of their age and their extent, terraced ricefields like them can be found almost everywhere in south-east Asia, and are indicative of highly-skilled and co-operative societies. The culture of *padi* rice is in itself an expert and demanding business. Without doubt the art of selecting the best-producing varieties must have begun a long time ago, and the custom of growing first in seedbeds then transplanting the young plants must be almost as old. There is nothing haphazard or careless about this. Each seedling is carefully placed so it is equidistant from its neighbours, resulting in a neat basketwork-like pattern.

There is evidence that this work was in some cases carried out under the supervision of a central authority. This was the case in the great Khmer empire of Cambodia. But in most cases it appears to have been undertaken by villagers for their own benefit. This required a considerable degree of co-operation between families, especially in negotiating the allocation of water resources, and indeed in building the elaborate irrigation systems so often used. It is also how complex systems of relationships must have developed, providing a stable, continuous set of rules necessary for harmony in close-settled societies. There were definite social hierarchies, favouring the old and presumably wise. Decisions, when necessary, were made by these councils of elders on a basis of discussion until consensus was reached – not on a majority vote, which would be regarded as socially crude.

There has always been a strong tradition of joint responsibility for all members of a group. People who are ill are looked after by their neighbours. If a family's house is burned down, the whole village will help build another. Care of children extends outside nuclear families to many other people and especially to the extended family, in which the bonds are very close.

All this is of much more than academic interest, not only because it is still the way things generally are now outside the cities, but also because consensus is an important part of national consciousness, and of politics. It is a major reason why Western-style democracy has not succeeded in Asia, indeed in many places it is politely condemned as being government 'by half plus one'.

How far such ideas go back is not known. It has even been postulated that the cradle of human civilisation was southeast Asia, or rather Sunda, the shallow seas linking the islands to the mainland which were dry land during the ice-ages. Stephen Oppenheimer, in his *Eden in the East* (1998), argues persuasively, though by no means conclusively, that when Sunda was flooded at the end of a glacial 14,000 years ago a civilisation which grew rice, perhaps even worked bronze, was displaced in several directions to create, or influence, those regions such as Mesopotamia and the Indus valley, which are conventionally regarded as the earliest civilisations.

The methods of growing *padi* rice are closely interwoven with animist religions – that is, worship of gods corresponding to and controlling the elemental forces of nature, together with a belief that virtually everything contains a life-force, a 'soul'. Later religions, coming from India, have not generally displaced these, but have simply added a top layer. Even in Thailand, where Buddhism is virtually universal and the state religion, the old animist beliefs are widespread. One such concerns a rice mother without whose approval the crops cannot succeed. Thai children are told about Mae Phra Phosop, and warned that if they don't eat all the rice given to them she may be offended, and refuse the life-giving rains for the next planting.

And this is not only the case in remote villages. Towards the end of World War Two the Thai Electric Corporation in

Bangkok reached the stage where it could no longer get the usual firewood and rice husks to keep its generators going. So it was decided to use surplus rice grain itself. Before this could be done a Buddhist religious ceremony, attended by two Cabinet ministers and other dignitaries, was held. The chief Buddhist official speaking at this function asked the permission of Mae Phra Phosop to use some of the bountiful grain for fuel. He begged her not to be angry and to visit them with her wrath.

'Mae Phra Phosop has always provided us with food,' he said. 'Now may she give us further blessings by supplying heat, wherewith we may get light, and power to drive the trams.'

The *Ramayana*, originating from the sixth century BC, makes references to what seem to be south-east Asia, but these could have been later additions, perhaps in the second century AD. The point indicates the vagueness of the evidence on which assumptions about this period have to be made.

The first detailed description of an Indianised state comes from a third century Chinese account. This was of Funan, located in the great delta of the Mekong River in what is now southern Vietnam, strategically on the trade route between India and China. Funan's capital, Vyadhapura, was a pirate base in flat, marshy country suitable for growing rice. It sprawled along the banks of mangrove-lined creeks, and here its many ships were moored. The Chinese record says the capital was a mudwalled city of considerable size, with dark, curly-haired people who were skilled artisans, making jewellery of wrought gold and silver and pearls. To the Chinese Funan was more a curse than a blessing. Often their merchant junks, which sailed as far west as Sri Lanka, were attacked by its fast pirate ships. Funan, which was probably a loose alliance of villages near the coast south-east of the present Phnom Penh, seems to have declined into obscurity in the sixth century. Other than this its history is debatable. It seems to have extended its influence beyond Vietnam into parts of what are now Cambodia and Thailand. Excavations there have revealed Roman-style medallions and ornaments. From a cultural and religious point of view its most important legacy was a belief in a line of rulers called the Kings of the Mountain, which persisted into later civilisations in several parts of south-east Asia.

During the decline of Funan its commercial monopoly was usurped by another estuary town called Shrivijaya, probably on the site of the present Palembang in Sumatra. Shrivijaya may have prospered under the patronage of China, which needed a strong 'tributary' state in this key area with enough strength to discourage piracy. A Chinese pilgrim named I-Ching who visited there in the seventh century said more than 1000 Buddhist monks lived there, and its rulers – once again Kings of the Mountain – had links with the Buddhist university at Nalanda, in India.

Shrivijaya has prompted much speculation as a major Indonesian naval empire, but this is based on very slender evidence. However, it does seem to have been a central point for trade in nutmeg, cloves and other spices, scented wood, especially sandalwood, and pearls, and a major intermediate port in the traffic, actually quite small, between Persia, India and China. It was attacked in 1025AD by the south Indian Chola empire, possibly because it made too exorbitant demands on Chola ships. Although it recovered from this, it finally faded into obscurity in the fourteenth century.

Another major kingdom flourished in central Java in the seventh century, and must have been appreciable because it built the tremendous monument called the Borobadur. This huge Buddhist shrine is a series of almost three miles of terraces built over a natural hill. The galleries of these terraces are flanked with stones on which thousands of bas-reliefs are carved with wonderful skill. There are some 400 statues of the Buddha, and the structure is crowned by a temple on the flattened top of the hill.

Other temples not far away, at Prambanan, show scenes from the *Ramayana* and were Hindu rather than Buddhist. However, these ancient Javanese societies are shadowy indeed, and on present available evidence are likely to remain so. They could scarcely have been 'empires' in the usual sense – they were more likely to have been loose regional alliances based on existing village structures.

In northern Cambodia, not far from the Thai border, are the ruins of vast buildings, painstakingly fashioned from intricately carved and jointed pieces of greenish sandstone, some of which weigh many tons. This city, Angkor Thom, was the capital of the Khmer kings, and is the remnant of what was south-east Asia's most impressive yet forbidding civilisation.

It is relevant that when the ageing king of Cambodia, Norodom Sihanouk, returned to his country in 1997 from a stay in Beijing, he flew directly to Angkor rather than to the capital Phnom Penh, to pray for peace between the warring factions in Cambodia. He did this because Angkor was the city of his ancestors – the reason also for the remarkable influence he still has in his country.

There is about these ruins a continuing presence which seems to have the power to stir even the most unimaginative person, although more than 500 years have passed since the builders deserted it. Over those centuries it has been locked in a losing fight with the jungle. Season by season, after the city was abandoned, the jungle advanced across highly-developed ricefields served by one of the finest irrigation systems ever built. Birds dropped seeds on the crumbling walls. Now great fig and belan trees, with broad, buttressed roots, perch fantastically over gateways, their roots grappling with carved faces. This whole fabric of slow decay is bathed in a green light of submarine aspect, filtering down through the canopy of leaves overhead. Yet the ruins convey a sense of utter futility. The narrow, forbidding galleries lead nowhere. There is nothing here that could be used as a habitation of man. Only a slave state of the grimmest kind could have forced men to shape and raise these huge blocks of stone. Teams of prisoners and slaves, impelled by the sword and the whip, built these.

A Chinese visitor to the Khmer court at the end of the

thirteenth century, Chou Ta-kuan, said that the tribesmen from the nearby hills were often caught and sold as slaves. He remarks that they were regarded as animals and that many families had more than a hundred of them. 'If they commit a fault, they are beaten,' Chou wrote. 'They bow the head and dare not make the least movement.'

Chou's account describes the wonderfully-developed rice-growing areas based on the two great artificial lakes, the East and West Baray, which flank Angkor, and an intricate system of canals using the water of the Siem Reap River.

Khmer society was based on a highly-organised aristocracy and a savage law. Often trial was by ordeal, and punishment of prisoners was summary and severe. The beautifully-carved friezes of the Bayon and Angkor Wat are still well-preserved and present a vivid picture of the life of Khmer society. They show cockfighting, men playing chess, slaves cutting stone, dancing girls, scenes of intimate family life, processions and battle scenes with warships, archers and elephants.

The Khmer people now became the masters of much of what is now mainland south-east Asia. Their influence extended east to the China Sea, westward through what is now Thailand to the Burmese border, and as far south as the Isthmus of Kra. The names of the Khmer kings, like those of certain Hinduised monarchs in Java, all end with suffix *varman*, which means protector. This gives an insight into their role, which was perceived as offering spiritual and physical protection to the rice-growing majority who served them.

Construction of Angkor began during the eighth century reign of Jayavarman II, who is thought to have been educated for kingship at the court of the Shailendra in Central Java. In the Angkor culture then, there is again evidence of the pervasive tradition of the Kings of the Mountain, enshrining the belief that the prosperity of the people is directly linked with the sacred personality of the king. Each king was required to create a temple-mountain, a building with terraces and towers in which he would be buried after death – a custom which is among the oldest known of the human race, discernible in the ancient kingdoms of Mesopotamia.

This belief resulted in the staggering assembly of huge buildings in the Cambodian jungles which are now regarded as one of the chief wonders of the world. The most famous is the vast Angkor Wat, a mile square, the largest religious building in the world. So well was it built in the twelfth century it remains virtually intact. Although the city itself was abandoned, Angkor Wat remained in use, and was a sizeable Buddhist monastery at the time the French became aware of it in 1850. The pictorial frieze along the inner sanctuary wall is carved with a remarkable artistry. Such things, of course, exist elsewhere. But the frieze at Angkor Wat, eight feet high, extends continuously for more than half a mile.

Few things here are lifesize. Even the carved hands of figures as so massive they are often more than a man could lift. It is probable that this mania for building finally weakened the kingdom so much it could no longer control its enemies. Here again, it is also possible that the *anopheles* mosquito, breeding on the great irrigation lakes, brought catastrophic plagues of malaria.

In 1431 a vassal people, one of the group called the Thais, who had come down into south-east Asia from south-west China, sacked Angkor after a seven month siege. In 1434 the capital was moved and finally established 150 miles south on the banks of the Mekong River at Phnom Penh, which is still the Cambodian capital. Military pressure from the Thais, who had built up a considerable empire based on the city of Ayudhya, and economic factors related to trade with China, seem to have influenced the decision to abandon Angkor. This was probably a considered, relatively gradual process, rather than the sudden dramatic catastrophe conjectured by some historians.

North Vietnam has had strong connections with China, which it borders, from at least the second century BC. Neolithic remains indicate a population of Indonesian type, but later bronze artifacts of considerable artistry are associated with a migration of Mongoloid people south from China into the Red River delta. The population grew steadily as the swamps of the delta were engineered to grow wet rice. In 111BC the region became a province of China called Annam, which means southern kingdom. Direct Chinese influence continued to shape north Vietnamese society for a thousand years, then the Red River delta region became independent as a result of the demise of the Chinese T'ang dynasty in the tenth century.

A glance at a map shows at once the geographic features which have several times resulted in Vietnam being divided into two, or even three, countries. The narrow coastal 'waist' bordering the mountains of Laos is as little as 40 miles wide, and separates two regions with marked historic, ethnic and cultural differences.

The south, consisting substantially of the plains and great delta of the Mekong River, was part of the empire of Angkor. The coastline north, along the narrow waist, was the considerable empire of a seafaring people, racially Malay. These were the Chams, whose society had acquired an Indian cultural influence as early as the second century AD, and which persisted for 1300 years. This was not an empire, but again a loose federation of river-mouth towns.

Champa traded in spices and ivory, but it was chiefly known and feared for its piracy directed at the passing coastal trade. This attracted considerable annoyance from the Chinese, whose ships were nearly always those attacked, and led to a number of punitive expeditions. Champa was also noted as a slave trading centre. Records of continual Cham wars with their neighbours were probably more often than not references to raids against neighbouring communities to obtain prisoners of war for resale. The point can be noted that, as with other south-east Asian kingdoms, power was linked to the possession of large numbers of people, rather than large amounts of land.

Judging from its architecture Champa had considerable cultural links with Angkor, with which, however, it was almost constantly at war. Constant military pressure came from China, too, after the Chams renounced Chinese overlordship in the sixth century. However, it was the Vietnamese advancing from the north who finally brought Cham influence to an end. They were virtually destroyed as a political force by persistent war with the north Vietnamese from the eleventh century onwards and a Mongol invasion in 1283. However, their descendants remain a distinct ethnic group in Vietnam and in Cambodia.

The Tran dynasty in North Vietnam not only attacked Champa, it was successful in turning back the Mongol invasion directed by Kublai Khan. Several centuries of intermittent wars with China followed, then with the fifteenth century came perhaps the most successful and the first genuinely Vietnamese dynasty. This was the Le, who, after inflicting a final defeat on the Chams in 1471, began to extend slowly into the Mekong delta.

At the time of the first contacts with Europeans, however, the Le emperors had become figureheads and the natural tendency of the country to divide had asserted itself again. Two families, the Trinh in the north and the Nguyen in the south, became the real centres of power. Cambodia, meanwhile, had dwindled both in population and influence, and had become a mere dependency of Vietnam.

5

China: The Eternal Nation

China's story is among the most remarkable of all human-kind; her river valleys have been the location of a society that has not only shown continuity and consistency for almost 4000 years, but was also the inventor of paper, printing, efficient merchant shipping, the grid-planned metropolis, firearms, credit banking and paper money, among many other foundations and tribulations of the modern world. The transfer of such things and the ideas that prompted them to Europe was slow but nevertheless consequential.

China's status as the most populous country in the world is nothing new. She has been so for millennia. All Chinese, including those living far from their homeland, are aware of this sense of continuity, of a culture that has withstood time and adversity as no other human institution has done, and are deeply influenced by it. China's Communist leaders are no exception. At the time of the new state's deepest financial need when it had been deserted by the Soviet Union, an option would have been to sell the immensely valuable solid gold and gem-encrusted artifacts in the Ming tombs near Beijing. But this was not done. Instead the tombs were carefully restored and maintained, all their treasures still in place.

The durability and individuality of Chinese culture has been due to a number of factors, of which geography is among the more important. China is removed from the mountain spine of central Asia and does not have the immediate vulnerability of the north Indian plain. These great mountains, together with the deserts to their north and the Pacific Ocean to the east, were a formidable barrier between China and the rest of the world, insulating her until the relatively recent development of efficient shipping. Trade contacts with the West before the nineteenth century were slight and the effects of them, especially on China, are often over-emphasised. Her mercantile contacts with other parts of Asia were more important.

North of the mountains are arid, lightly-populated plains and formidable deserts. These made overland travel and trade difficult. These outer regions were not, however, completely empty. Tribes of nomads moved through them, maintaining a constant pressure on China's borders and often invading her. The Great Wall was built and rebuilt or extended many times to keep them out. Yet unlike some of those who invaded India, the 'barbarians' who successfully occupied China had little effect on her. Chinese civilisation was able to absorb them, even when they were conquerors.

This cultural resilience was assisted by the fact that Chinese civilisation has a powerful binding force – a common written language and a body of literature of great antiquity that can be read anywhere in China, regardless of the many differences of spoken dialect. Much of this literature is concerned with the way people should live and behave. It has had a remarkable influence, which has extended beyond China, notably to Japan, Korea and Vietnam, and is the background to what have come to be called 'Asian values'.

The tenacity of Chinese civilisation also has much to do with its basic religion, ancestor worship. This ancient belief stresses the duty of sons to care for parents, both before and after death, when they are considered to have the same needs as in life. The welfare of the two human souls, a lower soul existing from conception, a higher one from birth, depends on the making of sacrifices, which can only be carried out by sons. If the souls are not tended, they can exert malign or unlucky influences on the living. An effect of ancestor worship was to make Chinese families strong, united forces, capable of great mutual effort towards common objectives. This clan and family resilience remains a significant quality of modern Chinese.

The earliest-known Mongoloid inhabitants of China lived in houses with earth walls, often partly dug down into the earth or bermed into the side of a hill. Millet was their staple, for the north-west region they inhabited is not rice-growing country. They probably entered the north China plain from the north-west and were attracted to the Wei and Huang (Yellow) River valleys by the light, friable windborne soil called *loess*, which is capable of cropping for many years before it becomes exhausted.

Formal Chinese history postulates a vague heroic age, involving three early dynasties, the Hsia, Shang and Chou. Hsia remains in the realm of abundant and hopeful myth, such as the reign of the Yellow Emperor, when the world was considered to be perfect, but a clearer view is possible of the Shang period. At the earliest time about which reasonable assumptions, based largely on archeological evidence, can be made, there was already within the great bend of the Yellow River an ordered society, recognisable as Chinese on the standards of later development.

The achievements of the Shang suggest a brilliant and quite sudden advance in art, technology and social order beyond what existed before. Early in the twentieth century, inscribed bones and tortoise-shells sold in Beijing for medicinal purposes were recognised as being very old. The inscriptions on them were of a strange and archaic pattern. These 'oracle bones', originally used for the prediction of future events, bore characters so related to present Chinese writing they could be considered its antecedents. As in contemporary Chinese writing this text did not use an alphabet representing sounds, but instead individual characters – pictures – for ideas, events, objects capable of description by words. Indeed it was writing already highly-developed. It was possible to establish the meaning of many characters, although some inscriptions are only partly decipherable. They supplied evidence of the existence of many rulers said in the traditional histories to have been of the Shang Dynasty.

Shang culture has left a large number of sophisticated and beautifully-worked bronzes, which are so far in advance of previous artifacts there can be little doubt Chinese culture made its first major advance in this era. When this became fully appreciated, a search for their origins began. Between 1928 and 1937 excavations at Anyang, in northern Honan Province, identified the later Shang capital of Yin, probably founded about 1300BC. From 1951 onwards further work in this region revealed an even earlier Shang city at Chengchow, probably dating to about 1800BC.

It had massive earth walls, up to 55 feet thick, surrounding an area about a mile square. In the pottery kilns inside were found clay stamps for decorating jars in patterns, like the dragon, trellis and square spiral, which would persist in future Chinese ceramics. There were also ox bones and tortoise shells with incised written characters.

Anyang revealed evidence of a wealthy and powerful ruling class, with impressive tombs, probably for the kings, in which have been found bronze weapons and ceremonial urns – also pits containing the beheaded bodies of humans, horses and dogs. Shang religious beliefs were animist, with gods representing the moon, sun, wind and other natural phenomena, but the beginnings of ancestor worship were already discernible. The king's role of conducting rites to guarantee agricultural prosperity was another Shang attribute to be carried forward into the future. The Shang army used bows and arrows with bronze heads, and horse-drawn chariots. Silk was used as a fabric, the silkworms being fed on mulberry leaves, as they still are.

The historical records have it that the last Shang king ended his reign in the eleventh century BC. The Shang were supplanted by a less-distinguished line, the Chou, who had been rulers of a border kingdom. They were feudal lords, maintaining only a formal authority over the families that had assisted the establishment of the dynasty. During the nine centuries of nominal Chou rule, the feudal families grew more powerful and the role of the kings ritualistic. Alliances and conquests led to the emergence of half-a-dozen major principalities, giving China a political organisation not unlike feudal Europe.

It was a time of tremendous growth, during which the Chinese states emerged from the primitive. Shang culture had been that of a small aristocracy, but now education and art became the preoccupation of a wider section of the community. A wealthy merchant class emerged in what must have been the world's largest cities of their time, with populations of over a quarter of a million. Huge irrigation works, involving hundreds of canals, were built. The first coinage came into use. At first metal tools – hoes, knives, spades were a means of exchange. These were soon replaced by small bronze replicas, which became China's first money. Iron was cast and forged into scythes, axes, saws, needles and weapons, well ahead of the rest of the world. Craftsmen working in jade used wire saws and diamond drills.

Writing flourished, and for the first time became more than flattery of royal houses. Textbooks, poetry, treatises on medicine, the arts, mathematics, political theory, were all part of a major intellectual flowering. The scholar, able to write and read, became, as he would continue to be thereafter, an object of respect and authority. This was the time of Confucius, said to have lived between 551 and 479BC. His name was actually K'ung Fu-tzu, of which Confucius is a Latinised version.

Many people know Confucius only because of his frequently-quoted *Analects* (actually compiled after his death) of which these are typical:

'The man who makes a mistake, and doesn't correct it, makes another mistake.'

'The mind of a superior man is conversant with righteousness; the mind of a mean man is conversant with gain.'

As with many great figures of history, the facts of Confucius' life are unclear. However, if the scholar-teacher lived today he would probably have been considered a dangerous radical, because of his basic admonition that the welfare of the people was more important than the privileges of a ruling class. The rulers of the small state of Lu, in which he lived, disliked such ideas, nor could Confucius, during many years of wandering, persuade any other leader to accept them. He insisted on his students studying poetry, music and history to broaden their minds, a tradition continued almost into modern times in the great Chinese civil service, the mandarinate. The fact that he was a dissenter, yet was held in reverence by his students, indicates that he was probably a man of considerable personal force of character, with an innovative, revolutionary mind.

It is ironical that later Chinese Confucianism was anything but these things. Of its enormous body of writing, remarkably little came from Confucius himself. Confucianism, so long the ethical system guiding China, was developed in the work and thought of a mass of subsequent commentators.

Mencius, who was active during the first quarter of the fourth century BC, was such a commentator. His view was based on faith in the ultimate goodness of human nature. To him is attributed a practical Chinese political device of some importance – the 'mandate of Heaven' concept – although there are hints of its development much earlier. This idea is one of qualification of the absolute power of the ruler. It is regarded as morally justifiable, even laudable, to revolt against a cruel, unjust, or even unlucky regime. In other words a government is finally justified by its success, its ability to maintain a reasonably prosperous and equable society; an emperor by his probity, his high moral character, since only such a man would be able to intercede with the forces of Heaven to ensure prosperity.

Rather than voting at elections, this became a means of bending governments to the will of the people. The recent concessions of the Chinese Communist party, especially its economic ones, are not inconsistent with this tradition. The habit of the Chinese Communist government of describing itself as 'correct' – that is, morally sound – may also have a connection. Contrasting with Mencius, a second important early commentator, Hsun Tzu, regarded human nature as fundamentally bad, in need of improvement through good government, the establishment of set rules of conduct, and the high moral example of rulers.

The Chinese world of this time consisted of a dozen or so large and small states grouped along the Yellow and Wei Rivers, which constituted Chung Kuo – the Middle Country – plus a number of others, on the western and southern fringes, which were regarded as having a lower culture. Beyond this lay the world of the 'barbarians.'

Of the fringe states the most significant was Ch'in, in the far north-west, occupying territory which was roughly the present provinces of Shensi and Kansu. Ch'in was traditionally a bastion against the hordes farther west that were a perpetual threat to the settled Chinese countryside and wealthy cities. Not for nothing was the most striking feature of Chinese cities their surrounding walls and defence outworks.

The ideals attributed to Confucius were suspect in his own time by those who held and influenced power, the energetic pragmatists who really decided the policy of states. Far from regarding humanity as noble and susceptible to an elevated moral example, they believed a rigidly-enforced system of law was the best means of government. This 'legalist' school reached its greatest influence in the state of Ch'in, which is not surprising. In Ch'in military effectiveness was considered of paramount importance. The entire population was subject to conscription without notice; the men to fight and the women and old people to carry supplies and labour at the fortifications. The army was equipped with elaborate siege machinery; tall, wooden towers on wheels, battering rams, mangonels and similar engines designed to hurl huge stones at the mud walls of beleaguered cities.

By the third century BC Ch'in had the barbarians on its frontiers under control, and was able to use its efficient military machine against its more cultured but less martial neighbours to the east. Under the joint rule of its young king and his chief counsellor, Li Ssu, it won every campaign. Not all were military, for Li Ssu was an intriguer of ability. His negotiating was a major factor in a series of victories that led to no less than the unification of China for the first time. The king of Ch'in now restyled himself Shih Huang Ti – the First Emperor – in 221BC.

His administrators had at least the virtue of energy, devoting themselves to a stream of reforms that transformed China – a name which, incidentally, derives from Ch'in. The width of carriage axles was standardised, a system of uniform weights and measures and coinage introduced, and Chinese writing reformed to make it more concise and practical, and moreover, standardised. The empire was linked by roads which must have been major engineering works even by today's standards. Ch'in also cut across the old feudal lines of authority, and established an efficient, if despotic, system of administration. China was divided into 36 provinces, each controlled by three specialised officials responsible to the emperor.

Efficient communications and a rigid discipline became the basis of unity. To further reduce the power of the great families the emperor called in all their weapons. The huge pile of bronze was melted down and cast into 12 statues, each reputed to weigh 70 tons, which were set up at the summer palace, A-fang. The building of A-fang is said to have involved a labour force of three-quarters of a million.

Li Ssu persuaded the emperor to issue an edict that books from the past, except a few specialist texts, should be destroyed. Anyone who failed to burn his books within 30 days would be branded and sent to forced labour. The case Li Ssu put to the king was not, however, altogether unreasonable. Pointing out that the feudal princes were continually at war, he argued 'Why should we follow them? The empire has been pacified, law comes from a single authority, the people have work, but the scholars continue to study the past, causing doubt and trouble.'

The books of the classics, compiled with great labour and almost irreplaceable, were bulky and difficult to conceal. Paper was not yet in use, and the books were mostly inscribed on ivory tablets, lengths of bamboo, and slabs of wood. At first some scholars defied the edict. More severe penalties were introduced. A huge pit is said to have been dug, and 460 scholars buried alive in it.

So Shih Huang Ti earned the hatred of succeeding generations of Chinese scholars as 'he who who burned the books and buried the scholars'. The story of this villainy has, no doubt, lost nothing in the telling, but the extent to which the First Emperor's reputation has been embroidered by later writers is not really known. Certainly a vast mass of stories, many fanciful, has grown up around his name. Myth has it that self-firing crossbows guard the underground passages into his tomb, and that rivers and lakes of mercury surround it.

While it is sometimes asserted that Shih Huang Ti built the Great Wall, much of it already existed before his time. However, he recognised its importance as a defence against barbarians, and greatly improved the older fabric. This involved forced labour by vast hordes of people over 12 years, during which it is said a million workers died. Labour on the Great Wall was a common and greatly-feared punishment. The existing wall is of later, Ming Dynasty construction.

An elaborate signalling system was used by the garrisons on the wall, to bring reinforcements to any point of attack. As soon as the fast-moving horsemen appeared out of a cloud of dust to the west, signal fires were lit. During the day bundles of damp straw were used to send up columns of smoke, and at night the fires were coloured using metallic salts – the basis of the Chinese invention of fireworks.

The harshness of Ch'in rule and the extent of the revolution it had visited on China foredoomed it. Long before his death the emperor lived constantly with fear and told no-one in which of his network of palaces he would spend the night.

His fear of death led him into a deep preoccupation with immortality and a search for a potion said to procure it. He died in 210BC while on a tour of his empire. Such was the fear that the fact of his death would lead to a revolt, it was concealed until his body – with a load of rotting fish – could be returned to the capital.

The extraordinary scope and power of this regime was confirmed by the discovery in 1974 near the city of Sian of the Entombed Warriors – a half-buried army of almost 8000 archers, infantrymen and cavalry made from terracotta and located in several huge pits which had been roofed with pine logs subsequently destroyed by fire. Bronze chariots and many other artifacts still being unearthed here confirm this is part of the mausoleum of Shih Huang Ti, on which three-quarters of a million artisans are said to have worked. Seven human skeletons also recovered may be those of Shih Huang Ti's children, murdered in the palace coup after his death, further weakening the dynasty.

Although the substantial hill believed to house the actual burial place of the First Emperor has not yet been excavated, other archeological work around the complex has revealed a very advanced technology for the world of its time. Blast furnaces were in use to make high-quality steel, and some of this steel, used for spear-blades, appears to have been rustproofed with chromium plating. Steel-making of this kind would not occur for another thousand years in Europe.

Here, too, appear to have been the origins of the alchemy which was to fascinate Europe a millennium later, and using much the same methods and materials. Like the alchemists, Chinese investigators of this time too often met an untimely end, either from poisoning by mercury, with which they were fascinated, or eating powdered jade, or mushrooms and fungi growing on high mountains.

Shih Huang Ti's heirs and supporters were not able to maintain the empire, and in the end his family was murdered to the last child. A period of confusion and civil war followed during which a general of peasant origins, Liu Pang, founded the dynasty called the Han. At first it had to struggle desperately to survive. To the north and north-west 'barbarian' armies of more than half a million men were waiting outside the Great Wall.

It was not until the half-century long reign of the Emperor Wu which began 60 years later that China's enemies were subdued and she became, for the first time, an empire of proportions and power significant in global terms. The Chinese call themselves the men of Han to distinguish themselves from minority groups in the outer areas. It is a dynasty particularly favoured as an historic model by the Communist government, perhaps because of the similarities between its origins and their own.

The Confucian classics reappeared and copies were made from odd fragments that had been secretly buried, concealed in chinks of walls or under roofbeams, or retained in the memories of old men. In spite of such painstaking efforts to recreate the past much had changed. Ch'in centralism had all but destroyed the old families, and the long wars during the early Han had impoverished China. The early Han emperors retained the provincial system and persistently interfered in the affairs of and supervised the former feudal states. It was largely this genius of the Han administration to divide and rule that allowed China the centuries of peace necessary to grow into a great power.

The population grew quickly and spread farther to the south. The increased use of irrigation, the building of canals and fleets of river boats made possible the growth and distribution of more rice than was needed for bare subsistence. Yet most of this additional wealth went to provide a luxurious lifestyle for the scholar-officials, most of whom came from the old feudal families. Records of the time indicate that life was generally desperate and precarious for the peasants, who were frequently in debt. Interest rates were rapaciously high and they were often forced to sell their land, and even their children into slavery, to survive. As a last resort men fled into the forests, compelled to robbery, or joining one of the bands of brigands greatly feared by travellers. As well as a month's labour a year required of the peasants to work on public enterprises they were also liable to conscription for two years in the army. They were provided with the necessities of life during this service, but were otherwise unpaid.

It was within the walled cities that the arts and graces flourished, based on an overall surplus there of commodities over demand. The first century historian Pan Ku claimed for the capital, Chang'an (the present Chinese city of Sian) that a wall a hundred miles long surrounded its offices, palaces and suburbs, with water gardens and parks featuring rhinoceroses from Kanji (south-east India), birds from Chaldea, and unicorns from Annam!

The Han empire became a first-rate military power, able to control the barbarians not only at the Great Wall, but far beyond it, pushing into the Tarim Basin and Tibet almost to the boundaries of India. It used armed cavalry, with long spears, to devastating effect. Probably the world's first largescale mass production industry equipped this army. Iron or bronze arrowheads were manufactured in millions, since individual soldiers would have at least 100 arrows for their crossbows. These weapons were highly-developed instruments, and remained more deadly and effective than firearms as late as the nineteenth century. Of particular interest was the standardised trigger and string release device, mass-produced in bronze to efficient and precise specifications.

However, these military expeditions were not designed to carve out an empire, but to subdue the nomad tribes, driving them far to the west so they would not be a threat to China. It became a confirmed Chinese attitude that control of neighbouring states was a prerequisite to the security of China.

As the Christian era dawned, China had its effect on the world of the West, even though both scarcely knew it. The world now had two great empires, those of the Han and of Imperial Rome, which was probably slightly the smaller. The Chinese census of AD2 lists 59 million people. There were trade contacts between the two empires, including an expensive and widespread fashion in Rome for Chinese silk, which at one time threatened to deplete bullion reserves. More significant was the displacement of the nomad tribes westwards, eventually to have disruptive effects in both Europe and India.

Major contributions to the Chinese tradition were made during Han times. One of the most important was a trend towards merit and education rather than birth as a qualification for high office. This was associated with the increasing power of the central government. Unlike in Europe, feudalism would virtually disappear at this early stage. There was also a major revival of Confucianism. These two factors, organised national government, increasingly by an intelligentsia, and the use of the Confucian classics to justify – even sanctify – the system of government, led on to the development of that great public service known as the mandarinate, the longest-lived and perhaps the most successful instrument of administration mankind has seen. Its influence and traditions are still apparent in the China of today, and may well become more so in the future.

In Han times the mandarinate had already developed many of its enduring characteristics, including examinations in the classics, and adoption of the Confucian idea that the educated man was to be guided by the force of example rather than driven by the fear of punishment. It had also developed a contempt for trade and what the west calls 'private enterprise.' To the Confucian scholars this seemed opposed to true moral values. Filial piety – the respect and support of sons towards fathers, the duties of wives to their mother-in-law – was a major Confucian idea, which was to permeate all levels of the society in time.

In spite of scholarly disapproval, there was almost unfettered capitalism and the accumulation of great fortunes by merchants. However these caused such convulsions of the economy, due to 'cornering' and speculation in food, and illicit coining of currency, that the Han state eventually curbed them. Large public works and much of the significant domestic industry and distribution systems came under state control.

Before controls were imposed, capitalists in the iron and salt industries were making huge fortunes. The government nationalised these industries and ordered their former owners to run them on behalf of the state. The association of capitalism and state control emerging in China now, in the late twentieth century is, then, a recurring theme in Chinese history, and ought not to occasion surprise. Indeed some of the economic problems with which the Han state wrestled were not too far removed from those emerging in China today.

The invention of paper in the second century was a major step forward. Writing became an almost universal occupation among educated men in Han times, and special attention was given to history. This was the time of the most famous Chinese historian, Ssu-ma Ch'ien, whose work became a model for succeeding generations. The art of paper-making spread slowly west, reaching Europe 1000 years later.

Under Han rule Confucianism developed its preoccupation with systems of complex rites and relationships in almost every area of life, a desire for an ordered harmonious universe, which, once established, would go on unchanged for ever. The idea of the ruler as a civilised, virtuous example to his subjects, a sort of moral pacesetter, became firmly developed. Already Confucianism was far from Confucius. It owed much not only to Mencius and Sun Tzu, but even to other sources; even to the seemingly antithetic Taoism, a philosophy from Chou times which saw men as simply part of nature, to whose mysterious forces they must adjust, changing what was about them as little as possible – forerunners of modern conservationists, among some of whom Taoism is again popular.

Music and philosophy were thought to be so closely associated that proper calculation of the degrees of pitch in the musical scale was considered essential to the proper functioning of government. Hence mathematicians and philosophers were assigned to the task of calculating them. This suggests the importance attributed to an overall harmony of the universe in human affairs. The movements of the moon, planets and constellations were also carefully studied for similar reasons. Mathematics was developed to a high degree, Chang Heng calculating the value of *pi* to be 3.1622 in the second century AD. He also invented the world's first known seismograph at that time.

A convincing example of the levels of Han craftsmanship came with the discovery in 1967 of the massive tombs of Prince Liu Sheng and his wife at Mancheng, in Hopei Province. Recovered intact were two funerary suits, the larger consisting of 2690 pieces of jade sewn together with gold thread. All the jade plates had been carefully shaped so they would fit together perfectly, with minute holes drilled at each corner to accept the gold thread.

The Han Dynasty commenced a slow decline after the death of the Emperor Wu in 87BC. It was so closely associated with Confucianism that the decay of one involved the collapse of the other. There was a massive revulsion from Confucianism, many people turning to the newly-arrived Buddhism and even more to the anarchic Taoism. Taoism lay behind the great second century peasant revolt of the Yellow Turbans, in which millions were said to have been killed and which hastened the decline of the Han. Flood, famine and poverty increasingly weakened the Chinese nation. The Hsiung Nu tribesmen took their opportunity, occupying much of north China. The Chinese fled to the alien, still lightly-settled south.

Meanwhile Buddhism, which reached China via the trade routes in the first century AD, had been rapidly gaining adherents. The form of Buddhism that came to China was the *mahayana* school, which is very different from the more orthodox *theravada* of Burma and Thailand. *Mahayana* Buddhism was a religion, already equipped with magic, gods and saints known as *bodhisattvas*, who deferred their translation to a state of divine perfection so they could intercede in Heaven on man's behalf. It postulated a paradise in which humans were given hope of a far better life. A universally-revered and characteristic Chinese *bodhisattva* is Kuan Yin, the goddess of mercy and examplar of feminine virtues. Certain aspects of Confucianism, such as ancestor worship and the cult of the family, were incorporated into Chinese Buddhism, which, as it has moved eastwards, has shown itself to be one of the more flexible and malleable human philosophies. It was in this sinified form that it began its further movement eastwards across the narrow seas to the islands of Japan.

6

....

Early Japan and the T'ang Dynasty in China

The original inhabitants of this small, sunny but cool group of mountainous islands off the coast of China were not the people now the Japanese. When the Japanese crossed the seas from the mainland, they found a people in the islands quite unlike themselves – short in stature, with heavy body hair, light skin colour and a language different from any other in the world. These people, the Ainu, were considered to be of Caucasian origin because of these characteristics, but recent genetic comparisons indicate links with the peoples of Russian Siberia.

The Ainus, who led a primitive hunting, fishing existence, nevertheless resisted the intruders ferociously. However the Japanese, originally settled in the southernmost island, Kyushu, eventually pushed these earlier inhabitants northward. Now only a small Ainu community remains on the northernmost island, Hokkaido.

Since the early Japanese were not literate and had no historical tradition, there is very little reliable information about this early period. When they arrived, just where they came from, remain conjecture. They were, however, Mongoloid, almost certainly coming to Japan from China via the Korean peninsula – although there are also intriguing signs of an ethnic connection with south-east Asia. There are links with Indonesian languages in Japanese, but the most striking resemblance is in the form of construction of Japan's oldest and most sacred shrine, that at Ise of the sun goddess Amaterasu, the chief deity of the Shinto religion.

For a temple that attracts such veneration the Ise shrine is unassuming – no more than a small wooden hut, of post and beam construction holding up a heavy, thatched, single gable, and mounted on about 50 timber piles. The shrine is believed to be an exact copy of the kind of house built by the Japanese when they first came to their islands. Every 21 years it has been pulled down and rebuilt in new, specially-selected cypress, so the copy and the original are identical. It is very similar to buildings still found in parts of south-east Asia, especially in the east Indonesian island of Sulawesi (Celebes), and in Sumatra.

This early Japanese society is called the *yamato*, named for the region inland from the big port city of Osaka on the island of Honshu. However, it probably originated in western Kyushu and then moved gradually north-east around the shores of the Inland Sea. It built large underground tombs in a variety of shapes, in which small terracotta figures called *haniwa* have been found. These figurines indicate that the *yamato* used the horse and armour, and that they were warlike.

This impression was confirmed by early contacts with Chinese civilisation, which were hostile. However, trade followed and a pact of friendship was concluded with two south Korean states, Paekche and Silla, in the fourth century. There was also considerable migration of whole extended families, and of craftsmen and scholars from war-torn Korea. Their loyalties were maintained in the new country and three or four of these clans became powerful enough to manipulate the imperial family. Written records appear only in the eighth century, when Chinese writing was adopted, hence the chronicles of earlier times cannot be taken as a reliable record. However, there can be little doubt that Koreans were a major influence forming Japanese society.

The briefest of summaries will serve to indicate all that is of any importance in the area of myth. The goddess Amaterasu emerges as the most important deity and her grandson, Ninigi, is said to have descended from the High Plain of Heaven to rule among men. Ninigi's great-grandson, Jimmu, is revered as the first of a continuous line of 125 Japanese emperors considered to be of the same semi-divine blood. Hence, while Chinese emperors were mortal and ruled only while they held the mandate of Heaven, Japanese emperors ruled by divine right, which they passed on automatically to their descendants.

The issue of the divinity of the emperor is not quite as simple as it seems. He was not regarded as a god in the Western sense so much as a human figure possessing, more than any other person or object, the quality the Japanese call *kami*, the crude meaning of which is elevation or superiority. *Kami* is a spiritual quality which persons and objects – even the islands of Japan – possess in differing amounts. The imperial line is considered to manifest the greatest amount of *kami*.

This concept is important because it represents a distinctive quality of the Japanese people – a belief that the main value of the individual is as a unit in the totality of Japan. It came to be expressed in the extraordinary loyalty, often tested to the death, of Japanese retainers to their lords, the willingness of Japanese *kamikaze* pilots to crash their bomb-laden aircraft on the decks of American ships during World War Two and, in recent times, the almost feudal relationships between the huge Japanese industrial complexes and their workers.

The main Japanese religion, Shinto, is essentially animist, although it has individual characteristics which play a major part in the thought and life of Japan today. One is an insistence on personal cleanliness as the necessary companion of holiness. Worship at a Shinto shrine involves purification in both the physical and spiritual sense. The first is achieved by washing in running water and the second simply by passing under a number of large ceremonial arches called *torii*, which span the paths leading to shrines.

Another manifestation of Shinto that has become part of the Japanese character is a refreshing preference for simplicity and restraint. Its shrines are usually small structures of natural wood, deliberately left unpainted, a key to the Japanese fondness for this material. There are no images or statues, the deity being represented by a symbol, often a polished bronze mirror but sometimes a sword or the *magatama* jewel, which represent the regalia believed to have been handed to Ninigi by Amaterasu. Only the emperor, certain members of his family, or his special emissary, may pass the silken curtain over the entrance to the Ise shrine, for its sacred symbols must always be screened from the sight of ordinary men. Some Shinto shrines are not buildings at all. Among them are a waterfall, a rock and a mountain.

The Shinto ideal of simplicity, at the same time shunning the direct, the obvious or ostentatious, is the mainspring of all its forms of art. Where westerners see beauty in massed displays of flowers, the Japanese purist would admire a single blossom. There are other aspects of Shinto which are not so appealing – a disregard for individual life and suffering, and a martial attitude involving great cruelty, much in evidence many times in Japanese history.

Japan is a mountainous country, with few large areas of flat land. Only 13 per cent is arable. Hence from the earliest times a remarkable intensity has had to be applied to cultivating the land, so the last possible ounce of food can be grown. The traveller through Japan sees at every turn, in the elaborate cultivated terraces on so many hillsides, the results of many generations of devoted labour. Early Japan did not have to face this constraint. It was a simple clan society, still quite small in numbers, when it turned to China for its first civilised model.

Although the first millennium of the Christian era saw Europe asleep in the Dark Ages, these were centuries of light in Asia, and nowhere more so than in China. Under the rule of the Sui and T'ang Dynasties China became the strongest, most populous and advanced society the world had yet seen.

The troubled years of disunity after the decline of the Han

gave place, in 589, to a brief preparatory dynasty, the Sui, which again united China. As with the Ch'in, Sui achievements were largely due to the qualities of the dynasty's founder, the Emperor Wen. His successor, the Emperor Yang, ruled less wisely, weakening China by the despatch of huge, disastrous expeditions to Korea. The emperor was murdered in 618 by his own courtiers, and a general of the north-west command succeeded him, commencing the T'ang Dynasty.

T'ang saw a pattern of administration in China which endured almost without change into the early twentieth century, and in which the system of recruiting the mandarinate through very difficult public examinations became confirmed. China had at various times during her long past experimented with codified law, and was aware of its deficiencies. The alternative was seen as entrusting decisions on legal and administrative matters to a corps of highly-qualified, broadly educated men, then controlling them rigorously with a system of inspectorates and by shifting them regularly from one post to another far away. This administrative elite were the mandarins, never numerous for a country of China's size but with immense powers in their regional bailiwicks. The 'law' they administered was based on custom and precedent. Reference to any Chinese dynasty as a government invites misunderstanding. Modern governments exist mainly to make and amend laws. The Chinese dynasties and their bureaucrats maintained law and order but their main purpose otherwise was to raise revenues.

More than ever the art of graceful and elegant writing was required of the scholar-administrator. The chief examination, for the *chin-shih* degree, which maintained its position into the twentieth century, tested administrative ability, but also literary skills – especially the composition of poetry. This tradition has not disappeared. Mao Tse-tung wrote poetry, as anyone who passed through Beijing airport in the nineteen seventies would know – a translation of his poem The Snow featured prominently on a wall.

T'ang was the age of perhaps the best-known Chinese poets. Its two most celebrated, Li Po and Du Fu, were contemporaries. Du Fu was a scholarly poet, highly regarded by the intelligentsia of the time, but the impetuous rebellious Li Po has had the greater international appeal over time. A rebel against constituted authority and one who could not be bothered with study, Li Po was a womaniser and a regular drunk, along with his companions, the Eight Immortals of the Winecup. Nevertheless the power and passion of his verse impressed even the emperor although its Taoist, nature-worshipping philosophy was directly antithetic to the Confucian ideal. Li Po is said to have drowned when, leaning from a boat, he tried to embrace the reflection of the moon in the Yangtse River.

China again became powerful militarily. All of Tibet, the Tarim River Basin, and even parts of Afghanistan, came under Chinese influence. Even though this led to skirmishes with growing Arab power, the overall result was to pacify Central Asia so thoroughly that traders could use the overland routes without undue fear of robberies or delays. This was the heyday of the Silk Road. A steady stream of horse and camel trains carried, among other things, paper, silk, gunpowder, spices, condiments and tea to the West. The journey was a long and perilous one, during which it was necessary to pass the dreaded thousand mile stretch of the Taklamakan Desert. Without the bad-tempered double-humped Bactrian camel, able to survive without water for two weeks at a time, this trade would scarcely have been possible. Beautifully worked Persian gold and silver, myrrh, precious stones, Turkish carpets, glassware came from the West into China.

There were also the beginnings of sea-trade, especially the longstanding position of Canton (Guangzhou) as a trading port. It was then regarded as uncouth, dangerous and unpleasantly hot, but it was a convenient point of entry into China for Persian ships, also large vessels, as much as 200 feet long, from Sri Lanka. Silk and china were the main exports.

This was a time of major cultural transfer to the Middle East and thence to Europe, both from China and the Buddhist universities in India. This transfer was not only one way. The capital, Ch'ang-an, became the principal metropolis in the world of the eighth century, and, probably also the most important repository of knowledge. It was certainly the largest, with more than a million inhabitants. There were many libraries in Ch'ang-an, and there is evidence of a knowledge of, and a lively interest in, other parts of the world and their thought – the cult of Zarathustra from Persia, Nestorian Christianity among them. Neither of these took hold in China but Islam, at the height of its missionary phase, eventually attracted millions of adherents among China's border peoples, many of whom are still Moslems today.

The world's first books were printed, using wooden blocks on which all the characters for a complete page were engraved. The Chinese experimented with movable type in the eleventh century, but abandoned it as impractical because of the large number of Chinese characters. (In the K'ang-hsi dictionary of 1716, there are 40,545 characters.) However, the Koreans later persisted for some decades with moveable iron type.

T'ang China had its rebels, its eccentrics and its non-conformists, which it was well able to accommodate, but generally it was an orderly, regulated society, based on state control of the economy and good communications. In more ways than one the old China was disappearing. The emphasis was going more and more to the south where the rich ricelands of the Yangtse valley were creating a new prosperity. Although enormous efforts were devoted to building canals and roads to take this new wealth northward, Ch'ang-an's days were already numbered. One of these waterways was the 1300 mile long Grand Canal, much of which is still in use today.

The Chinese belief that it was a religious duty to have many sons provided an almost inexhaustible pool of manpower for public works. Every ten miles along the road system radiating out from Ch'ang-an post stations were built, which provided horses and other facilities for couriers of the government.

The influence of this large, sophisticated neighbour on Japan was irresistible. As Chinese culture flourished the embassies from the *yamato* people became more frequent. An additional influence came from the regular stream of Chinese and Korean migrants to Japan from the fourth century onwards. They were educated and cultured far beyond the Japanese, and were welcomed as associates and advisors to *yamato* nobles. Many even established new noble families in Japan. Others, lower in the social scale, became scribes to *yamato* nobles. Gradually the Japanese nobles learned to read and write and adopted the Chinese script in spite of its difficulty and basic unsuitability.

Early in the seventh century the governing regent for the empress, Prince Shotoku, encouraged a major Buddhist missionary effort in Japan, and also introduced in the year 646 reforms known as the *taika*, or great change. The *taika* reforms were intended to strengthen the imperial bureaucracy at the expense of the regional clans. They closely followed similar changes in China, in which all land was vested in the emperor, reallocated among the peasants, and taxed. These modifications in Japan were carried out and policed by a public service modelled on the mandarinate. The custom of making compulsory military service part of the peasants' tax burden was copied. Since the Japanese army had no external enemy to fight, the conscripts were used as labourers on public works.

Such a project was a capital city, Nara, modelled on Ch'ang-an. The Empress Gemmyo began this work in 694, copying Ch'ang-an's layout of straight intersecting streets (which would eventually become a pattern worldwide), its styles of architecture and landscape gardening. T'ang music was also imported, and while it has disappeared in China, it has been preserved through the centuries in the Japanese Court.

Nara was the first big city in Japan even though its ambitious early plans were never completed, and has given its name to the succeeding era of sinification of Japanese society. The Emperor Shomu devoted his life and much of the energies of his people to good works inspired by Buddhism. Much of his work was to the benefit of the community – almshouses, hospitals, wayside halts for travellers, improved roads and bridges. Of less practical value was the building of a 53 foot high statue of the Buddha, the largest bronze statue in the world and still a major tourist attraction in Nara. This work became

Shomu's greatest preoccupation, at enormous cost to Japan. In 737 a plague of smallpox came to Japan from China which was so severe it inspired the emperor to build the statue in the hope this would ward off the disease.

At least seven big monasteries grew up in and around Nara. These quickly became centres of considerable influence and wealth. Abbots armed their monks as a means of protecting the monasteries against bandits, but later used these small armies aggressively, even demanding concessions from the emperor. It was probably Buddhist pressure that induced the Emperor Kwammu to move to a new capital in 794. At first it was called Heian, meaning peace and prosperity, but was later simply known as the capital – *kyoto*, the name it bears to this day.

The Heian period saw something of an exhaustion of the impetus given to Japanese civilisation by China. Regular contacts dwindled with the decline of the T'ang Dynasty, and ceased altogether in 894. The spirit of the *taika* reforms had, in fact, vanished much earlier. The bureaucracy suffered from being a slavish copy of the forms of the mandarinate while lacking its traditions. Japan drifted back into feudalism. One by one the provincial governors and other high officials obtained tax exemptions and used these to develop large estates.

The imperial family now came increasingly under the control of the Fujiwara clan. Fujiwara tactics, henceforward, were to marry regularly into the imperial family then force abdications in favour of heirs of tender years. This resulted in long periods of Fujiwara regency and the family became the effective rulers of Japan. This control of the nation by one of a number of powerful, competing cliques became characteristic of Japan, and is still manifest in the *ha* – factions – in modern Japan which make up so much of its political establishment.

Although Kyoto continued to be the capital until 1869, from this time on the emperors, with rare exceptions, were little more than prisoners – abstract symbols of inherited *kami*, too holy either to act on their own initiative or to be approached by ordinary men. The aristocracy grouped around the emperor drifted out of touch with the people, and, like the French Court before the revolution, devoted its time and resources almost exclusively to the pursuit of art and manners.

This society is described in clear and penetrating style in a remarkable novel called the *Tale of Genji*, written by the Lady Murasaki Shikibu, who was a resident of the Japanese Court, probably in the early eleventh century. Her diaries add to a picture of a shallow, amoral and luxury-loving society, at times capable of considerable artistic expression, but in the main occupied with, or bored by, trifles. The courtiers feared and disliked the crude ways of the rest of the country, and for an official to be sent from the Court to the provinces was regarded as a disgrace and banishment to a way of life virtually insupportable.

The truth was that the real power resided in the regions away from Kyoto. New areas of settlement and cultivation were opened up and the great feudal families grew more powerful. Among them were two dominating clans, both offshoots of the imperial line, who involved Japan in her equivalent of the Wars of the Roses. These two families, the Taira and the Minamoto, engaged in a struggle to replace the waning power of the Fujiwara, who had been weakened by internal dissension. At first the Taira had some success but finally their enemy, under the command of Minamoto Yoritomo, was victorious. He established, in 1185, a military dictatorship which called itself the *bakufu*, which means camp government. This regime was based far from Kyoto in the town of Kamakura, not far from the present Tokyo. So Japan was set on a path of feudal militarism that extended through into the twentieth century.

The great military clans had been strengthened because of what was regarded as the disgraceful defeat of Japanese armies during a particularly stubborn revolt of the Ainu minority in the eighth century. This defeat, in the year 790, was the last to be imposed on the Japanese army until the tide turned in the Pacific phase of World War Two more than 1100 years later. Widespread conscription was introduced to subdue the Ainu, who would never again be a threat to the Japanese.

By the middle of the tenth century this military tradition

had developed a code in many ways comparable with knight-hood during the so-called age of chivalry in Europe. In Japan it was based on an hereditary caste of soldiers, the *samurai*, which was to dominate Japanese society into modern times.

Although the Kamakura period was one of military rule, it had distinguished artistic achievements, especially landscape painting and sculpture, with the first signs of an emerging style significantly different from the Chinese. Typical is a vivid statue of the *kami* of thunder, Rai-Jin, which still stands in Kyoto. It surges with a crude and even a cruel vitality; mouth open in a snarl showing savagely-bared teeth; right hand raised ready to strike; staring eyes and bulbous nose – all these bear eloquent witness to the artistic force of the Kamakura era.

It was at this stage that military tradition merged with Bud-dhism, especially the Zen school with its stress on action and insistence on simplicity. It demands from its adherents a rigid discipline, hardship and great courage. It eschews logic – most of its few statements of belief are paradoxes. It is therefore not possible to describe Zen in words. The discipline, hard-ship, courage and long periods of calm meditation required of its adherents are designed eventually to create in them an in-ner experience which is beyond verbal description and which is the spiritual essence of Zen. This inner enlightenment is called *satori*.

Japanese architecture developed the simple, sparsely-ornamented style that remains typical today. In other arts, notably flower arranging, the formal tea ceremony and garden design, equal restraint came to be practised. One classic garden con-sists of nothing more than 15 carefully-placed stones on an area of raked, white sand.

In time, the spirit of the era seems to have inspired even the imperial family. The Kamakura government was ended in 1333 by the Emperor Go-Daigo. After some misadventures his forces were able to attack and defeat the *bakufu*. After taking, with much ceremony, the traditional small cups of Japanese rice wine, *sake*, the leaders and one thousand fol-lowers of the *bakufu* committed ceremonial suicide by the slow and painful process of disembowelling.

Go-Daigo did not, however, rule for long. His own general, Ashikaga Takauji, who had largely been responsible for the campaign against the *bakufu*, usurped power in 1338. A phase of almost constant war followed. The Ashikaga *shoguns*, or regents, were considerable patrons of the arts, but woefully inept at administration. Under their rule, Japanese society dissolved into civil war and banditry. In the fifteenth century Kyoto was sacked and burned. As almost all its buildings were of wood, much of the capital was destroyed.

During the confusion members of the imperial family had, at times, to beg and sell their calligraphy to stay alive. Two branches competed for the succession. Again there was something of a parallel with Chinese history, as society drifted off into anarchy. It was to wait a century for the strong men who would bring it back to order.

7

. . . .

The Awakening of Europe and the Challenge of Islam

Europe still consisted largely of small villages and somewhat larger castle towns, scattered through the forests. To this comparative handful of uneducated people Asia was little more than a legend. While a few scholars were dimly aware that great civilisations had flourished there, their concepts were largely of a region of queer, supernatural events, acted out by personalities either grotesque or larger than life.

Such a figure was Presbyter – or more commonly, Prester – John, a Christian monarch believed to govern, somewhere in Asia, an empire of fabulous wealth and power, administered by 72 subject kings. He was supposed to possess magical powers and devices, one of which was a mirror in which he could see events happening anywhere in his realm. It is symptomatic of the state of civilisation in Europe that such stories were accepted with apparent credulity, not only by peasants but even by scholars and kings.

Through the first millennium a tenuous link with Asia had been maintained. The Venetian empire, dominating the Adriatic, became the European terminus of three trade routes: a caravan track east from the Black Sea, an overland and sea route from Damascus, and another route through the Red Sea. Trade with the East was essentially small in bulk, because of the small size and slowness of shipping, and because the land

routes followed a scattered chain of oases, crossing formidable deserts and regions of predatory tribes. Only expensive
luxuries like silk, fine porcelain and spices were worth carrying in these conditions, but there was a steady and lively demand
for them that kept the trade alive in spite of all difficulties.
Spices, especially pepper, were in high demand in a Europe
which had no reliable way of preserving meat, to eliminate
traces of tainting during the long winters. Other spices were
highly regarded as medicines almost up to the modern era.

The efficiency of the overland routes depended a great deal
on political conditions. They were quickly affected by the advent,
early in the seventh century, of a new and militant religion
based on one god, Allah. This Islamic faith took a swift hold
in the Middle East. It was still regional at the time of its
founder Mohammed but grew rapidly under the control of his
lifelong friend and supporter Abu Bekr, who became Mohammed's first *caliph*, or successor.

Islam drove eastward through the wandering nomad tribes,
gaining adherents rapidly through its uncompromising offer
of conversion to the faith or death. It absorbed and adapted
the sophisticated Persian empire and penetrated to the borders
of China. To the west it occupied Spain, Portugal and half of
France, presenting a ringing challenge and a brilliant civilisation that helped to lift Europe from its apathy and ignorance.
Trade languished on the land routes: a flourishing sea trade to
Canton, in southern China, developed, largely in Arab and
Persian ships.

Nevertheless, the new Arab religion was not spread as far
as south-east Asia in its original form. It had been adapted
and liberalised considerably in Persia (now Iran), before it
was spread to northern India and then on to Malaysia and
Indonesia by merchants operating through the entrepot port of
Cambay. It is for this reason that there are major differences
in the modern world among Islamic nations, especially in regard to women. As far east as Pakistan they are discouraged,
if not forbidden to become educated, and are generally restricted to their homes, forced to wear the *chador*, the ugly

and cumbersome all-over robe, if they venture out in public. In Moslem Indonesia and Malaysia women endure no such restrictions. Indeed the Minangkabauer people of Sumatra are matrilineal, with women substantially controlling families and responsible for their finances and property.

Moslem culture was at its height around the end of the first millennium. It was Islam's capture of Jerusalem in 1076 that drew the European states into the great, if disastrous adventure of the Crusades. However, ultimately it was Mongol hordes who eventually destroyed the brilliant Moslem metropolis of Baghdad when they over-ran it in 1258.

Nevertheless, the Moslem dynasty of the Ottoman Turks continued to present an effective block to European sea trade with the east by dominating the eastern Mediterranean and the Red Sea from the fifteenth century onward. Indirect access to India and the Spice Islands was still to be had across the land routes, but these were slow and expensive. A sea route, especially one that could be travelled wholly by European ships, was much to be preferred.

In 1453 the Ottoman Turks captured and used for their capital Constantinople (now Istanbul), until that date the seat of the later, truncated Roman empire. For 50 years afterwards the Turks made concessions to one Italian state, Venice, which allowed her a monopoly of the Asian trade. The merchants of Venice waxed rich, so giving the other states of Europe an even greater incentive to break this monopoly. This anti-Venetian, anti-Moslem drive, combined with a half-religious, half-commercial ambition to make contact with the empire of Prester John, induced a lifelong effort in a Portuguese prince, Henry the Navigator, to seek a sea route east via the west coast of Africa.

Europe was beginning to recover from the appalling trauma of the Black Death in the fourteenth century. Probably pneumonic plague, it was the biggest known disaster in human history, reducing the population of the world by about one-third, and in some parts of Europe, by more than half.

Henry encouraged marine studies at Sagres, in the south-west corner of Portugal, where the half-forgotten maps, sailing directions and methods of navigation of the past were carefully re-examined. Portuguese shipmasters pored over the Guide to Geography prepared by the Alexandrian Ptolemy in the second century. Henry was assisted by the Genoese, anxious to supplant Venice.

The wooden ships, often as small as 40 tons and tragically unwieldy and topheavy, edged their way down the stormy leeshore of Africa. Many were lost, but the hard experience bought with the lives of ships and men led to important advances in naval architecture. A lighter, faster vessel named the caravel, and a bigger design, the armed carrack, were evolved and, in spite of their clumsiness, were able to survive the Atlantic storms. These larger ships also tended to make trade in bulk commodities, rather than lightweight luxuries, feasible for the first time.

In 1487 Bartholemew Diaz reached and rounded the southern extremity of Africa – the Cape of Storms. With much rejoicing, it was renamed the Cape of Good Hope. In 1498 Vasco da Gama reached India, and the eagerly-sought sea route to the east lay open. Portugal lost no time in exploiting it, despatching six expeditions between 1501 and 1505. The largest of these consisted of 20 ships manned by 2500 men, led by the first Viceroy of the East, Francisco d'Almeida. Efforts were made to drive away the interlopers, but the Portuguese won a major naval battle off the north-west Indian port of Diu in 1509. The following year the Portuguese established their base at Goa, and armed it as a fortress.

European infiltration of Asia had begun, and with it a new era. Profits on the early expeditions were so great that the share of the lowliest crew member could amount to a small fortune. A small consignment of pepper brought home by Vasco da Gama in 1499 paid for the entire cost of the expedition several times over.

Other nations of Europe were also resolved to seek adventure and fortune in the East. The dawn of the year 1520 saw the three small topheavy ships commanded by Ferdinand

Magellan four months and thousands of miles out from their home port of Seville. Sailing west, he made landfalls in the Philippines in March, and more than two years later one ship, *Vittoria*, reached home to become the first to sail around the world. By the end of the century a Spanish colony based on Manila in the Philippines was firmly established.

The Tudor monarchs of England built on the maritime tradition created by centuries of fishing in the stormy North Sea. Henry the Eighth brought in Italians to advise on the design of ocean-going ships, and offered a cash bounty to subsidise the building of new merchantmen. When Francis Drake returned in 1580 from his voyage around the world he brought a small package of cloves acquired at Ternate in the Moluccas, then known as the Spice Islands. On the last day of 1600 the East India Company was founded, with a Royal Charter giving it the monopoly of trade with the East.

Holland was next in the field. In 1602 she formed her own East India Company, with the then immense capital of more than half a million sterling pounds. In 1619 the Dutch established a base at a fortified village in Java called Jakarta. They called it Batavia.

The geographic advantage of the Atlantic nations over the Mediterranean, especially Venice, was to set the pattern for the colonial era. One of the great 'might have beens' of history was the failure to bring to fruition the 1504 consideration by the Venetian Council of Ten for a Suez Canal. If the canal could have been built then, instead of three hundred years later, Asia's major relationship with Europe would have been much earlier, and perhaps on more equal terms.

This period of exploration and trade expansion also brought the first crude enquiry into, and speculation about, economic forces. The earliest theorists, who maintained a persistent although diminishing influence for several centuries, were called the bullionists. They believed the prosperity of a nation was related to the amount of gold and silver bullion it was able to hoard. A further step was taken by the mercantilists, who held that this desirable accretion of bullion could best be achieved by having a favourable balance of trade with as many outside areas as possible – in other words, to take out more than was put in. One of the more profitable areas of commerce was the slave trade – around eight million forcibly seized and sent to America alone, plus perhaps two million more who died during transportation in the appalling conditions in the slave ships. Exploitation of other races soon found philosophic rationalisation, notably from the eighteenth century Swedish botanist Carolus Linnaeus. Linnaeus, who was highly regarded in Europe, firmly asserted the biological superiority of the white races, and this was at times used to justify the atrocities to come.

It is important to note this mercantilist theory, since it was the justification for a policy followed into modern times, which assumed colonies to be chiefly valuable as places perpetually milked of their wealth to the benefit of the conquering country. Autocratic political control, backed if necessary by armed force, was used to make sure the system was maintained. This, among other things, led to the Boston Tea Party and the loss of Britain's American colonies. Its effects in Asia were, ultimately, to be no less profound.

8

China: The Sung, Mongol, and Ming Dynasties

In 1206 a central Asian people, the Mongols, gathered in conference and elected a new leader, Genghis Khan. The choice was a wise one, for this man had already achieved a high reputation as a military planner among a people notorious for their ability and ruthlessness in war.

Under the leadership of Genghis Khan and his successors the Mongols built up the largest empire the world had yet seen, including the greater part of the Eurasian landmass; all except India, Western Europe, Arabia and a part of Indo-China. The Chinese section of this vast empire was ruled directly by the Great Khans, Genghis himself, and his successors. Regions farther west were virtually autonomous, but their rulers owed a token allegiance to the Great Khan.

The most detailed account of the Mongol Empire comes from the Venetian adventurer Marco Polo, who was in the service of the Great Khan, at that time Kublai. Marco Polo's view of the Great Khan and his empire is always favourable and often sycophantic, which is not surprising seeing he was Kublai's employee. He often exaggerates, his sense of geography is vague, and most deceptive of all, he attributes to Kublai a huge and sophisticated civilisation which was really the creation of the previous Chinese government. His book nevertheless gives a fascinating eye-witness account of Chinese civilisation in the thirteenth century.

The Mongol subjugation of China, then ruled by the cultured, refined and broad-minded Sung emperors, must be recognised as one of the major events of history. Although at the time of the conquest Sung China occupied only the southern half of the country, the population under its rule had already passed the hundred million mark, making it the largest nation in the world.

The simple fact of the conquest in 1279 after three years of bitter fighting was, then, a resounding event in world terms, yet it was even more so in its implications for the future. From this time onwards China was to diverge increasingly from the ideal culture it so much admired and which the Sung so closely approached. There was to be only one more native dynasty, the Ming, but powerful though it was it became bigoted, inward-looking and conservative. In the Mongol conquest then, was the seed of the great Chinese disasters of the nineteenth and twentieth centuries.

When the T'ang Dynasty crumbled early in the tenth century, five short-lived military 'dynasties' ruled successively in the north. There was a great deal of warfare and destruction, but the learning and traditions of China were preserved in the more peaceful south, especially in the Southern T'ang and the Southern Han, states founded by T'ang provincial governors who took control as the central authority declined. It is worth noting here a characteristic which is something of a constant in Chinese history, and which is still very much in evidence today – the considerable autonomy of provincial governments.

In 960 yet another general was acclaimed emperor, but the founder of this sixth dynasty, Chao K'uang-yin, was so able the Sung state he founded was not only more lasting than its predecessors, but also went on to an extraordinary brilliance for the world of its time. Chinese manufacture, especially the fine porcelain that came to be known as *china*, was in demand throughout the world and commanded an immense export trade by the standards of the time. Canton became one of the world's biggest ports. Book printing had become commonplace and many private citizens had libraries, with books printed in up to five colours, centuries before the production of the Gutenberg Bible, Europe's first-known printed book, in 1456. All of the arts flourished, especially painting and letters. The works of more than 1000 Sung poets are known.

The world's appreciation of its debt to Sung China is still increasing. There is, for instance, no known European record of the supernova explosion of 1054 which resulted in the Crab Nebula, even though the star grew so bright it could easily be seen in daylight. Yet, according to the British astronomer Fred Hoyle, modern science is much indebted to the careful records the astronomers of Sung China made of this event. Sunspots, studied by Europeans for the first time in 1610, had been observed and recorded in the Chinese annals 59 times during the previous 1500 years. This has made it possible for modern astronomers to calculate the solar activity cycle during that time.

Sung China had a relatively modern economy, using paper money and credit banking designed to facilitate inter-city trade. It developed inoculation against smallpox, maintained street lighting, street-cleaning, sanitary and fire protection services in the cities; provided hospitals, almshouses, orphanages and homes for the aged which were financed by trusts to ensure inalienable income; and encompassed a remarkable number of inventions ranging from hand grenades and repeating crossbows to hydraulic machinery in the world's biggest ironworks.

Major textbooks covered almost all areas of science – architecture, mathematics, geography, medicine, horticulture. There was a specialist book on growing citrus fruit and in 1242 the world's first known book on forensic medicine was published. The use of the so-called 'arabic' system of numbering was used in China at about the same time as it appeared among the Arabs, prompting speculation that it originated somewhere in Indo-China. There was an enthusiastic science of archeology researching earlier Chinese coins, ceramics and bronzes. The huge library at the Imperial palace housed four celebrated works – a literary anthology going back four centuries, a thousand-chapter encyclopedia, a vast collection of strange stories and fables, and a massive anthology of political texts and essays.

The system of recruiting the mandarinate by public examinations became fully-developed, so attempting an aristocracy of intelligence rather than of family and wealth. The fact that the ability of aspiring officials to paint and write poetry was tested has often been misunderstood. The examinations were primarily for administrative ability, but the mandarins were expected to be 'complete men' – accomplished in every way.

The lightly-ornamented and simply-styled porcelain, such as its green celadon, the delicate painting and understated poetry of the Sung have in the past been dismissed as 'primitive' by earlier Western critics, bred to the florid Victorian taste. It is only the modern West that has recognised in Sung art a sophistication it has itself approached.

One of the more eminent scholar-magistrates of the period, Su Tung-p'o, embittered by a series of reverses in his career, wrote this upon the birth of his son:

Families, having a child
Ask that it be intelligent.
But I, through intelligence
Have destroyed my whole life.
So I only hope the baby will turn out
Ignorant, stupid,
And end a peaceful life
As a Cabinet Minister.

The powerhouses of Sung society were its intensive and highly-organised agriculture, the great cities, some of more than a million people, along the rivers, canals and seacoast, and the world's largest merchant navy. Chinese ships had up to five masts, drop-keels, balanced stern rudders and watertight compartments, and could carry up to 1000 people. Experiments in other forms of boats, especially for inland waters, were various, and included crank-operated paddle wheels. Some had up to 25 such cranks, linked by metal connecting-rods. Accurate maps and charts listed depth soundings.

The cities provided every form of pleasure and indulgence, with playhouses, shadow theatres, acrobatic and performing monkey shows, wineshops, gaming houses, brothels open until dawn. Viewing the first plum blossoms, by the light of a spring moon, over snow fields, was a popular cult – indeed Sung poets and painters were virtually obsessed by the purity and simplicity of these flowers.

Zhang Zhi, a rich dilettante of the time, set out a list of what did and did not accord with plum-blossoms. Strong wind, continuous rain, hot sun, bad poetry, gossip about current events, discussing financial matters and erecting purple screens opposite the flowers, were no-nos. The list of things that accorded with plum blossoms included gentle shade, fine mist, early-morning sun, making tea, playing chess on a stone board (according to Maggie Bickford in an article in *Orientations*).

This era brought a revulsion against the power and wealth of the Buddhist monasteries, with purges and proscriptions in the ninth century that saw thousands destroyed, followed by a renewed interest in Confucianism. This neo-Confucianism set rigid patterns that persisted through to the twentieth century. Although it was designed to assert Confucianism as an ethic supplanting Buddhism and Taoism, in many respects it turned out to be a synthesis of all three. The new system was certainly far removed from the thought of its nominal founder. Indeed Confucius himself was virtually deified. To him, as well as to the sun, moon and certain nature gods, the second grade or 'middle' sacrifices were made.

However, Confucianism remained based on ancestor worship and the cult of the family. While having religious aspects, its main effects were ethical. The emperor was a father figure in a society that regarded the father as all-powerful in his own family. Filial piety became the outstanding virtue and family relationships were closely defined and regulated. This force for conservatism and respect for established rites and definitions of conduct led eventually to the narrowness of the official mind and disinclination for change so much responsible for the Chinese disasters of the nineteenth century. In spite of these reforms, which meant much more to the official class than the ordinary people, Buddhist influences persisted into Sung times and undoubtedly contributed much towards the liberality and broadmindedness of the dynasty.

The Sung state had a great deal of trouble with its army, in spite of spending vast sums on it. Soldiering was not highly regarded as a profession. During the period between the collapse of the T'ang and the rise of the Sung China had suffered greatly from the depredations of warlords and the mandarins were concerned to keep the military in its place. The army had become more used to plundering than to battle. It did not have the fine edge, good organisation and utter disregard for human life of the Mongols.

Mongol methods were total war to a degree seldom equalled before or since. When they conquered the northern state of Kin, which had already forced the Sung to retreat to the south, they virtually depopulated it. Its capital, Beijing, was almost wiped out, then burned. The Mongol troops were under orders to exterminate the population of cities that offered the slightest resistance and the fate of some of China's north-west cities was a terrifying example. Some of these have never again been populated, remaining desolate to this day. It is not surprising that the southern Sung capital, Hangchow, surrendered in 1276.

The populous and wealthy world of China presented an extreme contrast to the Mongols. They were largely illiterate and poor, and numbered perhaps three million. The victory brought into the conquerors' service some shrewd and able public servants, who were able to convince the Mongols they would be better off to maintain Chinese society as it was, and profit from taxing it. Not only was Chinese culture largely preserved, it was able to exert an influence on the Mongols that refined and educated many of them. The great Mongol leader so admired by Marco Polo, Kublai Khan, was sinified in this way and developed a liberality and interest in art and culture that would have amazed his forebears.

Thus the conquerors were largely absorbed by the conquered. Chinese ways spread outside China itself and became fashionable in other parts of the Mongol empire. The military discipline initially imposed by the conquerors even allowed China to grow physically. What is now Yunnan Province was a separate kingdom called Nanchao until 1253, when its Thai people were driven south into the valleys of Laos and other parts of south-east Asia.

Kublai was unable to invade Japan in spite of two great expeditions he sent against those islands in 1274 and 1281. Seasonal typhoons scattered his fleet, with heavy losses. This great wind, or *kamikaze*, was regarded by the Japanese as divine intervention. In 1945, as allied ships closed in on the Japanese islands, the same name was used for suicide aircraft that were deliberately crashed on the decks of warships.

By the early fourteenth century Mongol rule had already begun to weaken. Its parasitic nature had become increasingly obvious after the death of Kublai in 1294. In 1333 a series of unusually severe famines began and persisted for a decade. The reserve granaries were soon exhausted. Then in 1351 the Yellow River burst its levees, bearing thousands of acres of productive farmland down to the sea and destroying hundreds of villages. By 1356 paper money had become valueless and the printing of it was discontinued. The population fell, to perhaps 80 millions.

From early times the peasant revolt had been China's natural answer to tyrannical or inefficient government and also, grimly enough, to pressures of population. Over-population, combined with the failure of the central government, resulted in famine. This in turn led to insurrection. As society became further disorganised, the population was hugely reduced by starvation, massacre and sickness. When stability was resumed under a new regime the cycle recommenced.

Perhaps because of this a certain lack of regard for individual human life became a part of the Chinese tradition. Modern China, for instance, finds it difficult to understand the criticism it attracts for continued capital punishment. The Great Leap Forward, the attempt to force China into an industrial breakthrough between 1959 and 1962, is estimated by Jonathan Spence (*The Search for Modern China*, p. 503) to have caused at least 20 million deaths from famine caused by the ruthless seizure and export of grain to pay for imported machinery.

When the Chinese peasants were pressed hard enough to revolt, they organised within mutual assistance societies, which remained dormant for many decades or even centuries, only to become active when circumstances demanded. These societies were so firmly based even the mandarins hesitated to tamper with them. The oldest and most famous of the secret societies organising the peasants was the White Lotus. It appears to have played a consolidating role in the peasant revolts that ousted the Mongols.

The main impetus of revolt came from the south. Here Chu Yuan-chang, who would soon drive the Mongols out of China, began his career. He was an orphan of humble origins who rose to command of a rebel group through sheer force of personality and ability in the doubtful arts of intrigue. He concentrated on consolidating a significant area of power around the strategic Yangtse River city of Nanking, which he occupied in 1356. Twelve years later, when he dominated south China, he sent a huge army north to Beijing. The Mongols fled before it without a fight.

The humble peasant-adventurer now became emperor, giving himself the reign name of Hung Wu, which means 'vast military achievement'. The dynasty he commenced in 1368 was the Ming. As might have been expected from the nature of his career, Hung Wu's authority was direct, brutal and decisive. He is said to have had a furious temper and to have imposed the death penalty more or less on whim. Although he was an able administrator, his methods were a far cry from those of the Sung. Hung Wu refused to have a prime minister, as they had done, and when fairminded mandarins with a sense of duty ventured to remonstrate with him he had them beaten with bamboo clubs, often enough to death.

Hung Wu remained faithful to Nanking, which now became the capital. After his death the throne was inherited by his 16-year-old grandson, who was immediately challenged by his uncle, the Prince of Yen, a warlord based in Beijing and responsible for guarding the northern borders. He took Nanking in 1402, becoming emperor under the reign name of Yung Lo. Nineteen years later he moved the capital back to Beijing which, then on the edge of China, had a vulnerability that would ultimately prove dangerous and, finally, fatal to the dynasty. Situating the capital at Beijing not only placed it close to marauding tribesmen on the other side of the Great Wall, but also involved a huge cost in maintaining roads and canals to the south. Finally, it tended to encourage the persistent southern tendency towards autonomy.

Yung Lo had, however, inherited vast power. The empire was now larger and more populous than the whole of Europe, and its wealth and resources far greater. Even though she had diverged from her ideal of government China was now at the pinnacle of her material power. In no way is this more forcibly indicated than by the great sea expeditions sent out during the Yung Lo reign. Chinese ships ranged throughout Asia – indeed as far afield as East Africa – and by the end of the first quarter of the fifteenth century had brought home token fealty and tribute from scores of Asian principalities. A live giraffe from Africa was brought to Beijing, and presented to the emperor. Calling at Timor, the Chinese ships came very close to Australia. A significant comparison can be made between Chinese sea power and the Portuguese fleet that took d'Almeida to India in 1505. With its 20 ships and 2500 men it was the largest yet to sail to Asia from Europe. Exactly a century before, in 1405, the Ming Empire sent its first fleet to India. It consisted of 62 ships and nearly 30,000 men, and was only the first of seven such expeditions.

It is interesting to speculate on the possible shape of events had the ships of Europe, coming to Asia a century later, found it already controlled by a Chinese navy, policing a Chinese maritime empire. Looked at in this way, the cessation of China's great sea expeditions in 1433 becomes a fact of major importance in European as well as Asian history. Yung Lo had all the means at his disposal to dominate the world and lay the foundations of an immense empire except the will to do so. He used his great fleets casually, almost as toys. He looked, always with anxiety, to the north. The thought of permanent dominion in south and south-east Asia seems never to have crossed his mind.

The Chinese felt that in their world they had achieved perfection and came to regard all other nations with a casual arrogance and suspicion as 'barbarians'. The term 'Middle Kingdom' for so long used by the Chinese as the name of their country took on new overtones as they increasingly saw it as the centre of the world, with tributary nations arrayed around it. After 1430 Chinese were forbidden to leave her shores without special licenses.

In 1514 the first Portuguese ships arrived in China. Early encounters were often unfortunate, since the Portuguese almost always mixed trade with piracy. This confirmed Chinese suspicion of Europeans generally. When a trading post was set up at Macao in 1557 it was carefully policed by the Chinese, and Europeans were restricted to their remote base on an isolated southern peninsula.

Land contact with Europe came from the north-west, as the Muscovite Ivan the Fourth drove east from the Volga marshes, then the border of Russia. Within one more century Russian expansionism had given China a new and troublesome neighbour.

Whatever the shortcomings of the Ming, they presided over a vast, intensely productive state. Much of the antiquities the tourist to China sees today are of Ming provenance, including the dynasty's subterranean tombs on the outskirts of Beijing and most of the present fabric of the Great Wall.

The Ming Dynasty did not show serious signs of weakness until the reigns of the last four emperors. It entered its phase of most rapid deterioration between 1620 and 1627, when the T'ien-ch'i emperor reigned. He was only 15 when he came to the throne and was dominated by a predatory official, Wei Chung-hsien, who used his power to enrich himself and strike down any honest or courageous official who sought to oppose him. The architects of the Ming demise were a formidable army of eunuchs, probably as many as 70,000 of them towards the dynasty's end. Presiding over the elaborate and ritualised life of the court they used their position to accumulate wealth and power at any cost, including mass murder of their opponents, intimidation and at times covert assassination of emperors. When the last Ming emperor, Ssu-tsung, came to the throne in 1627 he made a last desperate effort to reorganise the government, but matters had gone too far for reform. The competent and honest men had already been destroyed and the pervading selfish and cynical factionalism had eroded the dynasty of support.

Away from the intrigues of Beijing, the people suffered from a breakdown in administration, an increase in taxes, and tyranny from officials that set an ugly pattern for the future. Already the peasants were in revolt. When one of their popular leaders seized the capital in 1644 the emperor, in despair, could see no possible course except death. He hanged himself, from a branch of a tree outside a graceful triple-tiered pavilion that still stands on Beijing's Coal Hill.

9

China: The Years of Decline

Power to replace the Ming was already waiting – to the north, as Yung Lo had feared. In 1583 a gifted leader called Nurhachi had persuaded a group of nomad tribes to unite in a largely military union, the Manchu confederacy. In 1644 Beijing fell to Chinese warlord Li Zicheng, one of many who exploited and exacerbated the social disorder and poverty in the country, and who lost no time in pillaging the capital. The Manchus took advantage of a last desperate struggle between Li and the Ming loyalists to invade China unopposed. When they entered Beijing with the support of the Ming generals they were at first cautious, insisting they were only there to support the lawful authority. But when a Ming prince was proclaimed in Nanking they made war on him and proclaimed their own child emperor ruler of China. Seventeen years later the Ming prince was forced into exile in Burma but the Manchu agents, fully aware of the dangers of a living Ming pretender, pursued him even there and killed him by strangling with a bow-string.

Manchu rule was not easily imposed in the south of China and never really accepted there. For many years, indeed, through the two and a half centuries of Manchu rule, there continued to be a persistent but small minority that affected to champion the Ming cause. Even today the slogan 'restore the Ming, supplant the Ch'ing' (Manchu) remains in the rituals of Chinese secret societies in Singapore. It is said that one of the first actions of Dr Sun Yat-sen, after the foundation of the Chinese republic at the end of Manchu rule in 1911, was to pray at the Ming imperial tombs.

The Manchus never allowed the Chinese to forget they were a conquered people. They required all men to shave the forepart of their heads and wear their hair in a queue – perhaps better known as a pigtail – as a sign of subjection. They also made efforts to maintain their identity, forming themselves into an administrative and military elite. Manchus were not allowed to work except as civil servants and soldiers and the Chinese people had to feed this large, non-productive group. Manchu garrisons were located in all cities and large towns. They were forbidden to intermarry with Chinese and the original Manchu capital at Mukden was maintained.

In spite of these precautions Manchu had by the nineteenth century become little more than a Court language and the invaders had become essentially sinified. The Chinese had again demonstrated their remarkable ability to assimilate a conqueror. This cultural merging was very evident at the end of the reign of the second emperor, K'ang Hsi, in 1722. A poet and a scholar with a deep interest in all aspects of knowledge, K'ang Hsi encouraged Christian Jesuit missionaries to live in China. Many of them stayed for years, even taking Chinese names, protected by the respect the emperor had for their knowledge and his gratitude, for the Jesuits had cured him of malaria by using cinchona bark – quinine – their order had supplied from South America. Nevertheless, when the Jesuits took exception to established Chinese rites, the emperor discouraged Christian missionary activity, which had virtually ceased by the early nineteenth century.

China expanded to its largest territorial extent in the eighteenth century, with the conquest of much of Sinkiang Province and renewed suzerainty over Korea and much of Vietnam. Tibetan opposition to a Chinese nominee as Dalai Lama led to an invasion in 1720 and the establishment of garrisons and a residency

there. Tibet remained under nominal Chinese control until the
Manchu collapse in 1911. Burma and Nepal were invaded.

The K'ang Hsi emperor's interest in European art and science was reciprocated in Europe, where many cultural and
artistic forms went through a phase of *chinoiserie*, an interest
in and copying of things Chinese. When the French novelist
and historian Voltaire wrote his *Customs of Nations* he devoted its first chapter proper to China. Although his account
was not accurate, it was in some respects perceptive:

> If one asks why so many arts and sciences have been cul-
> tivated uninterruptedly for so long in China and yet made
> so little progress, there are two possible answers: The first
> is the prodigious respect these people feel for everything
> which has been handed down by their fathers, and which
> makes everything ancient seem perfect in their eyes; and
> the other is the nature of their language, the foundation of
> all knowledge.
>
> The art of expressing one's ideas in writing, which ought
> to be something very simple, is something extremely difficult
> for them. Each word is expressed by a different character.
> A scholar, in China, is a man who knows most characters;
> some of them reach old age before knowing how to write well.

Although in some respects a reformer, K'ang Hsi maintained
the civil service examinations, now becoming increasingly
formalised, and fully supported the Confucian ethic. To all
outward appearances prosperity and order continued to be maintained during the rule of his grandson, who took the reign name
of Ch'ien Lung (Qianlong). During Ch'ien Lung's 60-year reign
China showed little sign of the collapse so close ahead. The
dynasty was now, for all practical purposes, Chinese. Ch'ien
Lung took pride in his support for the Chinese arts, especially
poetry, painting and calligraphy. He has left no fewer than
40,000 short poems of his own composition, and was a skilled
horseman and archer.

Only in the last decades of the eighteenth century did the

processes of decay become apparent. China was undergoing tremendous changes. The most significant was the huge growth rate of the population, which had reached 300 million. Populations were growing all over the world but in the West the challenge was met by a ferment of experiment and the rapid development of new skills and technology. The Chinese government, however, was chained by an arid conservatism. Faced with the great swirl of forces for change, only dimly recognised and undoubtedly feared, it looked steadfastly to the past and resisted any attempts at innovation.

A most serious consequence was a failure to improve agricultural methods. Overcrowding led to intensive cultivation of land until it became exhausted and would no longer bear crops. New land was often destroyed by erosion almost as soon as it was cleared. The Chinese were banned from the under-populated grasslands of Manchuria because these had to be preserved as the Manchu homeland.

The mandarinate also deteriorated, and was now far from its ideal of broad-minded, educated men administering wisely and with moderation. Instead, arrayed in their robes of office the mandarins travelled their domains in golden palanquins, escorted by men with whips who lashed out at any who obstructed the way or who failed promptly to grovel in obeisance. Unusual and cruel punishments became common, and were administered for trifling reasons. Death was not enough. Men were whipped on the soles of their feet until gangrene set in, or their heads confined in the cangue, a heavy wooden square which made it impossible for them to feed or care for themselves, then left to die slowly and painfully.

Manchu suspicion of the south led the government to forbid foreign trade except from Canton, which was badly located in relation to the sources of the main export products, tea and silk. The administration became increasingly lazy and effete. Pirates ravaged the coast, but little was done to control them. When Ch'ien-lung died in 1799 his favourite, Ho-shen, was impeached on charges of amassing a huge fortune looted from the administration, and forced to commit suicide.

Yet all these abuses, all the clamouring social and economic problems, did not lead to reform and correction, but rather to an even more repressive conservatism. Poverty grew year by year with the population, and famines of alarming proportions arose from quite mild seasonal variations. Rural poverty gradually developed towards its full horrors – the exposure of newborn girl babies in the fields at night to die, the selling of children into slavery, the growing rapacity of officials and landlords, themselves struggling on the edge of the abyss.

In 1795 poverty was so acute in Shensi, Hupei and Szechuan Provinces that the White Lotus Society raised a major peasant revolt that was not to be controlled for nine years. Two desperate attempts were made on the life of the emperor, in 1812 and again in 1814, and led to harsh reprisals.

China was not to be at peace for a century and a half. Bandits and Manchu armies alike, under the control of men who were warlords by nature and inclination, marched through the unhappy countryside, raiding and destroying crops, burning villages, pressing conscripts into their service. So the largest country in the world, the society that had prided itself on its superiority and civilisation, plunged into the trough. There had been such troughs before, but never with the same implications, for this one coincided with the reaching of the despised European 'barbarians' for the crest of the wave.

> Therefore, O king, as regards your request to send someone to remain at the capital, while it is not in harmony with the regulations of the Celestial Empire, we also feel very much that it is of no advantage to your country. Hence ... we have commanded your tribute envoys to return safely home.
>
> You, O king, should simply act in conformity with our wishes, by strengthening your loyalty and swearing perpetual obedience ...

In these words Ch'ien Lung addressed the choleric George III of England when, in 1793, the British government sent its first official mission to China to establish a resident at the

Manchu Court. The fiction that all foreign representatives came as bearers of tribute and fealty was maintained through this period of early contact with the West. Moreover, China could speak from the complacency of self-sufficiency. There was nothing she wanted from the outside world. A decision was taken to cease trade with foreigners altogether.

Britain, however, was anxious to trade more extensively, and pressures on China grew rapidly, especially after abolition of the East India Company's monopoly in 1833 brought spirited competition between a dozen companies for the lucrative trade in tea. This inevitably brought the two nations on a collision course. In June, 1840, a British naval squadron silenced the Chinese batteries on Tinghai Island, one of the group protecting the mouth of the Yangtse. Tinghai was captured by a task force of 3000 men and its inhabitants fled. Next the two large ports of Amoy and Ningpo were occupied. In alarm the regional authorities in Canton agreed provisionally to restore trade, but Beijing repudiated this and in January, 1841, the war was resumed.

The Chinese government had become concerned at the swift growth of the opium habit, especially when it began to drain silver reserves out of the country. The trade had been declared illegal in 1729 and its import forbidden in 1800, but it continued to flourish nevertheless. In 1838 Beijing had sent a mandarin, Lin Tse-hsu, as special commissioner to end the import of opium through Canton, which was still the only port foreigners were allowed to use. In that year opium imports had reached the massive total of more than 2000 tons a year, and the number of habitual users has been estimated as high as ten million. The fact that many of these were soldiers and officials increased the unease of the Chinese government.

Specially-built, fast ships, clippers like *Thermopylae, Nightingale* and *Cutty Sark*, raced from China to London at speeds as high as eighteen knots. Since these ships were built for speed rather than large cargo capacity, they required a commodity they could carry economically on the outward as well as the homeward-bound passages. Opium, with its high value for its weight and ready demand in China, suited this specification and was specially grown in India for the Chinese trade.

Commissioner Lin attempted negotiation to control the trade. He even wrote to Queen Victoria, saying . . . 'if there were people from another country who carried opium for sale to England and seduced your people into buying and smoking it, certainly you would deeply hate it and be bitterly aroused'. There being no response, Lin demanded the surrender of all opium stocks held in Canton. Hostilities began gradually, culminating in the arrival of the British expeditionary force in 1840 and actual invasion of China.

Britain's bombastic Foreign Minister, Lord Palmerston, had sought authorisation from Parliament for a punitive expedition to compel the Chinese to resume trading. 'The Chinese,' he said, 'must learn and be convinced that if they attack our people and factories they will be shot.'

William Gladstone, then an Opposition member, thought differently, saying . . . 'a war more unjust in its origin, a war more calculated in its progress to cover this country with permanent disgrace, I do not know, and I have not read of . . . our flag . . . is become a pirate flag to protect an infamous traffic'.

Parliament carried the motion for a punitive expedition by only nine votes.

The British warships were able to proceed up the Yangtse to the point, near Nanking, where the Grand Canal joins the river. With the southern capital defenceless under the guns of the foreign fleet and the batteries guarding the entrance to the Grand Canal silenced, the gravity of the situation could no longer be concealed from the Court. Among the British fleet was something new – the steam-driven ironclad *Nemesis*, whose shallow draught and manoevrability permitted her to do enormous damage.

China was forced to sue for peace and, as a result of the consequent Treaty of Nanking, agreed reluctantly to the resumption of trade. Britain had already seized Hong Kong Island as a base, and it was now ceded to her. Not only Canton but also four other 'treaty ports' – Amoy, Foochow, Ningpo and Shanghai – were to be opened to British shipping.

The opium trade flourished, imports doubling between 1830 and 1850. American merchants brought opium in from Turkey, and poppy plantations in China itself proliferated rapidly.

These events, and the fundamental injustice of forcing narcotic drugs on the Chinese, are a very important element of history taught to Chinese schoolchildren, and will continue to be in future. They also featured prominently in the celebrations and media coverage in China to mark the return of Hong Kong to China in 1997. Westerners dealing with China in any way would find themselves at a disadvantage if they betrayed ignorance, or lack of a proper appreciation, of the Opium Wars and their consequences.

The Treaty of Nanking proved unsatisfactory. The Chinese considered it to have been imposed on them by force, so they saw no reason why they should not evade its provisions if they could. The enforcement of similar treaties to the benefit of several European countries and the United States increased their anger.

Chinese intransigence resulted in a further war in 1856, designed to force her to comply. China was again defeated easily, and had to accept even more humiliating terms under the resulting Treaty of Tientsin (Tianjin). Now the importing of opium was legalised, foreigners were to be allowed to travel freely anywhere in China, and Christian missionaries were given freedom to operate wherever they chose. All these provisions were accepted by the Chinese, but with a bitter underlying hatred, especially for the final one, allowing the 'pale ghosts' to preach a militant Christian ethic to compete with Confucianism. Even though there were many converts and the missionaries did a great deal of good, founding hospitals, schools and orphanages for the thousands of girl babies left out to die slowly from exposure, a solid core of opposition to them persisted, and was covertly encouraged by the mandarins.

Resistance to the treaties brought war again in 1860. A joint Anglo-French mission – 38 men in all – had gone to Beijing under a safe conduct agreement to discuss the deadlock over the treaty terms. They were arrested on the orders of the Court, and 20 of them died in agony. They were tightly bound in new rope, then water was thrown on them, causing their bonds to shrink slowly.

A combined Anglo-French expedition marched on Beijing. Manchu cavalry, attacking at the charge, was blown to pieces from a safe distance by French artillery. Beijing capitulated and the emperor and his mother, the Dowager-Empress Tz'u-hsi (Cixi), fled. The beautiful Summer Palace near the capital was looted and destroyed in revenge for the death of the prisoners. One of the force that carried out this work was an English officer named Charles Gordon, later to become famous for his defence of Khartoum in the Sudan, and his tragic death there.

Gordon wrote to his mother: 'You can scarcely imagine the beauty and magnificence of the palaces we burned. It made one's heart sore to burn them. In fact these palaces were so large and we were so pressed for time that we could not plunder them carefully. Quantities of gold ornaments were burned, considered as brass.'

This was the last attempt by the Manchus to resist foreign domination overtly, and the Western powers now began to carve up China into 'spheres of influence'. Only jealousy between the powers, carefully cultivated by the Chinese, prevented the complete partition of the country. Nominally, it was allowed to remain independent. However Manchu rule was now on the foreigners' terms. These included foreign control of Chinese trade and revenues – the mainstays of government. An Englishman, Sir Robert Hart, was inspector-general of the maritime customs for more than 40 years from 1863.

Having secured the compliance of the Manchu dynasty, the powers now supported it against rival contenders, in particular the T'ai P'ing rebels. They were led by a visionary school-teacher named Hung Hsiu-ch'uan who, in 1851, proclaimed himself emperor of a rival dynasty. The new regime, which attracted enormous support throughout the anti-Manchu south, was based on ideas its founder had acquired from Christian tracts. The T'ai P'ing revolt was, in fact, a major civil war, similar to those which had led to the foundation of the Han and Ming dynasties. Some observers see in it the first large-scale manifestation of growing unrest and the desire for reform; a forerunner of the Communist revolution to come a century later.

Although it did advocate ideas of freedom, including the equality of the sexes and redistribution of land to the peasants, it is best not to regard the T'ai P'ing in too idealistic a light. For instance, recruits to its army had to memorise the Lord's Prayer and the Ten Commandments within three weeks on pain of execution; and the wives and children of the Manchu garrison in Nanking were burned alive after the fall of the city.

The T'ai P'ing achieved vast initial support. Its armies swept north to the Yangtse River and may well have overthrown the Manchu but for the support the dynasty got from European gunboats, artillery, and the 'Ever-Victorious Army', led by British officers.

It is worth noting, however, that the T'ai P'ing were not well-supported in north China, and lost much of their initiative after their capture of Nanking. Hung Hsiu-chu'an from that time onwards retreated into an ever more bewildering maze of religious mysticism, and religious oppression. The T'ai P'ing aroused wide opposition in the countryside by their habit of destroying Buddhist and Taoist temples. A notable victim was the nine storey, 250 feet high Porcelain Pagoda at Nanking, sheathed in white and gold tiles. The cost of the revolt and others – there had been an independent Moslem state in Yunnan for 15 years – to China was appallingly high; there could have been as many as 40 million dead. Many cities were destroyed and conditions rapidly became worse in the ravaged countryside.

So inefficient were the Manchu armies that efforts were made at improvement. Modern weapons were bought and German instructors recruited. But it was too little too late – these measures could not prevent China's defeat by Japan in 1894 in a war over the control of Korea, which had long been a Chinese tributary state. The resulting Treaty of Shimonoseki obliged China to surrender Formosa (Taiwan), the Pescadore Islands and the strategic Liaotung Peninsula of Manchuria. Japan now had a foothold on the Chinese mainland itself.

The decisive nature of Japan's victory led many Chinese intellectuals to believe China's only chance of survival as an independent nation was an urgent process of modernisation such as Japan was undergoing. One of these, K'ang Yu-wei, was able to persuade the young Chinese emperor to issue in 1898 a series of commands that would have started such a process of reform. Instead the dowager empress, supported by the mandarins, acted before the new measures could operate. The emperor was imprisoned until his death ten years later. K'ang Yu-wei escaped from China in the nick of time, but six of his associates were executed.

In 1900 came the last wave of violent reaction from the old regime – the attack on foreigners known as the Boxer Revolt. The Boxers, members of a society called the Righteous Harmony Fists, were encouraged by the dowager empress and some of her supporters in a final effort to 'destroy the foreigners'. In fact those to suffer most were the 'devil's disciples', the Chinese Christian converts, of whom 16,000 were killed. Armed Boxer bands attacked European missionaries in many parts of China, then converged on Beijing. They destroyed the German legation and killed the minister. All Europeans withdrew into the embassy quarter, which withstood a siege for nearly two months. In August China was invaded by an international force, including Japanese, which captured Beijing and relieved the embassies. The Chinese Court fled to Sian, in the north-east.

It was impossible that the old order should survive such events for long. It seemed to be maintained only by the iron willpower of the dowager empress. However even she could see the inevitability of change. In 1901 she ordered reforms in important directions, notably in methods of education. In 1904 the old civil service examinations, based on Confucian studies and the stilted, highly-formalised 'eight-legged essay', were abandoned. Western style schools were introduced and accepted eagerly by the Chinese. By 1910 there were 35,000

such schools, teaching more than a million pupils the rudi-
ments of a modern education. Many other Chinese studied
abroad, especially in Japan.

The younger men and women educated in this new tradition became deeply concerned for the future of their country.
The material of change was now in place, an explosive mixture awaiting the lighting of the fuse. Nor was this long in
coming. Late in 1908 the captive emperor died under mysterious
circumstances, probably poisoned by the Court mandarins, when
it became obvious that the aged dowager empress was near
her end. She died the following day, having nominated the
infant P'u Yi the tenth Manchu emperor. Only three years later,
still in early childhood, the last of the Manchus was deposed.

10

·········

The Three Makers of Japan and the Tokugawa Period

Japan as a unified nation was the creation of three opportunistic and treacherous men, artful enough to outwit and confuse the multitude of regional lords who in the sixteenth century controlled the country, and strong enough to set an imprint that would endure for many centuries.

The Ashikaga *shoguns*, acting as regents for the Imperial family, brought political chaos to Japan but, also – perhaps the one advantage of weak government – rapid advances in overall culture because of the freedom it gives to strong individuals and families. Although poor administrators, the Ashikaga were great patrons of the arts, which flourished surprisingly in conditions of almost constant war. This culminated in a bitter and largely pointless internecine conflict, the Onin wars, which commenced in 1467 a pattern of civil strife that would continue for nearly a century.

Many of the ancient families were destroyed and power became concentrated in the hands of a few powerful lords, ruling from fortified towns. These great regional leaders, called the *daimyo*, were to be an important factor in Japanese life from now on. Fortunes rose and fell rapidly and in this fluid environment the old feudal stratification of the community became blurred. In some cases bandit leaders rose from obscurity by sheer force of personality and came to command great influence. The capital, Kyoto, was burned, something which happened only too easily because its beautiful houses, temples and palaces were built of wood. The relaxation of central authority made it possible for the peasants to break free of their masters for a time and revolts were frequent. Some of these led to the creation of new regions of power.

It was this world of distinct, almost autonomous states controlled by the *daimyo* that the Portuguese found when they reached Japan in the middle of the sixteenth century. Generally speaking, the *daimyo* were willing to trade. They were intrigued with the matchlock musket and quickly saw the significance it could have in the struggle for power. Almost at once the Japanese learned how to copy these weapons and make them for themselves.

The heir to a small principality in the Nagoya region was one of the first to ponder the significance of firearms. This man, Oda Nobunaga, equipped an army with muskets almost as soon as he inherited his small estate. He used a skilful blend of force, intrigue, treachery and marriage alliances to extend his influence until in 1568 he was able to seize Kyoto.

He then consolidated his position around the capital. High on the slopes of a mountain he built a great castle – an almost impregnable stronghold of a kind not seen in Japan before. From this secure base he launched an attack on the centuries-old Buddhist monastery complex on Mount Hiei which, by this time, amounted to several thousand buildings – almost a city. Nobunaga destroyed it completely, and massacred 4000 monks, their families and dependents on a single day in 1571 without a shadow of pity, so bringing a time-honoured pressure group to an end. There is no evidence that Nobunaga was a particularly religious man. His dislike of Buddhism and his interest in Christianity sprang alike from political motives.

Roman Catholic monks of the Jesuit order had arrived in Japan hard on the heels of the Portuguese traders. Christianity flourished with amazing speed, and the number of converts soon ran into hundreds of thousands, representing all classes from the *daimyo* down. Nobunaga's support undoubtedly helped. Another great persuader was the association of missionary work with trade – often the monks actually controlled trading operations.

Oda Nobunaga was at the height of his power in 1582 and in his 50th year when he was treacherously killed by one of his generals, for reasons which cannot now be established accurately. He was avenged by another general, a vigorous, arrogant man named Hideyoshi. At first Hideyoshi ruled as regent for Nobunaga's infant grandson but within a year he had taken the leadership for himself. It was his role to build on the foundation Nobunaga had laid down, and he played this part with such vigour he commanded an army of a quarter of a million men towards the end of the decade.

Both Nobunaga and Hideyoshi were loyal to the imperial line, and at no time tried to usurp the functions of the emperors. In fact, both men did much to restore the pomp of the throne and freely conceded they ruled in its name. Hideyoshi also took other measures to secure a rigid social structure. Peasants were forced to hand in their swords, and the *samurai* were forbidden to work or own property. The *daimyo* in power at this time were reinforced in their positions and the *samurai* – about one in ten of the population – confirmed as a specialised military class which the unfortunate peasantry were compelled to support and obey without question.

Like his predecessor, Hideyoshi had been favourably disposed towards the Christians, but towards the end of the century his attitude changed. The new faith was perhaps growing too fast for his liking and he suspected the Jesuits of political ambitions. In 1567 he issued an edict ordering all foreign missionaries to leave the country within 20 days.

For ten years he enforced this new law only sporadically, but the problem of Christianity emerged again when the Japanese looted the wreck of a Spanish galleon blown off her course from Manila to Mexico. The Spanish captain objected vigorously, telling the Japanese about the mighty empire Spain had gained through the use of the Bible and the sword. When Hideyoshi was told of this he concluded that the missionaries might well be the forerunners of a bid for foreign political control of Japan. The following year, 1597, he crucified six Spanish Franciscan monks, three Portuguese Jesuits and 17 Japanese Christians after first torturing and mutilating them.

Hideyoshi was a swashbuckler of low birth, an adventurer, something of a *bon viveur* and an exhibitionist. He gave huge parties in the vast castle he built at Osaka, delighting in showing off its utensils – even its doorhandles – of pure gold. He seems to have felt the need for constant action to maintain his position. This was perhaps the reason for the expedition he launched against China in 1592, without any clear idea of the vast power of the Ming empire. The advance was made through Korea, which resisted the Japanese strenuously. China took a somewhat leisurely decision to send an army. It crossed the Yalu River early the next year and forced the Japanese to withdraw.

However, they were back again a few years later. Hostilities continued on and off until Hideyoshi's death in 1598 ended the pointless conflict. The Koreans, who were almost completely Chinese in their culture and outlook, bitterly resented this apparently wanton attack from the people they called the *wa* (dwarves), which caused immense distress and hundreds of thousands of deaths.

Like his predecessor, Hideyoshi had left an heir, his son Hideyori, who was in the charge of two regents. These men, however, commenced a struggle for power which ended in a great battle at Sekigahara in 1600, which was won by a Tokugawa named Ieyasu. The Tokugawa clan was now to control Japan for two and a half centuries, into modern times.

Hideyori, who had been betrayed in this way by the man into whose charge his father had given him, retreated with his supporters into the great castle in Osaka. Its eight-storied, many-gabled central keep was defended by a series of moats and walls – the outer one two miles long – and was virtually impregnable. Ieyasu besieged it for years, and finally took it by trickery in 1615.

He had promised Hideyori and his family favourable truce conditions and so persuaded them to weaken their defences. At the end of a treacherous surprise attack only one of Hideyori's family remained alive – his eight-year-old son Kunimatsu. Pitiless to the end, Ieyasu killed even this child, the last of the family of his former master.

So began the period known as the Tokugawa, during which the ruling elite imposed an iron conservatism and the rule of repression and fear throughout Japan. Measures were taken which froze Japanese culture so that, 250 years later, it presented a scene apparently medieval to the amazed eyes of nineteenth century Europe.

While in Kyoto Ieyasu lived within the moated, massive-walled Nijo Castle in a small wooden house distinguished by its beautifully decorated and painted colour panels and 'nightingale floors' – boards laid in such a way that they squeaked when trodden on, giving warning of the approach of a possible assassin. However, the later Tokugawa avoided Kyoto and instead based themselves on the little fishing village of Edo. The city which grew up there is now Tokyo, where the *shogun*'s castle walls still encircle the Imperial palace. During the Tokugawa period it became one of the biggest cities in the world, with more than a million people.

Urban life flourished under curious circumstances. The new *bakufu* – camp government – understood that its continued existence very much depended on the subjection of the great *daimyo*, especially those who had opposed Ieyasu at Sekigahara. Ieyasu required them to sign regulations limiting their power and permitting a close supervision even over their personal affairs. They were forced to leave their wives and families in Edo while they were themselves absent, and were required personally to spend a certain amount of the year in the capital. Along the great high roads, such as the famed Tokaido between Kyoto and Edo, guards working at special roadblocks checked constantly on the traffic, looking for 'women coming out and weapons going into' Edo.

An elaborate spy system was introduced to check on the great families. The slightest suspicion of disloyalty could lead to part, if not all, of the estates of the *daimyo* being confiscated. They were not allowed to enter into marriage alliances, build new castles or even repair old ones, without the permission of the central government. The obligation to spend regular periods in Edo led not only to the city's mushroom growth, but also helped to keep the *daimyo* too poor to cause trouble. Every great family had to maintain an establishment there. In fact, as the centuries passed, Japan was impoverished to pay for the infrastructure and amusements of the city.

The flood of money into Edo from the heavily-taxed peasantry created a wealthy merchant class and a varied entertainment industry – both new departures in Japan. A family originally occupied in brewing *sake*, the Japanese rice wine, branched out into rice distribution, the general retail trade, and then banking. A *samurai* named Iwasaki Yataro set up a shipping line which rapidly expanded after Japan again became open to the world. These were the origins of Mitsui and Mitsubishi, two industrial giants of today's Japan.

An entertainment complex called the *ukiyo*, 'the floating world' – tea houses, taverns, puppet shows, brothels, theatres, public baths and circuses – accumulated in Edo to serve the wealthy and leisured. There are restaurants in Tokyo that serve the same dishes – unchanged – now, as then. More specialised entertainment was also available – *sumo* wrestling and popular playhouses – the *kabuki* theatre. Because its productions were so often ribald and erotic the *bakufu* forebade the employment of actresses in *kabuki*, so female roles had to be taken by men. Bright-coloured costumes, lively music and dancing were all part of *kabuki* productions, which became enormously appealing to the ordinary people.

Then there were the bath girls and the *geisha*, a specialised female pleasure class. Particularly pretty small girls were sold to the *geisha* houses, and carefully trained in the social arts – flower arranging, the lengthy and formal Japanese tea ceremony, singing, dancing. Their occupation was then as paid companions for wealthy men.

The Tokugawa quite early considered any foreign contacts dangerous, and sealed Japan off completely from the outside world. A first step in this direction was to stamp out the major foreign influence – Christianity. Trade and missionary activity had earlier been closely associated. It was a time of intense commercial and religious rivalry between the Protestant and Catholic nations of Europe and Ieyasu could not fail to be influenced by this. Both factions tried to make him suspicious of the other. Finally he seems to have been impressed by the fact that the English and Dutch brought with them no organised religious activity like the Jesuits. The fact that many of those defending Osaka castle had been Christians increased his suspicions. In 1614 he ordered all foreign missionaries to leave Japan permanently.

However, it was the second Tokugawa, Hidetada, who began a major campaign of torturing and killing Christians extending over two decades. Many priests, and some of the congregations, accepted their cruel fate as martyrs and at least 3000 people died, in the most agonising ways. They were immersed in caustic water, thrown on to redhot gratings, dropped into pits of poisonous snakes, or most commonly, crucified upside down. People suspected of being Christians were called on to trample on a picture of Christ or the Virgin Mary, and were tortured until they agreed to renounce their faith or died.

The city of Nagasaki had become a focus for Japanese Christianity, nearly all the people in the city and its surroundings having been converted. It was here that the persecution reached its terrible climax. Bad local government and ruinous taxation led the people of this region to revolt in 1637, and the uprising inevitably became associated with the Christian faith.

The local *daimyo*, Matsukara, was a man of unusual cruelty and rapacity even for those times, notorious for his habit of boiling people alive in the hot springs of the region. The peasants were compared with sesame seed – the more they were squeezed, the more they would give. Almost everything was taxed – doors, shelves, candles among other things, and the appalling torture of the Mino dance was applied to those who could not pay. They were dressed in a bulky straw coat, their hands tied behind their backs, and set alight.

Desperate from the religious persecution and the ruinous

levels of taxation 37,000 Christians and their families gathered in an old fortress called Hara on the Shimabara Peninsula, and fought to the end a force of 100,000 Tokugawa *samurai* who besieged the castle for three months. The end came in April, 1638. Of those still alive in the fortress only one, a traitor imprisoned in the dungeons, was allowed to live. At Hidetada's request a Dutch ship had used her guns to breach the fortress walls. Fifteen thousand of the government's force were killed.

This terrible civil conflict, which is still well-remembered in popular arts in today's Japan, had two major effects. The first was to convince the *bakufu* that the only way to preserve Japanese society was to cut adrift as completely as possible from contacts with Europeans. Japanese were forbidden to leave the country. Those who did leave faced the death penalty if they returned. Shipbuilders were forbidden to construct anything bigger than coastal craft. After the Shimabara revolt the Portuguese traders in Japan were told to leave and warned that any further attempt to make contact would result in their death. At the time the traders were expelled, the Japanese still owed them considerable sums. A ship sent from Macao, on the south Chinese coast, in 1640 to try to collect the money was burned and 61 of her company beheaded. Thirteen who were spared were sent back to Macao with instructions 'to think of us no more, just as if we were no longer in the world.'

Spanish ships had already been warned away and England had abandoned its trading post in 1623 as unprofitable. Only the Dutch were permitted to remain and they were confined to a tiny, artificial island called Deshima in Nagasaki Harbour. Once a year they were allowed to leave this island to present gifts to the *shogun* in Edo. Normally they were treated with respect but sometimes they were forced to dance, jump and roll about as if drunk – these indignities apparently being designed to demonstrate the crudities of Europeans. Now thousands of Japanese visit a multi-million dollar 'Dutch' theme park in Nagasaki.

The second major effect of the extermination of the people

in Hara Castle was to cow down the populace to the extent that most would accept any privation, any indignity from sheer fear.

It is interesting to note that the *bakufu* made distinctions between European and Asian traders. Ieyasu encouraged trade with south-east Asia – in the first three decades of the seventeenth century some 400 trading passages were made by Japanese ships, which voyaged as far afield as the Thai capital of Ayudhya. That city had its own Japanese quarter, housing more than a thousand residents. Japan was a major exporter of silver, which was much in demand in south-east Asia.

Japanese society, now substantially removed from any outside influence, proceeded along the lines dictated by the *shoguns*. If restrictive, this at least enforced a kind of peace, although the heavily-taxed and much abused peasants revolted from time to time. The eighteenth and early nineteenth century saw severe famines causing thousands of deaths, but prior to that crop diversification and more intensive agriculture had resulted in a modestly expanding economy.

The autocratic nature of the government encouraged extremes of authoritarianism which are almost incredible, the most famous example being the measures introduced by Tsunayoshi, the so-called 'dog' *shogun*. He was worried by the fact that he had no heir and was told by a soothsayer that his childlessness would continue until a campaign of kindness was introduced to all animals, in particular towards dogs, because the *shogun* had been born in the Year of the Dog. Over the next 20 years a set of regulations forbade killing or ill-treatment of animals. Canine shelters were built outside Edo to house 50,000 dogs and all Japanese, when talking to a dog, must address it as 'Honourable Dog'.

In spite of the constraints of Tokugawa rule and their tradition of restrained and formal public behaviour, the Japanese people managed a certain wry and ribald vigour – an ambivalence still apparent today. By the late eighteenth century a deep respect for learning and letters had resulted in a relatively high rate of literacy. Towards the end of the Tokugawa close on half the boys and perhaps 10 per cent of the girls were attending schools. Book publishing was a flourishing trade, but because the modest incomes of most of the people made ownership of personal libraries prohibitive, lending libraries, often carried around on the back of their proprietors, were popular. There was a rigorous book censorship, interested especially in any criticism of the regime. When author Santo Kyoden published three popular satires, he was sentenced to 50 days in handcuffs and his publisher was heavily fined. Such happenings inclined most writers towards the fanciful, the ribald and the exotic. Fiction was very popular.

The Tokugawa used the *samurai* to enforce their orders – they even had the right 'to kill and go away', not to be brought to account by the law for murder. There has been a regrettable tendency to romanticise the *samurai* and *bushido*, their so-called cult of honour, in television programmes for children among other things, so a few balancing facts might not be out of place.

The appalling torture meted out, often to quite innocent people, indicates that a major motivation of the *samurai* was a sadistic desire to kill in as painful and prolonged a way possible. For instance, pirates captured in the Straits of Korea were boiled alive in copper kettles. The terrible deaths devised for Christians were carried out by *samurai*. *Daimyo* travelling between Edo and Kyoto would be accompanied by scores, even hundreds of *samurai* hangers-on. Any Japanese who did not prostrate himself abjectly enough in the dust beside the road was liable to be literally cut to pieces by the *samurai*. Hideously masked and dressed in leather and steel armour, the *samurai* were a specialised coercive force preying on their own people – probably unparalleled for their brutality anywhere else in world history. The main feature of the *bushido* code was the duty of the *samurai* to be faithful and even die for his lord without question. A political imperative designed to consolidate those already in power, its effect is still evident today behind the stage-show of Japanese democracy.

However, by the early nineteenth century the formidable image

of the *samurai* was much diminished. The class had not actually done any fighting since the Shimabara revolt of 1637,
and had become a caricature of its former self. While they
affected to despise the growing merchant and banking class,
increasingly the real power was moving to this mercantile sector.
The great *daimyo* and many of the increasingly corrupt and
idle *samurai* came to be deeply in the debt of the merchants.
So the coming of the nineteenth century saw strains and tensions
inside Japan which augured change in the not-too-distant future.

A small minority of scholars, who, from 1716, were licensed
to import Dutch books through the Deshima post, acquired a
purely theoretical knowledge of the advances Europe was
making. It was noted that more ships seemed to be appearing
off the coast. In 1805 a Russian ship lay for months off Nagasaki,
seeking permission to land an official envoy, but finally had
to sail away without achieving success. In 1824, the crew of
a British whaler landed, killed cattle, and generally seem to
have behaved in a lawless way. This led to a renewal, in 1825,
of the decree providing that any foreigner landing should be
killed. In 1837 a United States ship was fired on.

The Japanese were very much aware of and alarmed by
news of the Opium Wars and the unequal treaties that had
been forced on China. It was evident that the *samurai*, with
their antique weaponry and total lack of experience of war,
could not defend Japan against the feared Westerners. The
resulting public dissatisfaction with the regime was to be exacerbated by four years of disastrous weather and resultant
famines from 1833.

However much the Japanese wished the outside world would
go away, it was not to be denied. The isolated isles with their
Rip van Winkle atmosphere had become a source of intense
curiosity. In 1846 an American mission led by Commodore
Biddle was forced to leave without negotiating the trade treaty
it sought. So the next time the Americans came they made
sure it was with a suitable display of force. On 8 July, 1853,
Commodore Perry entered Edo's Uraga Harbour with a squadron
of two steam and two sailing sloops, the largest of 2400 tons

and carrying 16 guns. Under the guns of these ships Perry was able to deliver a letter from the President of the United States requesting that some Japanese ports be opened for trade. On 16 July the 'black ships' departed, leaving Japan in a confused ferment. Commodore Perry had undertaken to return the next year for the *bakufu*'s reply. This was affirmative, although cautious, and led to the opening of two small ports remote from Edo; a token gesture only. But America followed up by sending as its first official representative Townsend Harris, a shrewd, forceful but tactful man who, after much patient negotiation, succeeded in gaining audience in 1857 with the *shogun*, Iesada. This was followed by a comprehensive treaty, not only with the United States, but with other nations.

The centuries of isolation had ended, and with them all pretence that Japan's society was itself static – an illusion the *bakufu* was striving to maintain. Not surprisingly a major victim of change was the *shogunate* itself, supplanted by a restoration of the Japanese Emperor to a position of symbolic national primacy. This reversion to the past was engineered not by the wealthy merchants but by disgruntled *samurai*, leading Japan into half a century of unbridled militarism and aggression.

Part II
The White Man's Burden

11

The Dominators and the Dominated

The nineteenth and early twentieth centuries saw the development of imperialism on a scale never known before. This was due to the industrialisation of Europe, associated with a rapid growth in its population, and radical advances in the means of transport, notably shipping and railways, and naval power. A crucial factor in the conquest of empires was the development of deadlier light weapons. American farm machinery technician Richard Gordon Gatling developed a machine gun in 1862 that would fire 350 rounds a minute. This new device for mass killing was adopted by all the colonial powers. For the first time natives inclined to fight back could be – and were – mown down in hundreds.

By this and other means it became technologically possible for a single nation to dominate much of the world. At its maximum material extent during the 1920s the British Empire occupied nearly a quarter of the land surface of the planet inhabited by about 500 million people, then almost a quarter of world population. Wherever the eye fell on the map of the world, there were the daubs of red, marking the empire on which the sun never set.

This empire, like those of other major European powers, was substantially in Asia. The British colonies there consisted of what are now seven countries: India, Pakistan, Bangladesh,

Sri Lanka, Burma, Malaysia and Singapore. There were other smaller outposts, like Hong Kong, and also spheres of influence in countries nominally independent, but prepared to accept British advice.

The imperial dissection of Asia followed a definite geographic pattern. The British Empire was westernmost, extending east from India through Burma to small, lately-acquired possessions in Malaysia. Beyond Thailand, kept independent as a buffer state and twice lopped of some of its territory, was French Indo-China, now Vietnam, Cambodia and Laos. Holland controlled the western half of archipelago south-east Asia – what is now Indonesia. The 400 islands farther east became the Philippines, the colony first of Spain and later of the United States.

China was too big a fish for any single European state to swallow whole, or, indeed, to be permitted by its rivals to do so. Instead she became divided into 'spheres of influence'. The imperialist powers exacted important concessions in major ports along the Chinese coast, like Shanghai, Amoy and Foochow. These grew into big cities, centres of both a massive industry and a massive accumulation of human suffering, poverty and disease.

Japan maintained her independence only because she had 'westernised' her economy and industry with remarkable speed and energy and gained the respect of the dominators by becoming a colonial power herself, annexing Korea, Taiwan and Manchuria. Thailand, under the shrewd control of her Chakri kings, escaped colonial status by bending to the wind – surrendering territory where this seemed expedient and accepting European advisers.

This geographic organisation of Asia to suit the dominators, informed largely by an incessant, uneasy rivalry between them, had some strange and at times disastrous consequences. Everywhere one now looks in Asia anomalies remain – peoples divided between two or more nations, minorities cut off from the majority of their race, frontiers that defy the facts of geography. The tensions caused by these things are important, active influences in the Asia of today and will have unpredictable effects on future events.

But for colonialism it is likely that Indonesia would have been more than one country. Sumatra might have been associated with the Malay Peninsula which it neighbours and which its terrain and people so closely resemble. Java and Madura, with their dense populations and distinctive cultures, might have made up a second. The eastern islands and the Philippines could have comprised a third.

There are hilltribe people in north-east India who are ethnically identical with others now Burmese. The border between Afghanistan and Pakistan divides the Pathans. There is a substantial Malay minority in southern Thailand. The people of northeast Thailand are Laotian by language and tradition. India is showing indications of division into three regions of different interest, and throughout her history as an independent power regional influences have gained ground on those that seek to unify. Nearly all these anomalies resulted from the organisation of colonial empires, which successor states have insisted on as a basis for their own boundaries.

The dominators' manipulation of the economy of the colony to their own ends was facilitated by the association of soldier and merchant so typical of the colonial era (The British East India Company maintained distinct civil and military divisions) and by a policy of actively discouraging political development in the colonial peoples. The use and enforcement of monopolies was a typical economic practice. Those formed to sell opium are notorious examples. For instance, in 1867 the contribution made by the East Indies to the Netherlands Government was almost exactly the amount raised by government monopolies in opium and salt and the management of pawnshops. While Laos was a colony, even as late as 1945, its major export was opium, and during the Japanese occupation of Korea its production was legal. Throughout Indo-China opium, alcohol and salt were government monopolies so profitable they doubled colonial revenues in the first decade after their inception. Opium exports from India did not cease until 1909.

It has been estimated that the drain of money from south-east Asia alone in the form of profits from the colonies was $3007 million in 1930. In 1925, 51 per cent of all imports into India came from Britain, although Indian exports to Britain were only 22 per cent of her total. Imports from France represented 52 per cent of all into Indo-China. The economies of the colonies were manipulated so they could be a cheap, fruitful source of raw materials, while industrial development was retarded to discourage competition with the industries of the dominators. India, before the colonial era the world's major supplier of cotton fabrics, lost this position in the nineteenth century to the massive textiles industry that developed in the English Midlands.

Some interesting figures are quoted in *East and West*, (1998) written by the last British governor of Hong Kong, Chris Patten (p.130). He says: 'In the early decades of the 19th century . . . Asia still accounted for about 58 per cent of world GDP. By 1920 this figure had been more than halved. Over the following 20 years Asia's share fell further, to 19 per cent.' This enormous decline was no accident. While the industry and economies of the dominators boomed, those of the colonies were deliberately restrained.

These economic policies contributed towards major social changes in the colonies, the effects of which remain important today. The most significant were a massive turnover of land to export crops, rapid population growth and under-development – a lack of adequate material resources – and only a tiny and limited pool of educated people. These continue today to be common problems in most of the former colonies, and are the root causes of millions of avoidable deaths, especially of children, and of disease and poverty.

Unbalanced economies and a rising demand for cheap labour to work the expanding plantations resulted in increasingly rapid population growth. Java and Madura, with five million people in 1815, had twice that number a generation later, ten times as many at the time of independence, more than twenty times as many now. There were similar increases in all the 'plantation' regions of Asia.

Development of the human resource – education – varied from place to place but in none did it even begin to approach that in the dominators' home countries. At the end of the colonial era, when virtually the whole world outside the colonies was literate, the vast majority of the dominated peoples remained illiterate.

Much the same situation existed with material infrastructure. Some roads, railways, port facilities and cities were developed but these, paid for out of colonial revenues, were designed to suit the needs and interests of the dominator. Development was generally much below that achieved outside the colonies. In 1950 the three largest Asian nations, China, India and Indonesia had a total of 38,000 miles of rail track, compared with 217,000 in the United States and 237,000 in Europe. Statistics on roads, factories, power-generating stations and the other resources of modern states indicate equal or more serious under-development.

The fact that the colonies were regarded as the property of the master country is, then, central. The first objective of the colonial system was to make money. The colonies were businesses, run by businessmen, through most of their history, regardless of the Kiplingesque ballyhoo to the contrary. Only during the last decades before independence was finally granted was there much sense of responsibility towards the nations-to-be. Even then, this varied from country to country.

As late as 1913, J. Dautremer, the author of a standard book, *Burma Under British Rule*, wrote: 'The colonies are countries which have been conquered. They are the property of the country that administers them, governs them, and develops their riches for its own profit. Since the colony is the property of the nation, it has no right to be put on the same footing as the governing country.' These statements are typical of publicly-expressed attitudes at that time.

The colonial governments perpetuated a grotesquely-large disparity of wealth and privilege within the Asian peoples, a situation which persists in the modern nations.

It could be asserted Britain made the greatest contributions of value to her colonies, especially in the twentieth century. It is reasonably clear Dutch rule in Indonesia contributed the least. They left the huge archipelago only 3000 miles of railways, compared with 16,000 in India. The Dutch refused to recognise, even at a late stage, the possibility of the East Indies becoming independent, considering only a state within the Netherlands commonwealth to be governed by the 250,000 Dutch living there.

There can be little doubt that the relatively orderly history of India and Malaysia since independence, for instance, was due to efforts made during the later colonial era to educate some local people in business and administration, and to provide a reasonable administrative framework. That these were primarily to the benefit of the colonial business machine is beside the point.

On the other hand, the chaotic problems of Indonesia during her first decades of independence were due largely to a lack of such efforts to educate. This factor is difficult to over-estimate and one that those seeking to understand Indonesia should keep in mind. At the outbreak of World War Two, the virtual end of the colonial phase, the literacy rate was only seven per cent. Such educated men as there were had in most cases been sent to school overseas by their families. On their return to Indonesia they were employed only in subordinate positions.

The serious and enduring effect of this neglect is described in a 1998 report from UNICEF, *The State of the World's Children*, which noted that almost a billion people – 16 per cent of world population – could not read or write. Almost two-thirds of the illiterates were women. South Asia and Sub-Saharan Africa were the regions with the largest number of children out of school.

It is fair to add, however, that in Indonesia, as elsewhere, the nationalist movement came from among the tiny educated class. Also, research scholars of the colonial powers were largely responsible for bringing to the attention of these nationalists the glories of the past. French archeologists patiently unravelled the history of the vast buildings of Angkor and began the work of restoring the ruins of the great Khmer city. Dutch scholars did as much for Indonesia. The traditions of Shrivijaya and Majapahit, which came to mean so much to the nationalists, might never have been recovered, even to the present extent, but for the work of these Dutch enthusiasts. Later pre-colonial Indonesian society, for instance, had no inkling of the meaning of the great monument of Borobadur, simply shunning it as 'a place of ghosts'.

The nationalist movements were, then, organised and perpetuated substantially by a small minority educated in Western ideas of politics. For decades the language of the Indian Congress was English. Its leader, Jawaharlal Nehru, was English-educated and the Indian constitution was drafted on Western precedents. Ho Chi Minh was educated in Communism in France. Indonesia's Sukarno was literate in several European languages and widely read in European political theory.

But the future may lie elsewhere, as some Asian statesmen recognise. I can recall many years ago hearing a speech by the architect of modern Singapore, Lee Kuan Yew, in which he predicted the arrival of new, as yet unknown, political forces and the eclipse of Western-educated leaders such as himself. The beginnings of this process are now apparent.

A second contribution of colonialism was the rule of law. Europe obtained its basic concept of an impartial codified legal system, binding equally on all citizens, from the Romans. Attitudes towards law in Asia, with few exceptions, were quite different, the law being almost invariably customary rather than codified. In south-east Asian principalities law was generally such a savage, unfair instrument that people hesitated to use it. In China there was one law for the privileged, another much harsher code for the mass of the people, and, if the popular literature, classics like the *Chin Ping Mei*, can be believed, readily and regularly influenced by bribery. In Japan one class, the *samurai*, became virtually immune from the law.

During the colonial period most of the European powers imposed their own systems of law on the subject territories for long enough to train a significant body of local people in those legal methods. Places like Japan and Thailand, even though they were not colonies, found it expedient to accept advice on the setting-up of Westernised legal systems because if they had not done so, the much-hated principle called extra-territoriality, under which foreigners were immune from local law, would have continued.

Within the broad framework of law may also be noted the development of administrative procedures designed to see that public services, like roads, postal facilities, ports, health and education, were planned and carried on. Just how great was the achievement in this direction? On the whole it was much smaller than it might have been and a good deal less than what might be considered ideal.

Rapid growth in population occurred almost everywhere in Asia, with increases of between two and three per cent a year. This vast rise in population remains one of the greatest, if not the greatest, problem facing the world of the third millennium. The UNICEF report referred to above significantly notes that fertility drops sharply as education rises, illiterate women having an average of 6.5 children, mothers with secondary school education an average of 2.5 children.

12

South-East Asia: The European and Chinese Incursions, and Later History of the Mainland States

Many chapters could be devoted, without much profit, to the tedious dynastic successions, transitory empires, and constant wars which, over the centuries, punctuate the chronicles of south-east Asia. In some histories of the region they are. However, the source material deals almost exclusively with the affairs of ruling families, and frequently shows scant regard for truth; for instance, we are told that a Vietnamese king, Phat Ma, straightened a sagging pillar in a ruined temple simply by looking at it.

The real history of this region is the ebb and flow of village life; the succession of scores of generations of ordinary people, humble, unlettered but tenacious, without great possessions, patiently growing rice according to rituals already so old their beginnings have been forgotten, and just as patiently devoted to traditions and art forms of considerable significance. In the 1930s Europe became fascinated with these qualities in the Indonesian island of Bali – a way of life involving personal accomplishment perfected in one or other of the arts, a minimum of personal possessions, a disregard for any more money than is necessary, a proper regard for personal tranquillity and social harmony.

These things are in many ways typical of village south-east Asia in most of its diverse settings. To these, the real people, the struggles and ambitions of their warring masters meant trouble from time to time, but very little more. The figures of kings appeared almost Olympian; gods, whose actions, often tyrannical and usually unpredictable, were in some vague, magic way linked with the overall prosperity of the realm and the productivity of the soil.

Little has changed. Contemporary chronicles – the modern media – when they concern themselves with Asia at all, almost invariably report on the activities of the elite classes, living in capital cities that might make up, at most, five per cent of the Asian population. Beijing's ten millions, for example, are less than one per cent of the Chinese people.

Nevertheless, in the seventeenth century parts of south-east Asia passed through a considerable though restless phase of urbanisation, with several cities exceeding a hundred thousand population. Malacca was one of these prior to its occupation by the Portuguese in 1511. These merchant entrepots, which included Atjeh, Macassar and Ayudhya, were comparable with major European cities of that time. London had somewhat fewer than two hundred thousand people then. Significant location on the trade routes, or highly productive hinterlands, were the major economic reasons for this urban growth. Another was the diversion of much of the rural wealth and national manpower to the purposes of the rulers. In Thailand, for instance, the corvée could amount to as much as half the labour time of the peasants, to support a large bureaucracy and army and to carry out the physical construction of cities like Ayudhya.

Much of the population of the trading ports were transients, obliged to stay over for months at a time until the monsoons changed. They needed, and paid for, food, accommodation and other services during that time. They also provided the rulers of the city-states with a reliable source of income, since both imports and exports were taxed at rates between five and ten per cent.

This urban growth proved to be fragile. It depended tenuously on the authority of kings or emperors, which was frequently disputed, especially at times of succession. Bitter and protracted civil conflict at these times, and destructive wars between neigbouring realms, greatly reduced these mushroom cities, or even, as in the case of Ayudhya, led to their abandonment. Many of their population were slaves captured in war, or peasants forced into corvée labour or military service. Weakening or collapse of regimes inevitably and rapidly affected the entire urban structure. During its phase of occupation by the Portuguese, Malacca's population fell by two-thirds, and other cities later to be used as bases by the colonisers were similarly affected.

The evolution of nation-states in Europe did not then, have its counterpart in south-east Asia until recent times, although Burma and Thailand did achieve a kind of unity. At first sight it seems strange that relatively small numbers of Europeans were able to gain a foothold in countries which had a considerable and sophisticated cultural and economic past. The reason was that everywhere local petty lords were at each other's throats. They were only too ready to make concessions to European adventurers to use their guns and ships against a neighbouring rival. Often enough these concessions involved the critical but laborious bread-and-butter tasks of administration, such as tax collecting. Provided some money came to the sultan or rajah, it was a matter of little concern that vastly more was extorted from the unhappy peasantry by tax 'farmers'.

Parallel with the arrival of Europeans on the scene was another virtual invasion of foreigners, in much greater numbers and probably more significant in the long term. This was the advent of the overseas Chinese. Their descendants in south-east Asia now approach 20 million people. It is probable that if the Chinese government had supported its people in southeast Asia to the extent that European governments supported their's, the evolution of European colonial empires in Asia may have been greatly limited. But the Chinese government did not. The Manchus did nothing to help or support Chinese leaving for what became called the *nanyang* – the southern ocean – nor did it prevent them. It was a matter of indifference whether southern Chinese left the country or not. Deteriorating social and economic conditions in China provided a powerful incentive to seek a new life overseas and during the centuries of growing European influence the Chinese did so in millions. Everywhere they went they took with them their tradition of hard work and singleness of purpose, building ships, opening gold and tin mines, lending money to rulers, cornering rice markets, involving themselves in virtually every area of trade and commerce.

More than 600 junks arrived in Manila in the 30 years following its establishment as the Spanish colonial capital of the Philippines. There were 10,000 Chinese there by 1586, compared with well under a thousand Spaniards. The flood of Chinese was resented and resisted by the local people, with half a dozen massacres during the seventeenth century. Nevertheless the Chinese population of Manila had risen to 40,000 by 1750.

There was a large Chinese quarter in Ayudhya, which was perhaps the most solid and prosperous part of the city. The government used the Chinese as tax collectors and managers of state enterprises. Most of Thailand's trade at that time was with China, and the Dutch, French and English were unable to gain more than a foothold. This was an important element in Thailand's continued independence during the colonial era.

In Batavia (now Jakarta) Chinese control of commerce and manufacture became almost pervasive, and with the encouragement of the Dutch a large Chinese minority spread throughout Indonesia. By 1740 more than half the inhabitants of Batavia were Chinese. Many became wealthy through a system of taxation which granted the tax farmer the right to levy a range of taxes after he had offered the largest cash bid for the concession. Everything else he could wring from the populace was his – including taxes on ports, salt, opium, gambling, even duties on travel within the colony.

An important area of trade was opium, the use of which was uncommon in south-east Asia until the late eighteenth century, when the British growers of the poppy in Bengal and the Dutch adopted a deliberate policy of encouraging its use. The Dutch administration bought the opium in Bengal to serve its monopoly in Indonesia. They farmed out the distribution of the drug to Chinese dealers. It was enormously profitable, Anthony Reid (*Cambridge History of Southeast Asia*, p. 500) estimating that profits were three thousand per cent over the Bengal cost price.

There were several important consequences of the Chinese migration to south-east Asia. The first was the transplanting into the region of a large, widely-dispersed and permanent Chinese population. Singapore, for instance, a major independent city-state, is mostly Chinese. One third of the population of Malaysia is Chinese, and there are minorities in all the south-east Asian nations, often running into the millions. A second fundamental was the virtual domination of trade and commerce in south-east Asia by the overseas Chinese. While this has been resisted strenuously by the independent nations, it remains a major factor, with considerable portents for the future in the light of China's emergence as one of the world's largest economies. A third effect, deriving from the first two, has been a deep-rooted and violent resentment of the Chinese by the indigenous peoples. In thousands of south-east Asian villages the shopkeepers, moneylenders, and substantial landowners are Chinese, and are objects of suspicion, envy, and barely-suppressed hatred.

The destruction of the south China kingdom of Nanchao by Kublai Khan drove increasing numbers of the Thai people of that area southward. This migration established several important and related groups, who are now split up among several countries. These groups are the Shan tribes of north-east Burma, the Thais and the Laotians, and the people of Yunnan Province of China. National boundaries inherited from the colonising powers can be most deceptive. The Mekong River, for instance, on the map appears to be a logical border between Thailand and Laos; yet because the river is the main means of transport in areas with few roads and no rail links and because people who are ethnically the same and speak the same language live on both banks, it is a factor that tends to unite rather than divide them. As late as 1964 Thai government officials in Nongkai Province of Thailand near the Mekong found villages in which the inhabitants were firmly convinced they were Laotian and had pictures of the King of Laos on their walls as the object of their loyalties.

Thailand, then called Siam, became an independent country when a subject city of the Khmer Empire called Sukhothai broke free in 1238AD. So preoccupied was Angkor with wars on its other frontiers it was forced to accept the situation. A century later Sukhothai's people moved south, far into the fertile delta plain of the Chao Phraya River, where they built a larger city. This was Ayudhya, named for Rama's capital in the *Ramayana*.

Off to the west, the Burmese gradually welded together the northern section of their old empire, called Pagan, around a city named Ava, not far from the present Mandalay. This empire used Thai mercenaries, who ultimately set up their own king-doms in the north under hereditary lords called *sawbwas*. These kingdoms are the Shan states, which are still fighting to be-come independent from Burma.

Burma achieved significant territorial cohesion under the rule of her final line of kings, founded by a strenuous and ambi-tious soldier named Alaungpaya, who had been a village headman. He established an entrepot port in the southern town of Dagon, which he renamed Rangoon, which means 'the abode of peace.' Next Alaungpaya turned his armies east. In 1760, while directing an attack against the Thais, he was killed when a cannon burst near him. However, his army kept up the as-sault. It took the northern Thai city of Chiengmai in 1763. Four years later it sacked and burned Ayudhya at the end of a 14-month siege.

Burma was so strong militarily it was able to withstand attack even from China when the Ch'ien Lung emperor sent an army across the border from Yunnan State in 1766. Although the Chinese columns advanced several times from the hill passes on to the Irrawaddy River plain, each time they were driven back. In 1770 the Manchus were obliged to agree to peace terms with their small neighbour.

The Burmese were aware of British expansion in India and

both Britain and Burma knew a collision of interests must come in time. This was the more obvious following Burmese conquest of the Kingdom of Arakan on the Bay of Bengal towards the end of the eighteenth century. Early in the next century Burma occupied the big hill state of Assam, so gaining a foothold on India itself. Matters became worse in 1819 with the appointment of the assertive General Bandula as governor. There seemed no limit to Bandula's confidence and with growing alarm the British watched him prepare to attack Bengal itself.

Before he could act Britain struck the first blow. In 1824, a British fleet made a surprise attack on Rangoon and captured it easily. So began the first Burmese war. Bandula used spirited methods to try to defeat the British, but he had no idea of the scale of the resources behind his enemy. Like other British campaigns of the time, the execution of this one was criminally inefficient. Constantly plagued by disease and disorganisation, the British force pursued a slow motion campaign aimed at the conquest of the capital, Ava. At times, especially during the wet seasons, almost the whole army was laid low with fever and the death rate was appalling. Fifteen thousand British troops died, all but a few hundred of disease and infected wounds.

In the end the Burmese sued for peace. They paid an indemnity of a million pounds, although the war cost Britain 13 millions. Burma also lost – and Britain gained – a significant section of the Burmese coastline and it was agreed a British resident should be located at Ava, mainly to foster trade.

The Burmese were by no means anxious for closer relations, and the peace did not last long. It was reported back to India from time to time that British subjects in Rangoon were being treated with indignity, and feelings mounted on both sides. Matters came to a head when two British sea-captains were arrested on trumped-up murder charges.

The British Viceroy in India, Lord Dalhousie, sent a squadron to Rangoon under the command of a peppery naval officer, Commodore Lambert. In the river Lambert's ship, H.M.S. *Fox*, was attacked rather ineffectually by a shore battery, which made some holes in her sails. Lambert, acting with an energy and lack of discretion quite beyond his instructions, used the guns of *Fox* until he had sunk everything in sight that might conceivably have been a Burmese ship of war. So the opportunity for negotiation passed at once and war became inevitable.

Lambert's attitude – epitomising as it does the jingoist era of British colonialism – is evident in his letter to the Government of India: 'It is with deep regret that I have had to commence hostilities with the Burmese nation, but I am confident that the government of India and Lord Dalhousie will see it was unavoidable and necessary to vindicate the honour of the British flag.' In fact the government of India and Lord Dalhousie were not at all pleased, but had to accept the second Burmese war as an accomplished fact. Constantly under fire from the British Press, the dismal war dragged on, leading finally to the capture of Ava and the addition of several more Burmese provinces to the British Empire.

The resulting demoralisation did nothing to improve the ethics and standing of the ruling dynasty. The court at Mandalay became notorious for its violence, injustice and squalid immorality under King Thebaw, the last of his line, who succeeded to the Lion Throne after Mindon's death in 1878. Mindon had not nominated a successor and the resulting intrigue for power led to a horrifying slaughter of princes and princesses of the royal house, both adults and children. As in other parts of mainland south-east Asia, it was forbidden to touch the person of any of the royal line, and sacrilege to spill their blood. So the executions ordered by Thebaw were in the macabre tradition of the past. The victims were first sewn inside red velvet sacks and then despatched by breaking their necks with blows from sandalwood clubs. This atrocity deeply alarmed British residents in Burma, caused an outcry around the world, and brought the British government under strong pressure to put an end to Thebaw's misrule. Almost at once Thebaw began to intrigue with the French in Indo-China, with the idea of playing them off against the British. The British government now waited only for a suitable pretext for war, which Thebaw provided soon enough. A money dispute arose between the Court and a

big teak monopoly company, the Bombay-Burma Trading
Corporation. The British government intervened. An expeditionary force occupied Mandalay in 1885 and the following
year the monarchy was deposed. The conquest of Burma was
complete. Now it became a mere province of British India.

The burning of Ayudhya had destroyed one of south-east
Asia's most beautiful and populous cities – a source of mar-
vel to the European traders who visited it. However, a small
Thai army had been able to fight its way out of the ruins and,
in spite of four more Burmese raids, regained control of the
Chao Phrya River delta, the region's ricebowl. An army officer,
General Chakri, became king under the title of Rama I. So
began the dynasty that still reigns, as constitutional monarchs,
in Thailand today.

The destruction of their capital had taught the Thais a bitter
lesson, and Rama I was guided mainly by strategic consider-
ations in choosing a site for a new one. He decided to place
the broad stream of the Chao Phrya River between him and
his enemies, and found the site he needed at a village named
Bangkok. Foreigners still use this name, but the Thais call
their capital Krungthep, which means 'the city of angels.'

Old people who had known Ayudhya in its glory were called
in to advise the architects of the new city, for it was intended
that it should resemble its predecessor as closely as possible.
Ayudhuya had been situated on low land almost completely
enclosed by a great bend of the river, criss-crossed with hundreds
of canals, which are called *klongs*. This was how Bangkok
acquired the *klongs* which were such a distinctive feature,
although most have now been filled in to provide wider roads
for the city's hectic motor traffic.

The early Chakri monarchs continued to rule in the traditional barbaric and despotic fashion. The king was regarded
as a god. People had to enter his presence on all-fours, and to
as much as touch his person meant death. His title was 'lord
of life' and he held summary powers over all his subjects.
When he travelled outside his palace, which gleamed with gold-
leaf and multi-coloured tiles, the ordinary people shut themselves

away inside their houses, to avoid the risk of being seen with their heads higher than the king's, for this, even if inadvertent, was a capital offence.

In 1848 a young official, using the services of a marriage go-between, sought the release of a young woman from the king's vast harem so he could marry her. The mere intention was construed as treason. Not only were the young man and woman executed, but also eight other people, since they had known what was going on and had not informed the Court. Apart from protecting the interests of the king and aristocracy, the government took only the most casual interest in law and order. In civil cases especially, the law was so partial and illogical few people had the temerity to resort to it.

Fortunately the country was not then poor or overcrowded. Most people lived in little villages along the many waterways, vacant land was available to anyone who wanted to take it up, and the only serious burden imposed by the government was taxation. Under Rama III this burden became greater because the government let out to private persons the right to collect taxes – the so-called 'tax farming' system. These persons, who were mainly Chinese immigrants, bid for the right to collect taxes and were allowed to keep whatever they could realise above their bid. They were supposed not to oppress the people in the process but undoubtedly they did to a considerable extent, so helping to engender the dislike and suspicion of the Chinese still evident in Thailand today.

The tax system resulted in a large slave class, perhaps as much as a third of the population. Most of these were persons who had voluntarily gone into slavery for non-payment of debts. They were free to transfer themselves from one owner to another and could redeem their freedom simply by repaying the debt. Few chose to do so because slaves were exempt from taxation.

Rama III agreed reluctantly to a trade agreement with Britain in 1826. The Thais did their best to ignore or circumvent it, because they had no wish to follow the Indians and Burmese into the imperial maw. It was apparent to Rama III that every skill he could muster would be needed to escape colonial domination; this became the policy of the dynasty. It was served best by Rama IV, better known to the rest of the world as King Mongkut, because he is so described in the reminiscences of his children's English governess, Anna Leonowens.

It is a pity that the western image of this shrewd and intelligent ruler should have so much been formed by the film and musical comedy freely adapted from what were, even in their original form, rather inaccurate observations. Anna's main interest to history comes from the simple fact of her appointment. This sprang from Mongkut's awareness that his descendants might the more easily ward off the colonising powers if they spoke English. His judgment in this matter and many others greatly more important were major reasons for Thailand remaining the only south or south-east Asian country to stay independent through the colonial era.

Mongkut was a Buddhist monk for 27 years before he became king in 1851 at the age of 47. He undertook the reform of the Buddhist organisation in Thailand. Largely due to his influence it has become one of the best-organised and respected religious orders in the world. Mongkut's own character was formed by these years of monastic discipline and self-denial for, like other monks, he was enjoined to celibacy and could own no property other than his yellow robe, sandals and a few other necessities. He was polygamous as king because that was the custom; a custom inspired more by the political advantage of binding many families to the throne by the marriage alliance than by the personal desires of the monarch. He permitted members of his harem to marry others in certain cases and it has been recorded that a man who abducted one of them was let off with a fine amounting to about $5 ($ throughout this book are $US).

Thailand was set on the path for major reform under his rule, largely on his own initiative, for he was no reactionary forced into reforms by a nationalist movement. Indeed, he had to cajole and encourage his people into accepting liberality and change. His energies seemed to flow in every direction. He set up printing-presses, encouraged Christian missionaries, promoted education, issued a modern system of currency and democratised the monarchy by making himself far more accessible to the people.

He welcomed advice and help from the West and accepted advisers from many countries to assist in the reform of Thai law and institutions. There was a limit to what he could do in a 17-year reign, but in that time he gave his country a decisive push from the medieval into the modern world.

Mongkut was a man of considerable energy and intellectual curiosity, and even the circumstances of his death are typical. He died in 1868 as the result of a fever he caught when returning from a scientific expedition he had organised to view an eclipse of the sun. His epitaph might well have been the words of an English missionary who knew him in Thailand and who described his rule as 'the mildest and best heathen government on the face of the globe.'

The situation in Thailand's neighbours to the east, the Indo-Chinese states which are now Vietnam, Laos and Cambodia, was quite different. A group of French Jesuit missionaries had an early and major influence. They persevered in spite of considerable persecution and the Christian community numbered several hundred thousand by the end of the seventeenth century.

In the final quarter of the eighteenth century a major revolt broke out in the Tayson district in the mountains of Annam and then spread to the plains. It was an expression of mass discontent with levels of taxation and the rule of the mandarins, and was the beginning of the end for the two rival dynasties in the north and the south, the Trinh and the Nguyen. The Nguyen were driven out of Hue, their vulnerable and unstrategic capital sited according to the predictions of astrologers, and went into hiding in the far south, which was then largely unpopulated jungle.

They lived as outlaws on the islands of the Gulf of Thailand until, finally, their cause was taken up by the French Apostolic Vicar, Pignane de Behaine, who negotiated an agreement with the French government to restore the Nguyen to the throne in return for a trade monopoly and the cession of certain territories to France. At first de Behaine had difficulty persuading the French authorities in Asia to implement this agreement, but they eventually mustered a small French mercenary army which, using modern weapons, was highly effective. Not only was the southern kingdom recaptured but Hanoi was also taken in 1802. The conquest of the north was relatively easy, since the Trinh leaders had already been displaced by the Tayson popular movement. Unity of Vietnam under single rule was, then, largely the result of French exploitation of rival factions. A treaty was signed in 1862 ceding three southern provinces to France and permitting missionaries to work anywhere in the country. Six years later the French occupied three more provinces. They also established a protectorate over Cambodia in 1864, and 19 years later, over north Vietnam.

13

The Malay World: Majapahit and Malacca

The Javanese empire of Majapahit was one of the last of the major Hinduised states of island south-east Asia, and probably the best-remembered. In this lies possibly its greatest importance, for the Majapahit tradition has been adopted as part of its national heritage by modern Indonesia. Some Indonesians have seen in Majapahit a pan-Malay empire which might again be realised in the future.

There is a good deal of disagreement about how large Majapahit actually was. Tradition claims it extended beyond Java and Sumatra to most of Malaya, the Celebes (Sulawesi) and even parts of what are now the Philippines, possibly also to New Guinea and parts of northern Australia. Such contentions are based substantially on what is a suspect source – an account of the empire given by Majapahit's court historian, Prapanca, in a long panegyric poem.

Indonesia's independence leader and first President, Sukarno, referred to Prapanca's account of Majapahit during discussions, in the final years of the Japanese occupation of Indonesia during World War Two, about the form any future independent republic might take. At these discussions the Malayan Peninsula, Borneo, and New Guinea were mentioned as once having been part of the Majapahit realms. While it would be extreme to regard this as evidence of Indonesian expansionist ambitions to these territories, the vision of a 'new Majapahit' seems to have remained in the minds of some Indonesian leaders.

Apart from its contributions to the nationalist ambition, Majapahit has had important and lasting social consequences in East Java, which is still extensively Hinduised – especially the aristocratic, or *priyayi* class. This region has only a thin layer of Islam over much earlier animist and later Hindu influences, and Bali, which can properly be associated with it in this context, remains almost entirely Hindu. It is not without interest that President Sukarno's father was from the *priyayi* class and that his mother was Balinese.

Majapahit became in the fourteenth century the major co-ordinator of the spice trade to Europe, that trade being based on the port city, Surabaya, and Majapahit itself some distance up the Brantas River, on a rich, rice-growing plain. Any consideration of Majapahit's consequence needs to be tempered by the fact that it seems not to have been an empire at all, but rather a loose confederation of convenience between autonomous spice-producing states owing only token allegiance to Majapahit. Hence, far from being an empire derived by conquest, Majapahit appears more to have been a kingdom controlling East Java, Madura and Bali, with widespread reciprocal commercial contacts with the spice-growing Indonesian islands on one level; on another, trading relations with China and with Europe, via the Mameluke Empire of Egypt, which passed commodities on to Venice.

Majapahit appears to have been at its zenith during the prime ministership of Gaja Mada in the latter part of the fourteenth century. Whatever the facts about this, Gaja Mada is regarded as a national hero. One of Indonesia's largest universities, established in Jogjakarta during the struggle for independence from the Dutch, is one of many national institutions named after him.

Majapahit declined in importance after Gaja Mada died in 1364. We are told it was found necessary to appoint four ministers to do his work but in spite of their efforts the kingdom drifted into a phase of less competent government from which it never recovered. As always, a stronger enemy was ready to take advantage of weakness. It was probably a league of Moslem princes, based on the port of Demak, that conquered Majapahit about 1520.

The Moslems who spread the faith of Allah to south-east Asia were mostly Indian. When Islam reached Indonesia and Malaysia it was substantially modified from the stern ascetic faith of the desert, and because of this was more readily acceptable. The mystic Sufist school of Islam had elements of magic, and a certain flexibility which allowed the incorporation of ancient animist beliefs when it reached south-east Asia. And since Islam did not have professional priests, the missionaries were traders; adoption of Islam gave a definite commercial advantage to ambitious local rajahs.

These elements have important present-day implications, making necessary a large distinction between Islam in Indonesia and Malaysia and that in the Middle East, especially the fundamentalist branches. In the Middle East, Pakistan and Afghanistan, Moslem orthodoxy largely persists in restrictive attitudes, whereas in Indonesia the religion is much more pliable. Women have a high degree of personal freedom and independence, play an important part in government and business, and are not limited in their movements and freedom to gain an education.

The last of the larger Malay maritime empires was the first to be located on the Malayan peninsula itself. This was Malacca, a port on the straits which bear its name. According to a sixteenth century Portuguese observer, Tome Pires, in his Suma Oriental Parameswara, the founder of Malacca, may have been of Shailendra descent, of the same blood as the dynasty that had ruled Shrivijaya. Certainly development of the two empires was similar, and they both had the same commercial motive – domination of the Malacca Straits trade. Singapore is their modern equivalent.

Nowadays Malacca's river has silted up and is useful only as a haven for a few fishing boats. The sleepy town looks out over a shallow, muddy stretch of sea over which the monsoon drives an endless succession of short, steep waves. But 600

years ago both the river and the sea approaches were readily
navigable, providing a convenient port for sailing ships. The
weather is seldom stormy and the two monsoons, the trade
winds of this region, blow with remarkable regularity.

Because of this, Malacca was a useful stopping place for
the Ming armadas despatched by Yung Lo. Peace, and its location
on the main sea route through south-east Asia, permitted Malacca
to grow rapidly. Indeed China issued an order to Malacca's
main potential enemy, Siam, not to attack the city. In the two
decades from 1411, five Malaccan rulers journeyed to the
Chinese court. The Gujerati Moslems from India played a major
part in its brisk trade. They came to Malacca in hundreds,
using all the efficiency in trade and commerce that distinguishes
their descendants in India today. Indeed Indian cotton cloth
and spices were the major commodities traded. Malacca's revenues came from a six per cent duty levied on the value of all
cargoes brought in, and from a brisk entrepot trade.

The first Portuguese ships to arrive in Malacca, in 1509,
found the city at the height of its influence. The arrival of the
Europeans caused much uneasiness among the Gujerati Moslems,
who, from their experiences off the west Indian coast, knew
something of Portuguese methods. They anticipated a commercial
challenge in south-east Asia, and persuaded the rulers of Malacca
to agree to a sudden attack on the European squadron. These
ships were part of the Portuguese fleet that had so decisively
beaten the Moslems off Diu. Now the outcome was different.
The Portuguese were forced to withdraw leaving behind two
burning ships, many men killed, and 19 members of a shore
party held as prisoners. Revenge was not long delayed. Two
years later the second Viceroy, d'Albuquerque, arrived off
Malacca personally with a fleet of 18 ships, fresh from the
establishment of Goa on the west Indian coast as the head-
quarters of a Portuguese empire in Asia. At Malacca he demanded, at gunpoint, the return of the Portuguese prisoners
and compensation for the ships that had been destroyed.

Malacca decided to resist, and the Portuguese then took the
city by storm, after several days' hard fighting. The European

force was small – European forces in Asia usually were – but its discipline, superior arms and the supporting firepower of the ships allowed it to win the day. Also, resistance was far from general. Many of the traders living in the town had no real loyalty to its rulers. They were mainly interested in ending the fighting quickly so trade could be resumed. Following their usual custom the Portuguese consolidated their victory by building a strong, stone fortress near the river mouth. Its gateway can still be seen in Malacca, surrounded by green lawns in a park that looks over the sea.

The newcomers, who had arrived without women, readily intermarried with the Malays – a deliberate policy that helped the Portuguese to identify more closely with their colonies. A large Eurasian population descended from the Portuguese continues to live in Malacca, where surnames such as da Silva and Pereira are common. Most of these people are Catholic, and live in a poorer suburb of the present city. There is a curious story about them. It is said their present backwardness is due to a curse never to prosper by one of the earliest and most famous missionaries in Asia, St Francis Xavier.

The Portuguese had not been long in Malacca before its prosperity began to decline. Like most colonial powers, their primary objective was to make money, but the Portuguese set standards of rapacity never equalled afterwards, and so doomed their empire in Asia. Eventually they became so well-hated for their treachery, cruelty and greed that shipping began to avoid the port. Most of the Gujerati traders now went to ports in north Sumatra.

Another European power, Holland, was to be the Portuguese nemesis. Dutch ships bombarded Malacca in 1606, and from then on blockaded the port more or less continuously. Malacca's trade became almost non-existent, and eventually the town even ran short of food, for it was dependent on rice imports from Java. The Dutch, in an alliance with Malacca's former Malay rulers, attacked it in force in 1640 and six months later the fortress capitulated.

Malacca never recovered, because the Dutch did not allow

it to do so. Holland regarded it as a strategic fortress. While they held Malacca nobody else could reinstate its trading potential and so commerce was diverted to the East Indies (now Indonesia) in which the Dutch were more interested. Dutch military government in Malacca was harsh, and much misery resulted from the hostility between the Protestant Hollanders and the Catholic Malay and Eurasian converts. So the early promise of Malacca came to nothing. It became one of the first victims of the age of imperialism.

Although the kingdom of Johore, at the extreme south of the Malay peninsula, achieved a certain continuity of rule it, too, was riven with dissension and strife. The rest of the peninsula reverted to small, primitive river kingdoms, passing through restless alliances and perpetual, if sporadic, warfare between neighbours. The northern states became vassals of Thailand. For a time, dominance over much of the rest of Malaya was exercised by a race of sea-pirates, the Bugis of Sulawesi.

British merchants began to trade in a limited way with this small, under-populated Malaya during the eighteenth century. One of them was a sea-captain named Francis Light who, after much argument, persuaded the British East India Company to establish a port on Penang, the small mountainous island off the north western coast. This settlement, Georgetown, founded in 1786, was the first British foothold on Malayan soil. As usual, trade was the main consideration. The East Indiamen, as the company's ships were called, needed a base to break the long journey to and from Canton for tea. The China trade was fast expanding. Ship design improved and tea, unknown in England before the middle of the seventeenth century, was fast displacing coffee, and stronger beverages, in popularity, its appeal to the rapidly-developing British morality succintly described in the poet William Cowper's description of 'the cups that cheer, but not inebriate.'

Thomas Stamford Raffles, who had been governor of Java during the Napoleonic wars, landed in 1819 on a small, swampy island off the Johore coast, separated from it only by a narrow, shallow channel. This island of Singapore, inhabited only by a few fishermen, seemed worthless to the Sultan of Johore, who agreed to lease it in perpetuity. The new settlement quickly proved its value. As early as 1824, the date of the first official census, more than 10,000 people had settled there. In 1824 Dutch and British spheres of influence were regularised by treaty. Holland withdrew her objections to Singapore and exchanged Malacca for the only British post in the East Indies, Bencoolen, on Sumatra. Two years later Singapore was united with Georgetown on Penang and Malacca as a separate colonial territory, which came to be known as the Straits Settlements.

14
· · · · · · · ·
Indonesia: The Last Independent Kingdoms and the Extension of Dutch Rule

The merchant adventurers of Holland began that country's three and a half centuries of association with the fertile islands they called the East Indies under a haze of cannon smoke. They were treacherous, cruel and rapacious and from first acquaintance excited fear and hatred among the native people.

In these respects they differed little from their fellow European traders in this region. Journeys to and from the Indies were so hazardous that generally only criminals and others of desperate character and uncertain morality would take the risks. For many years an average loss of a quarter of the crews of ships trading to the Indies was regarded as normal. The first Dutch fleet of four ships to reach the islands in 1596 lost 145 of its complement of 249 during a voyage of 14 months. Many of these deaths were from scurvy.

Dutch exploitation might never have gone further than the casual mixture of piracy and trading typical of this earliest penetration of European influence had it not been for the ambitious vision of Jan Coen, who was appointed the first Governor-General in 1618. He foresaw a vast Dutch commercial empire in the east, with ramifications far beyond the Indies.

Coen achieved control of the trading port of Jakarta in West Java and built there a strong fortress and a miniature Dutch town. Its rows of small white houses huddled close together along the banks of muddy canals, with their brown-tiled roofs, leadlight windows and heavy shutters, were inspired by a keen homesickness for the Netherlands. In 1619 this town was given Holland's ancient name, Batavia. The small Dutch outpost did not, and could not, initially challenge the still-powerful rulers of Java. It successfully withstood some probing assaults from them, then signed agreements which technically acknowledged their overlordship.

Because of the remoteness of these islands from Europe, their spices had always commanded very high prices. At that time the Moluccas were the only place where cloves grew, and the nutmeg tree was found exclusively on Banda and Ambon. Jan Coen used a mixture of persuasion and force to secure a monopoly on this lucrative trade. He then consolidated his position by driving trade competitors, especially the English, from Indonesian waters. There were many obscure but violent incidents, of which the best remembered is the execution of a few English traders and their Chinese assistants at Ambon in 1623. In spite of a battle of words between the Dutch and English governments, the British East India Company was not interested enough to finance a lengthy war. The English disappeared from the Indies, maintaining only the single post at Bencoolen in Sumatra.

The Dutch applied rigid controls on the economy of the islands, for they were determined not to allow the price of cloves and nutmeg to fall because of over-supply. They forced the local people to cut down and burn their trees, until spice production had fallen to a quarter of the former crop. Villagers who resisted were ruthlessly hunted down and shot, and their homes burned. Coen's expedition against Banda to secure the nutmeg monopoly is one of the horrifying incidents of colonial history. The islanders fought back bravely, but were overwhelmed by the superior weapons of the Dutch. The survivors were forced to grow the spices for the Dutch under conditions little better than slavery. The company determined the price it would pay, and forced the growers to accept trade goods from Batavia in payment.

This barter system was very much to the disadvantage of the Indonesians. The prosperity of the islands diminished, and over the next century the population of Ambon declined by a third. So deep was the bitterness aroused by these policies that when world demand for spices increased in the eighteenth century even extreme measures could not induce these people to increase production of cloves and nutmeg. Finally the trees were successfully grown in India and the Dutch monopoly ended.

Meanwhile, the toehold on Java was precariously maintained. The last major Indonesian state prior to the colonial period was based on an inland capital, Mataram, in Central Java. It became large and powerful during the lifetime of an outstanding leader, Sultan Agung, who came to the throne in 1623. According to the Court records of the time, he regarded himself as the successor to the great rulers of Majapahit, even though he was a Moslem. By 1625 he ruled all of Java except for small areas at the eastern and western tips of the island, which were controlled by Bali and the state of Bantam. Bantam was a vigorous state based on the west Javanese pepper trade. It is probable that some of the great Hindu-Javanese families of Majapahit had fled east to the island of Bali. The society they led there maintained a well-organised opposition to both Mataram and the Dutch, keeping their own island and the small enclave on Java independent.

Between 1627 and 1630 Agung made determined efforts, both by treachery and direct assault, to put an end to Batavia. The armies of Mataram attempted to trick the Dutch into unwariness. They placed a dam across the river that provided the fortress's water supply, and when all else failed, instituted a siege involving thousands of soldiers. However, this massive army soon ran short of food. Dutch naval power was vastly superior – the Dutch ships destroyed a fleet of 200 boats carrying rice – and within weeks the starving army of Mataram was forced to retreat. A treaty followed guaranteeing Batavia's continued existence.

In many ways Mataram followed the traditions of Majapahit and was probably representative of even earlier Javanese kingdoms. It is consequently of some interest because there are many written descriptions of it by European observers. Social changes are slow in Asia. Mataram resembled in a number of ways the Indian kingdoms of more than a thousand years before its time – the first of which we have independent accounts. The observations of the Greek Megasthenes about the Mauryan empire in north India in the fourth century and those of Dutchmen who visited the *kraton* – the palace complex – of Mataram, bear witness to this continuity of tradition.

One similarity was the king's guard, composed of women armed with spears and lances, who were the only people allowed near the ruler when he appeared in public. Far more basic was the actual sacral role of the king, his place as an intermediary between the people and the feared and worshipped forces of nature, which are impressive enough in Java, with its active volcanos and sudden, violent thunderstorms, in some places occurring on more than 300 days a year. Only the king, supported by the spirits of his ancestors, could negotiate with these forces, on which the common prosperity and safety so much depended. There are links with East Asia in the *pusakas*, or sacred objects, on which the welfare of the kingdom was believed to depend, hidden away in a secret place deep within the *kraton*.

The Sultan of Mataram's life, and that of all Javanese princes of his tradition, was surrounded by magic and mystery. He was believed to possess sacred weapons, such as swords, that could make him invulnerable; he would spend nights near the graves of his ancestors, gathering magical influence, and was believed to obtain dynamic power from the soil itself, from thunder and lightning, and other manifestations of nature. In spite of being educated and well-read in European political theory Indonesia's independence leader, President Sukarno, consciously followed this tradition.

The sultan was above and beyond the law. If he behaved in a peremptory, brutal, even, at times, hideously criminal fashion, this was seen by the ordinary people as a manifestation of divinity in him. The ruler was expected to live in a more extravagant, dynamic and flamboyant way than ordinary men – to be a great user of women among other things. Because of this belief in his superhuman qualities, the rulers had absolute powers of life and death over even the highest-born, and these seem never to have been questioned.

The Indonesian people, although apparently very gentle, have hidden qualities of violence and can be suddenly taken with a killing frenzy, described by the word *amuk* – mad. European observers were shocked when Agung's commander ordered the summary execution of 800 of his soldiers because they had failed in the attempt to take Batavia. The aristocracy, made up of princes of the royal house and of associated states, had to live in the *kraton* with the king and could be, sometimes were, killed at a word from him at the slightest suspicion of disloyalty.

Royal wrath was visited on high and low alike without mercy. The peasants suffered, as peasants did in every feudal state, and in much the same ways. They were taxed and sweated to support the *kraton* and regularly conscripted to fight the king's wars. As elsewhere in south-east Asia such armies could number a hundred thousand or more, and casualties among them were often high. The relatively small population of the region before 1800 has been ascribed to this.

Nevertheless, Mataram did have a considerable prosperity and a definite system of law. Dutch observers say the region around the *kraton* was intensely cultivated, with hill after hill built up into a complex of terraced, irrigated ricefields. Several million people lived under Mataram's rule, in perhaps 3000 villages of 100 families or more, each surrounded by their fields. It was an organisation of rural life still typical of much of Asia today.

Although Agung was a Moslem, he did not base the law of Mataram solely on that of Islam. The religious courts existed, but the law was a mixture of the Islamic and the traditional Javanese customary code, called *adat*, which retains considerable force today.

The *kraton* itself was a rambling collection of red brick, stone and timber buildings, gardens, pavilions and courtyards.

Certain parts of it were semi-public. Much of the rest housed the king's retainers and the nobles who were kept constantly under his eye so they might have no opportunity to plot rebellion. Other parts of the *kraton* were never open to visitors or any but the highest officials. Building work for the ruler was a constant occupation for much of the community because new *kratons* were required constantly. There is an interesting echo of Angkor in the fact that every new ruler was expected to build a new *kraton*. Sometimes the residence was shifted after the passing of a certain number of years, or if the old *kraton* were defiled for any one of a number of ritual reasons.

Those who reflect on the limited nature of Indonesian democracy, the privileges assumed as of right by its rulers and their families, the vast economic advantages they have over the ordinary people, the ruthless decimation of whole communities, as in Irian Jaya and East Timor, might also consider the extent to which these things are simply part of a continuing tradition.

The rulers of Mataram did not regard the Dutch as superiors, or even as equals. Initially they were welcomed because competition between them and the Portuguese drove up spice prices. However, the sultan treated the Dutch with contempt, because they were merchants, and forced them to wait for hours in the hot sun. On the other hand the officials of the company treated the rulers with deference, offering regular gifts imported from Europe.

Nevertheless, during Agung's reign the Dutch had been able to consolidate. The third Governor-General, Anthony Van Diemen, took Malacca from the Portuguese. This, with the eviction of the British, left Holland as the major trading power in the Indies. Van Diemen and Agung died in the same year, 1645, and the relationship between the company and the state of Mataram began to change. Agung's successor, Amangkurat, was a less formidable man than his father. In 1646 he concluded a new treaty which made him dependent on the company for much of his personal income. He reined in the power of the religious courts and is said to have killed 6000 Moslem 'priests' in a single massacre after calling them together in conference. This reaction against Islam, and his desire for absolute control of the empire, caused dangerous trouble in the outlying vassal states. The ruler of one of these led a revolt that dethroned Amangkurat. His *kraton* at Mataram was burned, his treasures looted.

Amangkurat died shortly after he escaped from the ruins, but before he did so he advised his son to seek a closer alliance with the Dutch. Amangkurat II, who was said to be of weak character, was restored to power by a Dutch army. The price was control of the Mataram empire by the company, which now had troops stationed permanently at the new *kraton*. With Mataram subject, Bantam's years of independence were numbered. The Dutch took advantage of a royal quarrel there to manipulate the succession and control the state.

So the eighteenth century began with the Dutch empire greatly extended. Although the old kingdoms had lost their power, the Dutch did not disturb their traditions and essential social organisation. The rulers and the aristocracy remained in their traditional positions, but were not permitted to make war on one another. The Dutch in fact used them as agents. The nobles became 'regents', responsible for exacting a certain amount of income from the peasants, which they must pass on to the company. The worst features of the independent states remained – but added to them was the burden of tribute going to the Dutch. Thus the old social relationship was maintained into modern times, the privileged position of the *priyayi* still remaining an essential feature of Javanese society.

Batavia itself was afflicted for a hundred years with a contagious fever – probably malaria – which caused a high deathrate among the Dutch settlers. The large numbers of Chinese who had settled in Indonesia now became increasingly influential. The 'regents' apppointed by the Dutch were usually lazy and inefficient, and had a contempt for the details of commerce. Chinese immigrants were ready to act as intermediaries, provided they saw a good profit in it for themselves. Internal highway tolls, another burden on the ordinary people, were often 'farmed out', like other forms of taxation, to the Chinese.

Because of this direct relationship with the people in what came to be an extortionate role, the Chinese came to be despised and hated. This attitude is still strong today, and lies behind anti-Chinese violence since independence.

Like all institutions that exist for a long time without change, the Dutch East India Company gradually deteriorated. The Chinese made money but, increasingly, the company did not. It was dissolved in 1799 because of its heavy losses and overheads and a bad record of corruption among its officials. Direct rule by the Dutch government did not mend matters significantly. Holland became embroiled in the Java War, which dragged on for five years from 1825. It was caused by Dutch interference in the succession in Jogjakarta. A prince named Diponegoro, the eldest of his family, was passed over by the Dutch, who installed a younger brother as sultan. Diponegoro led a revolt that combined many different hostilities, including those of the aristocracy against the Dutch and the ordinary people against the Chinese who were their immediate oppressors. Vague and mixed though its motives were, the war was intense and destructive. It resulted in the loss of 15,000 Dutch soldiers and the death of perhaps a quarter of a million Chinese and Indonesians – mostly civilians not actually concerned with the fighting.

From 1830 Holland was involved in war at home – a nine year revolt of her Belgian provinces that completed the exhaustion of the Netherlands Treasury, already depleted by the Napoleonic Wars. To restore her finances Holland imposed on the Indies the cultivation system, requiring the planting of one fifth of all agricultural land in a crop dictated by the colonial power. This crop became the property of the government. Added to existing burdens this resulted in such a severe 'squeeze' of the peasants that there were major famines in Java. This cultivation system introduced new crops to the island – sugar, coffee and indigo, and later tea, intended entirely for export.

The vast sums pouring out of Batavia made up close to one-third of the entire Netherlands Budget over a period of 50 years. Yet barely half this revenue came from the cultivation system. A further large sum came from land taxes, customs duties, and monopolies in salt, opium and pawnshop operation. Little was provided in return. No attempt was made to develop a basic education system of any consequence, nor to train Indonesians in the professions. Introduction of universal basic schooling was considered once or twice, late in the colonial period, but dismissed as being too expensive.

15

....

India under Two Masters: The Grand Moguls and the East India Company

After the decline of the Gupta empire no other unifying force comparable with it emerged for nine centuries, leaving north India at the mercy of any marauding band that chose to ride down through the passes. Revealed instead are cruel and extortionate north Indian kingdoms, like those of the sultans of Delhi, and the petty empires of scores of warlike princelings, each the predator of a tract of country dominated by a central fortress. Although incessantly pre-occupied with war, these rulers, the Rajputs, contributed to their country's defencelessness by their quarrelling, lack of a common purpose, and retention of old-fashioned if romantic military methods against enemies who had cannon and had advanced the use of cavalry to an exact science. Reckless, indeed suicidal, bravery was no effective answer to these things. It was a tradition of the Rajputs, when one of their fortresses was doomed to fall, to burn all their women and children alive on a funeral pyre while the men sallied out to meet death at the hands of their enemies.

Many of the invaders who drove down from central Asia were simple destroyers, like the Huns – probably the ancestors of present-day Hungarians – who were execrated in India just as they were in Europe and China. Later 'barbarians' were more cultivated although just as cruel. They were Moslems, practising a form of Islam derived through and influenced by the civilised and artistic Persian (Iranian) culture. To these people the ornamented architecture of the Hindu temples, their many statues of gods and goddesses, elaborate rituals and use of music for worship, were evidence of an idolatry the removal of which, by fire and sword, was a religious duty. It was one that associated itself conveniently with looting.

Buddhism in India was hastened into decline by the Moslem invaders, who slew its peaceful monks in thousands and destroyed the great teaching monasteries. This phase of conquest and brutality is balanced somewhat by a blending of indigenous and Moslem art, notably painting and architecture. The delicate building of this time, with its shady courts, fretted walls, water gardens, and tall graceful minarets, owed much to Persian influence and the dislike of the conquerors from the clean air of the hills for the hot mugginess of the Indian plain in the months before and during the monsoon rains. It is a style still very much alive, and one which spread far beyond India, as the railway station in Kuala Lumpur and the extravagant marble mosque in Brunei can testify.

Order and authority returned to north India with the advent of the Moslem dynasty Europe called the Grand Moguls. They added glamour, pageantry and a strange collection of legend to the world's story but, more than that, brought a unity and established methods of government that, in many respects, foreshadowed the patterns of today. At best, it was a remarkably able administration for its time. Many of its methods, even when in ruins, were admired by later British officials.

In 1525, with a force of only 12,000, the first Mogul emperor, Babur, marched through the Khyber gorges to conquer India. He met a defending army of 100,000 on India's traditional field of decision, the plain of Panipat, 50 miles north of Delhi, and won decisively. Babur's victory was due substantially to good discipline, highly-trained cavalry, and possession of an artillery train. The people of north India were accustomed to these periodic raids from the north. When Babur pushed on from Delhi to Agra, the Indians sought to placate him with the gift of an enormous diamond, thought by some to be the great stone now called the Kohinoor.

But unlike his forerunners, Babur did not return to the mountains of the north. In Agra he laid out a garden, and made other preparations for a permanent stay, in spite of complaints in his memoirs that India lacked interesting fruits, baths and graceful buildings, and that it was steamy, hot and unattractive. Although capable enough of harsh, even cruel, actions by the standards of today, Babur was moderate and cultured for his time. He was reflective and thoughtful, with considerable powers of personality, which were fully engaged persuading his homesick followers to stay in India.

According to a chronicle of the time Babur's eldest son Humayun became seriously ill. Babur followed a custom of his people in offering his own dearest possession, his life, in exchange for his son's restoration to health. He is said to have walked three times around Humayun's sickbed and to have pledged his own life in exchange. Humayun recovered, but Babur died at the age of 47. Humayun, heavily addicted to opium, had little of his father's powers of leadership and came close to losing the empire. He spent practically the whole of his life on the move, intriguing against, fighting with, or running away from his enemies. His son Akbar was several times taken hostage before his father's death made him emperor at the age of 13.

Against all expectation all the powers of his grandfather, and more, returned to the dynasty. Akbar brought a rare genius to the task of controlling his difficult heritage. During his reign of nearly 50 years, to 1605, the Mogul dynasty was firmly established, and even integrated with the older elements of Indian society. Although he was a Moslem for most of his life, Akbar went out of his way to win the respect and assistance of the traditional Hindu leaders and, as the decades passed, even the intolerant and wild Rajput princes came to serve him loyally. Akbar was astute enough to see that pride and self-esteem were the mainsprings of their lives, and he won them over by allowing them what would be called, today, status symbols – the right to sound their drums in the capital, which was a privilege of royalty, or to enter the royal audience chamber fully-armed.

Akbar used them in his civil service, which was organised with fixed, graded salary scales so officials did not have to depend on bribery and extortion for their incomes. This, his regularisation of taxation, standardisation of weights and measures, and improved legal code, made the Indian society relatively peaceful and prosperous under his rule. Taxation of the peasants was limited to a third of gross product. Unfortunately his lively mind turned to a restless mysticism as he grew older. Akbar established a new religion, a court cult based on the assumption of his own divinity, which sought to blend Islam and Hinduism. He even went so far as to wear the caste-marks and sacred thread of the Hindu twice-born. This alarmed the orthodox among his Moslem followers, and a period of reaction set in after his death.

It was an added misfortune that his heir, Jehengir, was cruel by temperament, and reverted to such forms of punishment as flaying alive and impaling. During Jehengir's reign, in 1615, Sir Thomas Roe led a British embassy to the Mogul court. The gifts it brought were scorned as trifles, and Sir Thomas was not able to achieve as much as he had hoped. However, Jehengir formed an admiration for the quietly courageous Englishman, who stubbornly refused to knock his head three times on the floor before the Mogul, the required form of homage. Roe was able to make some trading arrangements and consolidated the first British trading post, established by Captain Will Hawkins in Surat in 1609.

The extravagant wealth of the dynasty was at its most lavish during the reign of Jehengir's son, Shah Jahan, who is remembered chiefly because his great and lasting passion for a woman inspired one of the world's most beautiful buildings. The emperor was wholly devoted to his wife, Mumtaz Mahal. When she died, Shah Jahan set 20,000 men to work for 22 years to build her memorial, the Taj Mahal at Agra, the most famed and lovely of all Indian monuments.

He also created the Peacock Throne, perhaps the most extravagant and expensive single object the world has ever known. One of the thousands of jewels adorning it was a ruby three finger-widths long by two wide. The three steps approaching the throne were encrusted with gems as carelessly and lavishly as if they had been mere pebbles, according to the French jeweller and traveller Jean Baptiste Tavernier, who inspected it at firsthand.

The last of the Moguls to hold more than a shadow of power was a devout and bigoted Moslem, Aurangzeb, who damaged the empire through the narrow-minded religious zeal that marked his reign from 1659 to 1707. Aurangzeb failed to control the ever-present Moslem extremist faction, which sought to persecute the Hindus. They seized the opportunity to loot and burn Hindu homes and temples, and to force Hindu officials out of office. Aurangzeb quickly lost the support of the Rajput princes, on which the empire so much depended. His most persistent enemy was the Maratha confederacy from the mountains of west India, led by a warrior chief called Shivaji. His name is important because it was later used by Hindu extremists as a symbol of their opposition to Indian Islam. In spite of his wealth and pomp, his 800 war elephants and huge army, Aurangzeb steadily lost ground against the rebels.

In 1701, six years before his death, the emperor had granted the British East India Company the right to collect revenues from land near Calcutta, and their influence in the trade of Bengal increased steadily from then on.

During the next 40 years eight Mogul emperors, increasingly out of control of the empire, sat on the throne. Over these decades the realm split into fragments as, one by one, local officials or governors set up virtually autonomous states. So began the princely states, which were to endure into the twentieth century. The largest of these states became as populous and wealthy as some of the world's leading powers of the day, the greatest of them the central Indian state of Hyderabad, whose hereditary rulers, the Nizams, became the richest men in the world.

Then, in 1739, came another sudden raid from the north, this time led by the Persian adventurer Nadir Shah. After a whirlwind attack on Delhi he carried off treasure said to be worth $60 million. Among the loot that accompanied him back to the mountains were the Peacock Throne and the Kohinoor Diamond.

The Moguls and their administrators were, of course, a super-structure above, and supported unwillingly by, the real India, which was very different. Eighteenth-century Europe spoke in glowing terms of the treasures of Ind, but in reality the flam-boyant prosperity of the Moguls was based on the exploitation and poverty of the mass of the people. After Akbar's death, the villagers suffered acutely. Mogul taxation was increased to as much as half of all produce, and even this does not take into account additional amounts extorted, less formally, by tax gatherers and local lords. The peasant was exploited as much as possible without actually being starved to death. Virtually all the national income that came into the hands of the govern-ing class was spent on high living, paying retainers and the creation of private buildings, tombs and monuments. Public works like irrigation canals, roads and bridges, which would have improved the lives of the villagers, were not seen as a state responsibility. Instead local officials exacted highway tolls at strategic points, such as river fords and crossroads, for their own benefit.

In the eighteenth century there were still large tracts of jungle, swamp and desert in India. There was also a great deal of petty crime and banditry. Travel was difficult and dangerous. From time to time bands of travellers might be joined by strangers of innocent appearance who, however, killed their victims late at night by strangling them with a silken scarf. These silent killers, who worshipped the goddess of death, Kali, made a point of efficient disposal of the bodies of their victims. The practice was known as *thuggee* and has given English the word 'thug'.

Villages, then as now, stood dirty and impoverished, an untidy network set on the dusty plains. Their people were poor, vul-nerable to the vagaries of the seasons and the cupidity of their rulers alike, limited in their ambitions and almost all suffering from one or more debilitating diseases. Women, worn out by bearing large families when they had scarcely left childhood themselves, were lucky indeed to survive their twenties. Those who died young were perhaps the most fortunate, since widows were frequently burned alive on their husband's funeral pyre. Men became old in their thirties.

The caste system was by then fully developed. It divided Hindu society into a myriad of small groups, each of which sought to maintain its special position or privileges. In many respects the caste amounts to an exclusive society, with established rules and discipline imposed on all its members, and designed to serve their interests. Often membership of a caste group is associated with occupation, as guilds were in Europe, with work skills passing on from father to son.

Castes do not intermarry except for rare individuals, who then face becoming outcast. Members of one caste will not eat in the same place as certain others, or suffer them to use the same utensils or the same wells. In some cases, even the shadow of a member of another caste is regarded as defiling. Extreme though all this must seem to those brought up in the relative social mobility of the West, it is possible to see reasons for it in the conditions of Indian society. The system seems to have evolved to its present form prior to and during the later Mogul period, and is consistent with the necessity for small social groups to maintain their identity.

Yet to say no more than this would be strongly to underestimate India, which in spite of its problems and staggering social disproportions, has evolved a remarkably diverse and vigorous culture, a reflection of a society full of subtleties and surprises. Its dance and music are distinctive, highly-developed and formalised. They have also been pervasive, to the extent that the same arts throughout south-east Asia are plainly derivative. The elegant dancing performed on the steps of Angkor Wat, and in Bali, have evolved from Indian forms. Indian art is a part of life, intimately linked with the everyday life of individuals, rather than a separate 'package' as in the West, where appreciation of the arts tends to be a spectator sport.

Perhaps because of this much Indian art is ephemeral – one gets the feeling that its great works have survived almost by accident, usually because their original intent was decorative. There is a strong sense that it is the act of creation that is important, rather than the finished work. Frequently, large amounts of time and effort are put into displays for processions, carnivals or religious occasions, using temporary materials, that are destroyed or disregarded soon after they are complete. It is very much art of the moment, using colour, form, sound, light, fire to create as vivid, often as bizarre, an effect as possible.

A further dimension of Indian culture is the mysterious, even the miraculous, based on meditation and prolonged mental training. This can manifest itself in apparently impossible physical events – people who can walk on fire without being burned, who have been buried alive for long periods, withstood what would be for most people terrible injuries amounting to torture, the stopping of the heartbeat and breathing for long periods. How much of this is genuine and how much trickery is difficult to determine, and is a constant area of controversy.

During the Mogul period the first European trading posts were established in India and continued to exist in a small way, more or less on sufferance. The merchants neither exercised political power nor sought it. Their motive was trade, their ambition to amass enough capital to retire at home in comfort as soon as possible. These nouveaux riches *nabobs* excited some resentment and curiosity when they retired to the English countryside, not the least for their habit of bathing regularly.

Just as the Dutch were predominant in Indonesia and the French were later to be in Indo-China, Britain's main zone of interest in Asia was India. During the seventeenth century three major posts were established by her East India Company. These, in the order of their founding or acquisition, were: Fort St George, later to become Madras (Chennai), on the Coromandel, or south-east coast; Bombay (Mumbai) on the central-western coast; and in 1691, Fort William on the Hugli River in the Ganges delta of Bengal. Fort William was later to become Calcutta, (Kolkata from July, 1999) one of the world's biggest cities and the place from which Britain's empire in India was largely to develop.

The struggle to inherit Mogul power was intensified with the coming of the eighteenth century. At first circumstances seemed to favour the Hindu Maratha princes, but they were too self-seeking and disunited to take advantage of the situation. Some modern Indian historians look back on the Maratha campaigns at this time as a patriotic Hindu uprising against Islam. The Marathas cannot be really viewed in this way after the death of their leader Shivaji in 1680. They became more interested in plunder than politics, and their power was broken in a battle with a coalition of Afghan raiders and the Moslem princes of Delhi. The Afghans emerged from this battle, at Panipat on 1761, as the strongest single force, but they had no ambitions for empire. Hence there was no Indian power left that was strong enough, and anxious enough, to take over government of the country.

At this stage the British also had no desire to rule India; indeed, the East India Company's policy was to avoid involvement in local politics if possible. This was not necessarily the view of its officials on the spot, who understood the value of political power in promoting trade. Their influence had a far-reaching effect. One of them, Robert Clive, began the chain of events that led on to British India when he first eliminated a French foothold on the Coromandel coast, for reasons of commercial rivalry, then intervened in the succession in Bengal.

An inexperienced ruler of Bengal – he was only 19 – attacked the British settlement at Calcutta. He is said to have had more than a hundred people locked in a small room, 18 feet by 15 feet, through one tropical night. Most of them were said to have died in this 'black hole.' The apparent enormity of this event, prominently featured and coloured in almost all British histories of India written during the imperial period, depends on a single suspect source – the account of one of the survivors, one J. Holwell. Now the 'facts' are disputed by several modern historians; the emotive term 'black hole' was in fact British army slang for a barracks prison.

Clive led a punitive expedition, regained Calcutta and defeated a much larger Indian army at Plassey in 1757. The East India Company was now in a position to control Bengal. It did so through local officials it appointed and kept in office, then consolidated its political power when in 1765 it exacted from the puppet emperor the right to collect the revenues of Bengal, Bihar and Orissa, worth $4 million a year. Anarchic conditions through much of the country made further increases in British power almost inevitable. The three rapidly-growing ports under British rule and British law were islands of relative peace and order amid chaos, and attracted business of all kinds.

One of the fatal weaknesses of the Mogul empire had been its inability to foster a flourishing mercantile class with rights and influence of its own, like the sturdy British middle class even then laying the foundations of empire. The Moguls and their provincial governors dominated manufacture and trade and forced artisans and craftsmen to work for them almost as slaves. Even though merchants acquired wealth, they had no standing and no privileges. These mercantile families, who wanted only to trade fairly and lawfully, flocked to the British enclaves in thousands.

Bengal, in 1769–70, suffered a famine of such intensity that one third of its inhabitants died – probably as many as eight million people, often in the most atrocious circumstances. After this huge disaster there was such a severe labour shortage as to disturb the whole balance of land ownership. This was perhaps the blackest period of British exploitation of India, since the forcible extraction of huge sums in tax from the peasants was maintained in spite of the extent of the famine. Tax revenues were £1.3 million for 1769/70, while famine relief offered by the company was less than £10,000. The British enclaves prospered and grew rapidly. The Indian population of Calcutta was over a quarter of a million in 1788, with Madras and Bombay not far behind.

The East India Company remained a commercial undertaking, based on trade and exploitation. High prices were paid for posts as company officials at the courts of Indian rulers, and large fortunes were made through 'tax-farming' the unfortunate people. The ostentation of these returning 'nabobs' continue to attract unfavourable comment at home. Clive, who became the first governor of Bengal, and his successor Warren Hastings drew widespread criticism because they had made large fortunes through the exercise of their influence. Clive was forced to defend himself on the floor of Parliament in 1772 and, after an all-night debate, was exonerated. Two years later he committed suicide in London. A similar controversy marred the repute of Warren Hastings.

Mainly as a result of these scandals the British Government passed, in 1773, a regulating act which brought the operations of the East India Company under the surveillance of the Crown. While the company maintained its trading monopoly for another 40 years, political control was henceforward to be a matter for a council of directors in London, and a governor-general in India, responsible to Parliament. A period of consolidation followed. The real beginnings of that devoted, honest, competent and unbelievably self-righteous band of Britons, the Indian Civil Service, came with the establishment of a staff college in England to train recruits. Of these Rudyard Kipling wrote:

Take up the white man's burden
Send forth the best ye breed
Go bind your sons to exile
To serve your captives' need.

Unshakably convinced of their mission to govern, they were at least constructively reformist. Widow-burning was outlawed in 1829, although it continued illegally long after that. The more responsible British thinkers and statesmen began to feel the wider implications and responsibilities of their vast dominion. In 1834 the celebrated historian and essayist Thomas

Macaulay, who had taken a seat on the Supreme Council for India the previous year, argued successfully for a system of education, based on the English language and European traditions, to produce 'a class, Indian in blood and colour, but English in taste, in opinion, in mind and intellect'.

This education minute has been severely criticised, especially its assertion that 'a single shelf of a good European library is worth the whole native literature of India and Arabia'. Yet English as the official language and vehicle of education, from 1835 onward, gave India, for the first time, a single language that was understood throughout the country. To some extent Persian, the Court language of the Moguls, had met this requirement but it was used only by a small restricted class. A very much wider range of people learned English and India's debt to it as a unifying agency is recognised by most thoughtful Indians.

Education in the historical traditions of Europe during a phase of liberal revolutions also brought to the evolving Indian intelligentsia some new and disturbing concepts – nationalism, democracy, the freedom of the individual. Up to this time no one had seriously thought of India as an entity, a possible nation.

However, imperial reforms caused serious misgivings among both Hindu and Moslem traditionalists, who could now be in no doubt of British intentions to transform Indian society. Some historians regard the Indian 'mutiny' that broke out in 1857 as a consequence of this disquiet. *Sepoys*, Indian soldiers in the Bengal army, turned on their officers and their families. Although the scale of the revolt was relatively small and its duration brief, the horror of it, especially that of the killing of English women and children in Cawnpore, made a tremendous impact in England. It should be recorded that British retaliation was equally brutal and a good deal more extensive, involving the destruction of whole villages, and the extermination of whole families, often completely innocent of any involvement in the rebellion.

Christopher Hibbert's *The Great Mutiny*, largely derived from carefully-documented contemporary accounts, presents army officers, especially the notorious Colonel James Neil, in a very unfavourable light. When Delhi was occupied by the British, it was virtually destroyed by indiscriminate burning and looting. Thousands of the people were hanged, shot, or bayoneted. Another account describes how villages were surrounded by cavalry, the women and children brought out and all the men burned alive in their houses. If they tried to escape the flames they were 'cut up'.

While it seems doubtful there was really any significant nationalist element in the Indian mutiny, it is a convenient point at which to observe the declining influence of many of the old Hindu and Moslem aristocrats. British land reforms, designed to make tax collection more efficient, disturbed the old, interdependent communal nature of rural communities and instead substituted definite landlord and peasant classes. In general the energetic and businesslike became landlords, rather than the traditional ruling class, which was too proud to appear to jostle for financial gain. In many respects influence was going over to the mercantile middle class, the new class of British-educated, based mainly on the three big cities of British India, but especially on Calcutta.

In 1876 Queen Victoria was proclaimed Empress of India, leaving no doubt about how the Britons of that generation saw their imperial destiny. An impartial and codified system of law, well-adapted to and largely based on local traditions, did much to reduce oppression and injustice. Even if the devout deplored railways because they jostled all castes together in shocking proximity, Indians did not hesitate to use them. Also the trains were able to move food quickly, and this did much to mitigate the intensity of famines. In 1883 a famine code was developed that placed the responsibility squarely on the government to provide adequate famine relief. After the turn of the century these proved reasonably effective, with one massive and disastrous exception – the Bengal famine of 1943.

16

Gandhi's India: The Struggle for Liberty

Universities teaching the Western humanities were founded in the three main Indian colonial cities, Calcutta (Kolkata), Bombay (Mumbai) and Madras (Chennai) in 1857, the same year as the 'Indian Mutiny'. Of the two events the first was arguably the more significant, since Indian nationalism developed largely among the graduates of those universities. During the next 30 years nearly 50,000 Indians passed the entrance examinations, which themselves required literacy in English, and 5000 achieved the Bachelor of Arts degree.

Christianity was an important influence on Rammohun Roy, the first Indian reformer of consequence. It was he who led a vigorous campaign that persuaded the British Government to overcome its reluctance to interfere in religious customs and prohibit the custom of *suttee*, which obliged, and often forced, a widow to be burned alive on the funeral pyre of her husband. Roy had watched his own sister die this way. In 1828 Roy founded the Brahma Samaj, which sought to reform Hindu society by introducing into it the Western ideals he so much admired, and by abolishing the caste system. His ideas interested the increasingly large middle class of officials and professional men who owed their opportunities to the British.

There was also concern for the depressed and unhappy position of widows. They were condemned to a life that was almost a living death, unable to remarry and forced to live out the rest of their lives in sterile seclusion. Their hardships were the greater because for a variety of religious and social reasons girls entered into arranged marriages very young. Normally their husbands were older, and in a society which then had a life expectancy of about 30 wives frequently became widows younger than the average Western girl becomes a bride – sometimes as young as eight or nine.

The issue was, of course, important in its own right. However, it also brought into view another consideration that was to cast a long shadow on India's future. This was the immediate conflict between the reformers and the forces of Hindu religious conservatism, and the revelation that the latter were easily the stronger. The educated reformers talked a great deal, but flinched from actual defiance of caste discipline. There were a few exceptions. One, a champion of women's rights named D.K. Karve, actually married a widow. Both were ostracised. Nobody would sit or eat with them, they were barred from the family home, and evil gossip was circulated about them. Such courage was understandably rare.

The second wave of reform was based on a political and social revival of Hinduism itself, as revealed in the ancient epics. This came with the founding in 1875 of the Arya Samaj by Dayananda Saraswati, an Indian sage who spoke no English and had no Western education. He went back to the 'Aryan' epic, the *Rigveda*, for his inspiration, and attempted to identify a 'pure' Hinduism free from the contamination of later influences. The Arya Samaj movement was of lasting importance. It influenced many Indians to oppose social reforms introduced by Britain on the grounds that it was best for Indians first to achieve political influence and reform their society afterwards. Hence a revivalist Hinduism became a central theme of nationalism. Politics until then had revolved around parochial issues and had lacked such a major unifying influence.

The dusty brick mounds of Harappa and Mohenjo Daro were still enigmatic. Half a century would pass before these ruined cities would be recognised as the remains of the first important Indian civilisation, and no hint of their significance was available to the Hindu revivalists. Accordingly they looked back for a tradition to the epic writings of the later Aryan-speaking invaders of India, and so attributed to the beginnings of Indian society a pastoral simplicity quite unlike the sophistication and urbanity the Harappa ruins indicate.

Even after the discovery of Harappa, these early ideas tended to be rationalised, and still persist in the modern Indian's sense of national identity. They constitute a further major influence of the Arya Samaj – its definition on behalf of modern India of a 'golden age', long before India came under the domination of foreigners, in which happiness and simplicity were thought to have prevailed.

There were also material facts that gave impetus to nationalism. From 1837 on a selected number of English planters were allowed to take up land and settle in India. Even though they were subject to certain conditions – for instance, they must live on their holdings – the very fact that they were there at all was a source of uneasiness to Indians. Another influence was the growing pressure of poverty and landlessness among the villagers. The British themselves did not usurp land to any major extent, but they did introduce a land tenure system open to abuse. In many cases tax assessments were unfairly high and there was inadequate supervision of Indian middlemen. This forced hundreds of thousands of peasants from their land, which passed into the ownership of moneylenders who foreclosed on mortgages. Famines persisted, in spite of relief measures introduced by the government.

A sense of competition between the two major communities, Hindu and Moslem, induced both towards political organisation. An educated Moslem, Sir Seyed Ahmad Khan, warned his people as early as 1883 about the nature of the communal problem. 'If the British were to leave India,' he said, 'Who would then be the rulers? Is it possible that two nations, the Moslem and Hindu, could sit on the same throne and remain in power? To hope that both would remain equal is to desire the impossible and the inconceivable.'

Sir Seyed was the leader of a movement to raise Indian Islam from the apathy and disunity into which it had fallen after the collapse of the Mogul Dynasty. Due to his efforts the Anglo-Oriental College was founded in 1875 at Aligarh, near Delhi, to provide a place at which 'Moslems may acquire an English education without prejudice to their religion'. Almost all the national leaders of what was to become Pakistan were educated at Aligarh.

The first organisation with the declared objective of Indian self-government was the Indian National Congress. Its political offspring, the Congress Party, was to lead India to nationhood in 1947. However the first Congress, in 1885, was far from being a political party in the modern sense. Of its 72 delegates only two were Moslems, and there was a solid commitment to establishing Anglo-Saxon political institutions in India.

However, a militant anti-British nationalism was also developing. It emerged first in Bombay and was founded not only on the Hindu revival, but more specifically on that of the Maratha people who, under their great leader Shivaji, had successfully defied the Moguls in the seventeenth century. The movement gained terrorist overtones. In 1896 bubonic plague spread from Bombay south to Poona. Strong measures were needed to control it. A British official named Rand used soldiers to evacuate houses thought to be infected and to destroy property, if necessary at bayonet point. The following year an extremist murdered Rand and an associate.

The extremists found renewed opportunities during the autocratic term of office of Lord Curzon, the Viceroy from 1898. Curzon, a dedicated Conservative, was a man of restless energy and efficiency. Almost constantly in pain, for he had to wear a leather and iron harness because of a back complaint, he was overbearing and tactless to the point of rudeness. He had no patience with 'political Indians', and stated his objective of 'assisting the Congress to a peaceful demise'. Two unpopular measures towards the end of his term led educated Bengalis to oppose him. The first restricted their influence on university administration, the second partitioned the huge state of Bengal to provide better government for its predominantly Moslem eastern section, the present-day Bangladesh. This resulted in riots and demonstrations. A campaign called *swadeshi* was organised to boycott British goods, especially textiles, and remained a favourite tactic of the nationalists from this time onwards.

World war in 1914 became as much the end of an era in India as in Europe. More than a million Indians were recruited into the Imperial forces – the influence on them of the European war is perhaps most graphically illustrated by a work of fiction, John Masters' *The Ravi Lancers*, which describes the profound disillusionment with European ideas caused by the senseless carnage of the war. The war effort seriously weakened British administration in India. Bubonic plague swept the country in 1917 and the following year came an even greater scourge – the world epidemic of influenza. It killed 12.5 million Indians.

The consequent unrest and rioting were aggravated by the extension of wartime laws to control revolution and sedition. The Congress in 1916 negotiated a remarkable accord in which Moslems and Hindus pledged themselves to support the common cause of home rule for India. The Congress, until now the compliant and willing partner of the imperial government, was henceforward to be its antagonist. Against this tumultuous background a new player would enter the stage, a figure of enormous significance not only in India, but throughout the world.

Mohandas Gandhi, a Gujerati who went to England in 1888 for an education in law, was admitted to the bar at the Inner Temple in London three years later. Subsequently he went to South Africa and acquired an international reputation as leader of a movement which resisted discrimination against the Indian expatriate minority there. World attention was attracted not so much by the cause itself as by Gandhi's novel methods of mass passive resistance. Patient and non-violent acceptance of an adverse situation had long been a tradition of Hinduism, but Gandhi, impressed with Tolstoy, added to it the firmness of the Russian's concept of a more militant non-co-operation with the evil and destructive. He was 45 when he returned to India in 1914 to work for the Congress, becoming its unquestioned leader in 1920.

The extension of the wartime anti-sedition laws triggered serious opposition. Gandhi rallied support against these repressive Rowlatt Acts. His intention was for a day of fasting and prayer and a business strike, but that event on 18 March, 1919 led to severe rioting in Amritsar, the holy city of the Sikhs, in which five Europeans were killed and a number of buildings burned. On 12 April a British army officer, General Reginald Dyer, issued a proclamation warning that any public assemblies in Amritsar would be fired upon.

Two factors bore on the situation. One was Dyer's order that all Indians passing through a street in which a European had been attacked should crawl, and the second, noted in the report of the later investigating commission, was that in many parts of Amritsar Dyer's proclamation had not been read. Hence a large proportion of the population was unaware of the warning.

The following day a large crowd gathered in an enclosed square called the Jallianwalla Bagh, which could be entered and left only through a few narrow gateways. Although the crowd was unarmed, and listening peacefully to a speaker, General Dyer ordered 50 Gurkha riflemen to start firing on them. They continued until they ran out of ammunition. The people inside were unable to escape the deadly, individual marksmanship, which was so effective that of 1650 rounds fired almost all found a mark, since 379 people were killed and more than a thousand injured. Many were women and children.

The brutal overkill of the Amritsar incident and its consequences are of immense importance, for they destroyed any remaining feelings of goodwill and faith in Britain so many educated Indians had had. The world-renowned Indian author, Sir Rabindranath Tagore, renounced his knighthood. Gandhi described British rule as 'Satanic'. These reactions were due not only to the massacre but also to the fact that so many influential Englishmen approved of Dyer, the House of Lords supporting a public subscription which delivered him a considerable sum. The repercussions were still considerable as late as 1997 when Queen Elizabeth, making a visit to India, was told she would not be welcome in Amritsar.

In 1920 the Congress issued an ultimatum – complete self-rule within a year or massive civil disobedience. When this was ignored Gandhi called for civil disobedience throughout India. Outbreaks of mob violence, notably the burning alive of 20 police inside their station at Chauri Chaura, shocked Gandhi so much he withdrew from the campaign, retiring in 1925 to a religious retreat to meditate. The rest of the decade passed without major event. One ominous tendency was the steady deterioration of relations between Hindus and Moslems, with a growing number of deaths from communal violence.

During Gandhi's absence from active politics the nationalist cause was led by a successful lawyer, Motilal Nehru, who had given up a life of wealth and privilege to follow Gandhi. Motilal Nehru died in 1931. He was succeeded as leader of the Congress by his son Jawaharlal, then aged 40.

Born in 1889 of blue-blood Kashmiri stock, Jawaharlal Nehru had all the advantages of a privileged birth and environment. A *brahmin* by caste, he was educated at Harrow and Cambridge and was admitted to the bar in 1912. Like his father he renounced his career and former way of life to work for the nationalist cause but, nevertheless, remained essentially a product of Western ways of thought and an English education. Throughout a long life of immense influence he was impatient of Indian traditionalism and caste barriers. Although he fought bitterly for Indian independence, his influence on its final form was almost entirely derived from Western political traditions.

The younger Nehru and Gandhi were close friends and associates, and with the advent of Jawaharlal to major influence, Gandhi left the spinning wheel and looms of his secluded *ashram* to return to the political battle. Within a year came a further call for independence and a civil disobedience campaign. Gandhi began this with an inspired gesture – one of protest against the much-hated government tax on salt that applied to all, rich and poor. In March 1930 he began a 240 mile walk to the coast. Gandhi, then aged 61, led the procession, which grew steadily in volume during the 24 days before the Arabian Sea was reached. There he scooped illicit salt from the beach. Now, all over India, thousands began to make it illegally.

The incident was typical of Gandhi's genius, which reached the hearts and inspired the enthusiasm of the vast mass of the Indian people. The peasantry, who had formerly not been involved in the nationalist struggle had, indeed, for centuries regarded themselves as too humble to be concerned with matters of power. Gandhi fought ferociously for the poor and downtrodden, and especially championed the cause of India's millions of untouchables. This deep concern for the under-privileged permitted Gandhi to act as a bridge between the people and the intelligentsia.

The defiance of the salt tax was vigorously repressed. By May, 1930, 60,000 people were in prison, including Gandhi, Nehru and most of the other Congress leaders. Not long after Gandhi was imprisoned two and a half thousand Indians marched on the government salt factory near Bombay where, according to a European correspondent, Webb Miller, 'scores of native policemen rained blows on their heads with steel-shod *lathis*. Not one of the marchers even raised a hand to fend off the blows. They went down like ninepins. The waiting crowd of marchers groaned and sucked in their breath in sympathetic pain at every blow. Those struck down fell sprawling, unconscious or writhing with fractured skulls or broken shoulders. The survivors, without breaking ranks, silently and doggedly marched on until struck down.' Miller reported that two men died and 320 were injured.

Incidents like this attracted attention and sympathy throughout the world for the nationalist cause. From now on Britain was never allowed to forget it. Limited provincial self-government was introduced in 1937. It resulted in the training of a pool of experienced Indian administrators that would stand the new nation in good stead after independence. There were also special provisions designed to encourage the princes controlling the 600 large and small states outside British India – governing a quarter of the total population – to enter an Indian Federation. Bickering, selfishness and apparent lack of wider vision made it impossible for them to avail themselves of this last chance to unite and form a significant area of power. A few years later they passed out of history largely unlamented, shorn of political power but with some even now enormously wealthy and influential within their own territories.

Part III
The Modern Nations

17

The South Asian Nations: India, Pakistan and Bangladesh

The south Asian nations, with over a billion people, may soon outstrip China to become the largest fraction of humans on the planet. They also face greater and more fundamental problems than the rest of Asia – an uncomfortably high rate of population growth, one of the world's lowest percentages of literate people, and one of the highest incidences of fatal or disabling diseases.

Their societies all have a small wealthy class and a great majority of people who live in crowded, sub-standard housing, who lack clean drinking water, who are not fed adequately and who can call on only the most minimal medical services. One would hope for signs of an eventual improvement in all these things, and the government at least in India is working in this direction. However, a visitor to the region can see scant evidence of this, probably because of the sheer magnitude of the problems. The ramshackle slums that make up most of the larger cities seem to be more crowded, more broken-down, than they were 20 years ago. While there is now a growing and modestly-prosperous middle class, the industrial growth that has fostered it has been disastrous – heavy blanketing of smog from factory chimneys and increasing motor traffic, choked roads and streets, and a constant clangour of noise. The beautiful Taj Mahal in Agra, surrounded by slums and a whole landscape of bleak industrial buildings from which a hundred tall chimneys belch smoke, eloquently characterises India's urban problems.

The countryside is little better, made up substantially of arid fields in which the productivity of the soil is steadily declining, villages which every year have to house more people in the same wretched conditions, to share food resources which become more and more limited. Five per cent of village dwellers own as much as 40 per cent of the available agricultural land – in Pakistan four per cent own 36 per cent of the land. This represents close on a doubling of the alienation of land to the rich since independence.

Another common characteristic of the region is that its people are more religious than most other human populations. The two main religions, Hinduism and Islam, are similar to the extent that they deeply influence the individual and social life of most people. In other respects they are antithetic, to the extent of provoking violent reactions which have already caused millions of deaths in the region. Recent political and social developments indicate, if anything, that these religious tensions are increasing, and that the anger and violence they prompt are growing because of the misery and frustrations caused by the lifestyle of the great majority.

Mohammed Ali Jinnah, a Western-educated lawyer, is sometimes considered the sole architect of Pakistan, but this is not borne out by the facts. The vision of a separate Moslem homeland in India was that of Pakistan's honoured poet-politician Mohammed Iqbal, who was president of the Moslem League from 1930 until 1936. In 1938 the Moslem League actively considered various proposals for a separate state, Jinnah agreeing to lead personally a special committee to investigate what might be gained from partition. The investigations appear to have convinced him. 'Pakistan is inevitable,' he said soon afterwards. Gandhi's acid comment that the idea was absurd served only to redouble the efforts of the Moslem leaders on its behalf.

Meanwhile war came to Europe in 1939, and Britain had little leisure to consider the shaping of political forces in south Asia. Nehru had foreseen the war, and had told the 1936 meeting of the Congress that 'it becomes necessary for the Congress to declare clearly now its opposition to India's participation in an imperialist war'.

Congress demanded immediate self-government on a basis to be decided by a constituent assembly of Indians. In 1942 Britain sent a Socialist member of her War Cabinet – Sir Stafford Cripps, long known as a supporter of Indian nationalist aspirations – to Delhi. Cripps brought with him a plan for an independent India with Dominion status and the right to secede from the Commonwealth, to be established immediately after the war.

Congress turned down these proposals categorically, apparently at Gandhi's initiative. He is said to have described the Cripps' proposals as 'a blank cheque on a failing bank' and wanted all Commonwealth forces out of India so a possible Japanese invasion could be opposed with a passive resistance campaign. The two words 'Quit India' suddenly appeared in white paint, scrawled on walls and hoardings. A major campaign of civil disobedience was to be used to force Britain's hand. However, the British authorities acted at once. All the Congress leaders were gaoled and remained in prison until 1945. The Congress was declared an illegal organisation. The first riots and sabotage began in Bombay and quickly spread to other parts of India. Public buildings were burned down, railway and telegraph lines damaged, and there was some sabotage of military installations.

So rose the sudden bitterness that was to cloud the last years of British rule – a sad blot on a record that contained much of value. More than 1000 nationalists were killed, 3000 injured, and 60,000 arrested before the 'Congress rebellion' was put down. But worse was to come. The year 1943 brought fresh horrors with a catastrophic famine in Bengal, the worst since 1866. The famine, little publicised at the time because of wartime censorship, and, inexplicably, still ignored by many modern histories of India and most standard reference works, killed at least two and a half million people – some estimates of the ultimate toll are as high as four million. It was one of the major tragedies of World War Two. On any estimate, its death-toll was far higher than British Empire military and civilian wartime deaths, which totalled around half a million.

The 1943 famine is the subject of a recent book, *Jane Austen and the Black Hole of British History* (1998). Its Australian author, G.M. Polya, speaking on a radio programme early in 1999, said: 'Although there was plenty of food potentially available, the price of rice rose ... driven by a number of factors including: the cessation of imports from Japanese-occupied Burma; a dramatic wartime decline in other requisite grain imports into India, compounded by the deliberate strategic slashing of Allied Indian Ocean shipping; heavy-handed government action in seizing Bengali rice stocks in sensitive areas; the seizure of boats critically required for food acquisition and rice distribution; and finally, the "divide and rule" policy of giving the various Indian provinces control over their own food stocks. Critically, cashed-up, wartime, industrial Calcutta could pay for rice and sucked food out of a starving, food-producing countryside.'

Several of the factors mentioned above suggest a British 'scorched earth' policy designed to deny assets in Bengal to the Japanese, at a monstrous cost, should they successfully invade India. Those consequences severely indict British policy-makers of the time, and the failure to investigate and acknowledge them is to the discredit of all subsequent British governments.

So great was the industrial output from India during the war that it not only cancelled out all Indian indebtedness, but actually gave India a credit balance in London of over a £1000 million. Consequently, the end of the war saw the disappearance of any economic justification for British rule. In July 1945 the wartime government of Winston Churchill was defeated and Labour, which had been critical of the India policy for some time, embarked on the task of making India free. The Labour Prime Minister, Clement Attlee, intended to grant independence without reservations and was little deterred by Churchill's comment that this would involve 'the clattering down of the British Empire with all its glories'. Even so, the task proved not so simple. In India strikes and demonstrations continued well into 1946.

Amid this confusion a dominant influence was the Moslem League, driven forward by Jinnah, its leader, who insisted on a separate Moslem nation. 'We will either have a divided India or a destroyed India,' he said. 'We have forged a pistol and we are in a position to use it.' Jinnah called for a direct action day on 16 August. It was to be an ominous and tragic occasion, resulting in the death of 12,000 people, 5000 in Calcutta alone, under conditions of appalling brutality. Nineteen forty-seven came with India on the edge of civil war. Attlee admitted that Britain could no longer control events and urged Indians to 'sink their differences'.

Partition was now accepted as inevitable. New boundaries were drawn with little chance to consider local interests and loyalties with any care. Yet the line had to be drawn, and quickly. Inevitably it split village and clan groups, cut off irrigated land from its sources of water, among a myriad of other problems. This crude surgery led to another disaster, compared with which all the communal horrors of the past four years dwindled into insignificance. India and Pakistan became independent dominions within the British Commonwealth on 14 August 1947. At once both countries faced an explosion of communal violence on an unprecedented scale. In the border regions of the Punjab, which was partitioned, millions left their homes while Hindu, Moslem and Sikh fanatics preyed on them in a nightmare of butchery and destruction. Entire families died inside their homes as hundreds of villages were burned and the chaos prevailing on both sides of the new border cloaked every kind of atrocity – some barely imaginable. Crowded trains were found stopped on the line without a soul still alive in them.

No accurate estimate has ever been possible of this terrible disaster, but as many as a million people are believed to have perished. In what was probably the largest single shift of population the world has ever seen, seven million people crossed from India into Pakistan and slightly more migrated the other way.

Consideration of these events leads to a ready understanding of the bitterness and mistrust between the neighbouring south Asian states, which has led to war on a number of occasions, a host of minor military clashes, a confrontation along one of the most heavily militarised frontiers in the world, and an immoderate spending on weapons – including nuclear technology – by both nations – money urgently enough needed to ease the poverty and deprivation experienced by the vast majority of their people.

While Pakistan is generally considered part of south Asia, geographically and culturally it is a borderland between the Middle East and Asia. It shares a frontier with Iran, its main city and port, Karachi, is located on the Arabian Sea and the official language, Urdu, is closely related to Arabic and Persian. Pakistan has close ties with the oil-rich Middle East states, especially Iran, which provides economic assistance.

However, the most important link is Islam. Virtually all Pakistanis are Moslems, and the country is an Islamic state. This means that the teachings of the Koran, including religious law, deeply influence all aspects of life. Islamic religious law, the *sharia*, which prescribes severe penalties for offences, such as the amputation of a hand for theft, is not yet universal, although there have been official moves in that direction.

Pakistan has remained poor and backward throughout its half century of existence, with some three-quarters of its people subsistence farmers, and at least the same proportion illiterate. The correspondence between these two figures is not a coincidence, since education is expensive and not compulsory. Most rural families need their children to work at home or in the fields and cannot spare them the time to go to school. There is a small but dominant privileged class, closely connected with government administration and the armed services.

Many more boys than girls are educated, because it is widely considered that since women will go straight from virtual seclusion in their parents' home to the same condition in their husband's, there is no point in educating them. From an early age boys and girls are segregated. There is strict observance of the Moslem instruction that women should avoid being seen by men outside their own family. For this reason they must wear heavy clothing that covers the whole body except the face, whenever they appear in public. Most women emerge from their homes rarely, and there is strong orthodox religious feeling that they should not be trained in the arts and professions. Marriages are arranged, and the future husband and wife are not permitted to meet alone until after their wedding, although the *qazi*, the Moslem priest officiating at the wedding, is required to obtain the bride's consent at a private meeting with her.

In 1947 Pakistan consisted of two areas of territory separated by almost a thousand miles of India – the present-day Pakistan, and the preponderantly Moslem section of Bengal which is now Bangladesh. This curiously-divided nation faced immediate problems. Because previous administration had been based on Delhi, there were no organised transport or communications services.

Matters were not improved by the death from tuberculosis of Jinnah only a year after independence. In 1951 the succeeding prime minister, Liaquat Ali Khan, was assassinated before the basic principles of a constitution for the new nation could be established. The attempt at parliamentary democracy failed in conditions of growing political instability, and the army leader, General Ayub Khan, took over in 1958 after a military coup, continuing as president with wide powers for the next seven years.

A brief though savage war with India followed in 1965 and again in 1999 over the state of Kashmir, which became Indian because it had an Indian rajah, although most of the people are Moslem. War came again with the revolt of East Pakistan against control from the far-off west. India entered the conflict to help the rebels. The Pakistani forces were defeated and in 1971 the east became a new nation, Bangladesh, substantially on the flat flood-prone plains around the mouths of the Ganges, criss-crossed by more than 2000 waterways.

With 130 million people, Bangladesh is one of the most heavily-populated regions on earth. Much of its land is only a few feet above sea level, and subject to regular flooding as the Ganges, Brahmaputra and Meghna rivers are swollen by the melting snows in their headwaters. Flooding in Bangladesh has taken millions of lives. Late in 1970 a cyclone and tidal waves killed half a million people. A similar disaster four years later inundated almost half of the country, leaving millions of homeless and hungry people. Confined in camps outside the capital, Dacca, they began dying in thousands. A virtual civil war ensued between these desperate, starving people and the police. Sections of the army turned against Sheik Mujid Rahman, the prime minister, who only three years before had been feted as the nation's independence leader. In August, 1975, he and several of his immediate family were murdered by elements of the army. Government by several military regimes has followed, with intermittent attempts at parliamentary democracy.

Flooding of record proportions, covering more than two-thirds of the country, drew world attention to the plight of Bangladesh again in 1988, and in 1998. The fact that flooding in Bangladesh continues, and even becomes worse as the decades pass, is a reproach to the world. The problem has been studied and it is known the floodwaters could be controlled by reafforestation of the upper reaches of the major rivers, and by a series of dams and hydro-electric schemes, which would incidentally provide cheap power to the entire subcontinent. Such a development would save millions of lives, and improve the lives of tens of millions more. Its high cost, in the billions of dollars, would nevertheless be only a small fraction of what the world spends on armaments.

Other problems have emerged over the years. After Bangladesh became independent massive aid programmes were provided to deal with the almost universal incidence of waterborne disease. More than three million deep tubewells were bored. The water from these was for some years considered safe, but during the 1990s a further grave problem emerged – contamination of tubewell water with arsenic, causing skin keratosis, cancer and eventually death.

Village life – that of 80 per cent of the people – is primitive and hard, with as many as a dozen people living in single-roomed mud houses – walls and a roof, but lacking all other amenities. Life is a desperate battle to grow enough food and gain small amounts of money by labouring in export agriculture industries growing jute, sugar and tea. Most children must work at least five hours a day from the age of six or seven. There is little time, and few facilities, for schooling, hence the literacy rate is barely 20 per cent. As in Pakistan, girls are especially disadvantaged, for much the same reasons.

In Pakistan in 1977 yet another general, Mohammed Zia ul-Haq imposed martial law – the second such episode in Pakistan's short history. Zia arrested and hanged the former prime minister, Zulfikar Ali Bhutto, so commencing a brutal dictatorship which allowed for no dissent or political activity. Bhutto's family, including his daughter Benazir, were kept under house arrest and later exiled. Benazir returned from exile in 1986, immensely popular among the people. Following Zia's death in an air crash in 1988, she was elected prime minister.

Oxford-educated, Benazir Bhutto is nevertheless a woman, in a country traditionally opposed to any exercise of power by women. She faced an almost impossible task to reform Pakistan's laws and society. Indeed it proved to be impossible, and the country drifted into a renewed phase of political and economic anarchy, directed by and to the benefit of influential groups of 'businessmen', who have not hesitated to intimidate and murder those who attempt to oppose them. In 1999 Benazir Bhutto was sentenced to five years in prison on corruption charges which she insists are false and politically motivated.

Pakistan has intruded substantially in the affairs of its northern neighbour, Afghanistan, arming and organising the fundamentalist Moslem organisation, the Taliban, who controlled most of that country by 1998 after 15 years of almost constant civil war which killed more than half a million people. The young zealots of the Taliban were mostly trained in the *madrassas*, Moslem schools in Pakistan. As the Taliban consolidated its hold, there were increasing signs of its extended influence in Pakistan. Meanwhile Pakistan's economy continued to deteriorate, with a third of the budget devoted to the armed forces, a further third to interest payments on national debts. A third military coup overturned parliamentary government in October, 1999.

Following the communal tragedy in 1947, Gandhi, at the age of 78, began a fast to exact a promise from the Congress leaders that the lives and property of the 40 million Moslems remaining in India should be respected. Five days later Nehru and his colleagues gave this undertaking.

It was the last triumph of the man who, though he himself disliked the title, had become universally known as the *mahatma*, the 'great soul'. On 30 January, 1948, as he walked out of a house in Delhi, an assassin fired three pistol shots at the old man. The fatal gun was held, not in the hand of some Moslem fanatic, but in that of a *brahmin* member of the Hindu extremist party, the Mahasabha. Hindu orthodoxy thus at last exacted its penalty from the man who had fought so hard to free India from its ancient hatreds, superstitions and prejudices.

India's more recent history can best be summarised – and perhaps broadly understood – by looking at trends rather than a huge mass of political detail. The early decades after independence, years of firm control by the Congress Party and a doubling of food grain production in the two decades from 1965, showed promise. However, more recently new 'green revolution' plant varieties have proved less useful, and this, combined with losses of soil fertility in many places from overcropping and the relentless growth of the population, has increased problems of poverty and disease, both in the villages and the burgeoning slum areas of the big cities.

Nevertheless there has been growth in the industrial sector, resulting in a larger and relatively affluent middle class, and also a strident noisiness and very evident pollution in the cities. India's literacy rate, under 40 per cent, compares with more than 70 per cent in China; life expectancy at birth in China is 67, in India, 52, due substantially to higher infant mortality.

Communal violence has continued in India between Moslems and Hindus, regularly causing more than a hundred deaths a year and almost four hundred in 1980. A more recent development has been conflict between advantaged and disadvantaged caste groups, incidents over five months of 1985 resulting in the death of 275 people in Gujerat State, with less serious conflicts in most other states. This violence recurred in 1998 and 1999, and extended to attacks on Indian Christians, who make up only two per cent of the population.

Politically the tendency has been for greater regionalism, lack of strong national leadership and a gradual but definite increase in influence of Hindu nationalism. Especially after the decline of the Nehru dynasty – two presidents of that family, Indira Gandhi (not related to the Mahatma) and her son Rajiv, were assassinated – the influence of the Congress Party dwindled. Although it served a later term of office, the tide began to run against the Congress as a result of severe repression associated with a state of emergency imposed by Indira Gandhi in 1975 during which more than 30,000 people were imprisoned without trial. This followed a year of strikes, some of which involved as many as a million workers. A campaign against the union movement was widely seen as government support for the big industrial conglomerates, like Tata and Birla, that dominate Indian commerce and industry.

Congress was defeated in elections in 1977, and India was handed over to the uncertain leadership of a loose rightwing alliance, the Janata Party. By 1980 Janata had split into irreconcilable factions, and Congress regained power in elections that year. Mrs Gandhi was to survive only four more years. Late in 1984, following a bitter and bloody dispute with the Sikh community she was shot down by machine-guns in the hands of two of her guards, who were Sikhs. This led once more to communal killings, directed against the whole Sikh community, on an appalling scale, whole families burning to death inside their houses. Her son Rajiv succeeded her, until he too was assassinated in 1991 by a Tamil extremist.

An election in 1996 was inconclusive, necessitating another in 1998. That election brought the Hindu nationalist Bharatiya Janata Party – the BJP – to power. This election, probably the most significant in recent Indian history, did not, however, give the BJP a clear authority. The party and others likely to support it held 19 seats short of the 272 needed for an absolute majority. However, the decision of the voters in the world's largest democracy confirmed a continuing downward trend in support for Western-style politics, as evidenced by the Congress Party, which won only 140 seats.

Instead the people have preferred a party based on the Hindu traditions and ideas of the past, with strong organisation and support at the grassroots level, and with a major commitment to local industry rather than multi-nationals. The BJP has been criticised because of past links with communalism, a criticism which extends to its leader, Atal Behari Vajpayee. Many of its members also belong to the Rashtriya Swayamsevak Sangh (RSS), a fundamentalist Hindu youth organisation founded in 1925 which has been described as a cross between the Boy Scouts and Hitler Youth, and which has been strongly implicated in past violence against the Moslem community.

In May, 1998 India heightened regional tensions with five nuclear weapons tests, including that of a fission trigger hydrogen bomb. Within days Pakistan responded with a similar test programme. Both nations indicated their possession of missile delivery systems for atomic weapons, prompting worldwide fears of a dangerous nuclear arms race. Further testing, this time of launch vehicles, occurred in 1999.

Early in that year a Parliamentary vote of no confidence in the BJP succeeded by only one vote, resulting in the necessity for India's third election in three years in September, 1999, at a cost to the nation of more than $200 million. The Congress Party, led by an unlikely candidate for the Indian prime ministership – Sonia Gandhi, widow of Rajiv, who is Italian-born and Christian, had its worst result ever. The BJP also failed to win a clear majority. Its dependence on an alliance of smaller parties and strong votes for regional candidates again raised the prospect of indecisive government in India.

18

China: Two Revolutions

In 1896 there was a curious happening in England. A 30-year-old Chinese doctor, who had graduated only two years before from the medical school in Hong Kong, was kidnapped from a London street and secretly imprisoned inside the Chinese Legation. He was held there for 13 days, but before he could be spirited away to China for execution a warning note was smuggled to an English friend, and he was released by the British police.

The kidnappers were agents of the Chinese Dowager Empress Tz'u Hsi, and the prisoner, on whose head the Manchu officials of her court had placed a price of £100,000, was Sun Yat-sen. An exile, a Christian, Western-educated, he was typical of the new class of Chinese looking for reform. The kidnapping episode did not deter him. In 1905 Sun formed in Tokyo an organisation called the T'ung-meng Hui, half secret-society, half political party, which would develop in 1912 into the Kuomintang (Nationalist) Party.

In 1911 a plot against the government by officers of the military garrison at Wuchang, on the Yangtse River in Central China, was prematurely discovered. As the news of the Wuchang revolt spread more and more cities, especially in the south, declared against the Manchus. Sun Yat-sen, who was fundraising in the United States, returned to China as quickly as possible and in the first days of 1912 took the oath as president of a provisional republic. The following month an imperial edict announced the abdication of the emperor.

Sun held his office for only 44 days. In order to maintain the republic, he was obliged to hand over the presidency to the army commander, Yuan Shih-kai, who had the confidence of the foreign powers. However, the following year Yuan, a man very much in the warlord tradition, disbanded the provisional government and declared the KMT illegal. His assumption of personal rule followed the classic pattern in which new Chinese dynasties have begun – even more so when Yuan announced he proposed to declare himself the new emperor. This was forestalled by his death, apparently from natural causes, in 1916.

Virtual anarchy followed as the warlords – many of whom had been Yuan's officers – and the KMT struggled for power. The infant Manchu emperor Pu Yi was suddenly restored to power, and as quickly deposed again. Sun Yat-sen renewed the declaration of the republic in 1917, but it controlled only a small part of south China when Sun died in 1925 of liver cancer. Meanwhile a number of Marxist groups had come together and, inspired by the Russian revolution, formed the Chinese Communist Party in 1921.

Chiang Kai-shek became the next leader of the KMT with the support of the army, and, for the time being, the Communists. In 1926 he led the KMT army out of Canton (Guangzhou)* on the Northern Expedition, which was to unify China within two years and make the republic a reality. Chiang's task was to coerce or persuade the regional warlords into accepting KMT government. Some of these men, like Chang Hso-lin in Manchuria, controlled what were virtually whole nations, and others little more than circles of ricefield bounded by the horizon as seen from the drum tower of a central walled city. This picture of a group of military autocrats gains interest as it is

---

* Wade-Giles transliteration has been used where it is likely to be most familiar to readers; modern *pinyin* is added in brackets where this seems useful.

approached more closely. Their foibles and methods have re-sulted in a mass of anecdote, still to be found in the yellowing pages of the writing on current affairs of 70 years ago.

Feng Yu-hsiang, a Christian, was said to have exhorted his men with sermons before battle, and to lead them singing 'Onward Christian Soldiers' as they marched. However, John Gunther, who recounted this story, added it was not true that, as a contemporary legend claimed, Feng baptised his troops with a firehose. When General Yen Hsi-shan was shaved, a soldier held a revolver at the barber's head in case the man had been bribed to cut the general's throat. Six foot tall Gen-eral Chan Tsung-chang, by origins an illiterate coolie, was reputed to have concubines of 26 different nationalities, each with a washbowl marked with her flag. Quite different was the courtly Confucian Marshal Wu Pei-fu who, according to Bertrand Russell, won a battle while it was raining and then, because this was considered unorthodox, informed his enemy he would retreat to his original lines and fight it over again in the sunshine.

Chiang Kai-shek's Northern Expedition succeeded largely because the KMT army had a sense of discipline unusual in China at that time. But a breach with the Communists was not far off. Chiang was suspicious of them, and strong pres-sures were brought to bear on him – including a reputed payment of three million pounds by Chinese and foreign interests – to break with those he came to be persuaded were dangerous revolutionaries. Chiang, after making a triumphant entry into Shanghai in 1927, suddenly attacked the Communists, who had assisted the capture of the city by paralysing it with a strike. Hundreds of Communists were killed in Shanghai, and the purge was extended to other areas. From Shanghai the Nationalists, moved on from success to success, establishing their capital in Nanking (Nanjing).

However, the Communist Party had not been destroyed. The more important leaders escaped, including Mao Tse-tung (Mao Zedong), a quiet, tall man of peasant antecedents from Hunan (Henan) Province. Mao had been trying to convince the other leaders that classic Marxism, the revolt of an urban group, was not appropriate in China just because it had succeeded in Russia. Mao's position in history depends considerably on his realisation that China's essential problem was a rural one, that only a revolt based on the peasants could succeed. It is a curious irony that Chiang's purge of the Communists in 1927 brought Mao's ideas to the forefront. By eliminating so many orthodox Marxists, it diverted the Communist Party to a more realistic course that would deliver it government of China only two decades later.

Chiang was to find that he had no sooner resolved matters in the north than his old enemies, the Communists, had re-grouped in the south. Mao and his ragged army killed landlords and redistributed their holdings to the peasants. Because of the extreme poverty of the peasants the Communists quickly gained support and recruits. Mao, a military planner of ability and imagination, established a fundamental principle of Asian Communism with his insistence on guerilla warfare, defined in his maxim: 'When the enemy advances, we retreat; when he retreats, we pursue; when he is tired, we attack.' However, in 1934 the Red Army allowed itself to be trapped into a disas-trous 'setpiece' battle in an 'encirclement campaign' by three-quarters of a million Nationalist troops. Towards the end of the year, when it had been reduced to half its former strength, the survivors slipped through the surrounding Nationalist block-ade under cover of night.

So began the legendary Long March. The Communists' objective – more than 1000 miles away – was a remote part of Shensi (Shanxi) Province in the northwest. Here there was already a substantial Communist presence, and Mao planned to join forces with it. But since strong Nationalist forces stood between them and this possible refuge the Communists were forced to march around the borders of China for almost 6000 miles. The Long March took an appalling toll. Of more than 100 thousand people who set out, barely 15 thousand reached Shensi. Almost every family, including Mao's, lost some mem-bers, for wives and children accompanied the men. The journey took 368 days, during which the Communists fought 15 major battles and 300 skirmishes. This epic of suffering and endurance has become Communist China's most important body of legend, well-known to every schoolchild.

The years in Yenan saw a phase of experiment that set most of the patterns the new Communist government would use later throughout China. Membership of the Communist Party grew from 40,000 in 1937 to 1.2 million in 1945. The problem of land reform was tackled seriously, if, in the end, brutally. The party was carefully organised into a pervasive network of authority, leading and guiding even at the village level. Under Mao's control the Communist Party became a consistent, carefully woven thread in the fabric of Chinese society. It owes much of its present authority to the fact that it remains so today.

Meanwhile Japan had seen colonial opportunities in the divided China. She occupied Manchuria in 1931 and set up there a puppet state named Manchukuo, over which she recalled to the throne the deposed Manchu emperor, P'u Yi, much later to end his life as a humble gardener in Peking (Beijing). Open fighting began between China and Japan near Beijing in 1937. The tide of invasion swept across China, marked by a series of brutal atrocities against civilians by the Japanese. The Communists did not escape these. They attempted an offensive against the Japanese in 1940, which led to severe reprisals – Japanese orders to its troops to 'kill all, burn all, destroy all.' This became the fate of entire villages. Some who tried to escape this fury by digging underground refuges were killed when the Japanese pumped poison gas into these tunnels. The Communist Eighth Route Army was reduced by 100,000 killed, wounded or deserted, the population under their control halved to 20 millions.

The Nationalists fared little better. They eventually lost all of the coast and were forced back to Chungking (Chongqing), west of the Yangtse gorges in the fertile and readily-defended basin of Szechwan (Sichuan) Province. Here they remained throughout World War Two. Chiang Kai-shek had done little to remedy China's poverty and despair. John Gunther's *Inside Asia* claimed: 'About a million people die of starvation in China every year. In 1935, a normal year, 29,000 bodies were picked up off the streets of Shanghai alone, of men, women and children, dead of hunger. Many were female infants, left by their parents to starve.' Other accounts tell of seeing from the trains, running on lines elevated above the flooded surrounding country, people clinging in trees until they fell into the water, exhausted, and drowned. No attempt was made to save or help them. People trapped in flooded rivers were likewise left to drown, since it was traditionally believed unlucky to deprive the river gods of their prey.

Unfortunately adversity did not improve the Nationalist government. It relied increasingly on terror and autocracy and its secret police came to be hated and feared. Men were conscripted to Chiang's armies who were so weak from malnutrition they could hardly walk. During the war over a million died before they could even reach the battlefields. Money power was concentrated almost entirely in the hands of four families. One was Chiang's and another was his wife's. The Communists awaited events in the north, in rugged country too remote and poor to interest the Japanese. However, despite difficulties they were able to replace the Nationalists as *de facto* rulers of much of north China, regions inhabited by 95 million people.

When Japan was defeated in 1945 Chiang emerged from his battered refuge in Chungking nominally ruler of all China. At once he began planning a major campaign against the Communists. In the north Mao also took a more extreme line, confiscating property owned by landlords and rich peasants. These two classes now became automatically proscribed, no longer 'people'. Whole villages met to indict the wealthy, and landlords were frequently beaten, tortured or killed by angry mobs.

The Communists gained popularity because of harsh and inept rule by the Nationalists in Manchuria after the Japanese had left, and their membership grew rapidly. By contrast the Communists handled with efficiency an outbreak of bubonic plague in the city of Harbin, introducing immediate vaccination and quarantine measures. The plague, which killed 30,000 people, was caused by the deliberate release by the Japanese at the end of the war of rats they had infected with plague in biological warfare experiments.

Both the Western powers and the Russians were anxious to see a settlement in China. But these efforts proved fruitless. In the spring of 1947 the war began in earnest. Chiang lost heavily in decisive battles in Manchuria in 1948. Almost half a million Nationalist troops surrendered, deserted, or were killed, handing over vast quantities of United States-supplied weapons to the Red Army. Barely 20,000 escaped.

Simultaneously the Communists thrust south and by February, 1949 had assembled a huge army on the north bank of the Yangtse River, poised to invade China's heartland. In April nearly a million Communist soldiers crossed the river on a 300-mile front centred on Nanking. The fall of the traditional Nationalist capital brought any organised opposition to an end. By autumn Chiang, with the remnants of his armies, had retreated to the island of Taiwan.

19

Modern China: The Communist State

The Communist victory saw the world's most populous nation at one of the lowest points in its long history. The currency was worthless, the great mass of the people illiterate, only a shadow of internal organisation remained, the exhausted soil was eroded and treeless, and everywhere profound social, medical and economic problems clamoured for solution.

The decades of struggle had hardened the new government to the pitch of discipline and ruthlessness necessary to attack these things. The party's executive arm is its elite corps of fulltime executives, the cadres, the effective successors of the mandarinate. Many of them are descendants of former scholar-officials, who were substantially the only group sufficiently educated for the tasks of government.

Indeed, after a phase of 're-education' the bulk of the intelligentsia and former 'upper classes' seem to have been able to accommodate themselves to life under Communism. Not all, however, were permitted to adapt so readily. Edgar Snow, in *The Other Side of the River*, says that Chou En-lai (Zhou Enlai), himself of mandarin origins, had stated that 830,000 'enemies of the people' had been destroyed up to 1954. The Nationalists put the figure at nine million dead. The draconic removal of these classes from their traditional influence and land ownership permitted redistribution of their property among the landless. As early as 1952 almost half of China's culti-vated land had been distributed to 300 million peasants.

This savage elimination of the 'landlords' ran parallel with campaigns to raise the standards of health, education and overall prosperity and to create at least the beginnings of the indus-trialisation the Communists saw as essential. Russian experts went to China to advise on the evolution of an industrial base that would provide the essential tools of a modern nation – good communications, cheap and plentiful hydro-electric power, and heavy industry, especially steel mills.

One of the most challenging tasks was to tame the Yellow River, long described as 'China's Sorrow' because of the flood-ing and drowning of millions of people when it regularly broke its levees. In 1954 the Yellow River Planning Commission set about the work of building 46 dams along the 2000 mile course of the river, a task undertaken, in a phrase popular in the Western media, by 'blue ants' – millions of blue-clad coolies using picks, shovels, and wicker carrying baskets. The scheme was planned not only to control seasonal floodwaters but also to produce more than 20 million kilowatts of power.

A major afforestation scheme was started in north-west China to provide belts of trees that would hold back the sand and dust brought in by storms from the Gobi and permit the re-claiming of huge regions of semi-desert. This planting of tens of millions of trees was a remarkable achievement in world terms, and has created forests again in a country almost de-nuded of them for fuel only 50 years ago.

Mass immunisations were undertaken to control China's traditional scourges – smallpox, cholera, plague, typhoid and typhus. Leprosy and malaria control programmes were insti-tuted where necessary. Since it was not possible to train fully-qualified doctors quickly enough a large corps of 'mid-dle' doctors and nurses was organised into travelling teams to complete immunising programmes as quickly as possible. These people later became known as barefoot doctors, although all I have seen were most correctly garbed, including shoes.

China was back at war again only five years after the suc-

cessful Communist revolution. When World War Two ended
the Soviet Union occupied the north of Korea. The Communist state established there launched a major attack on South
Korea in June, 1950. A United Nations force arrived just in
time to save the south, driving the north Koreans back over
the *de facto* frontier, the 38th parallel of latitude. The war
was then continued within North Korean territory, in spite of
a Chinese warning that she would not tolerate this. A week
later China launched a major offensive that drove the United
Nations forces south of the parallel again. More troops became involved, mostly Americans, and the line was stabilised
at the parallel once more. Negotiations for peace to end this
futile and costly stalemate were commenced in July 1951, but
Korea remains divided and the two halves of the country still
face each other over one of the world's most heavily-militarised
frontiers.

There were other important consequences of the Korean War.
One was the policy of neutralism adopted by governments
representing three-quarters of the Asian peoples – the five
principles of peaceful co-existence. It is an intriguing possibility that another took place thousands of miles away on China's
western borders when on the same day, 7 October 1950, that
the United Nations authorised its forces to cross the 38th parallel, the Chinese despatched a small army to occupy Tibet.

Tibet had been a Chinese tributary state over lengthy periods
during her history, and a Manchu residency was maintained
there until 1911. The population at the Chinese invasion was
about one and a half million, of whom perhaps ten per cent
were Buddhist monks occupying some 3000 monasteries, the
largest of which housed thousands of monks.

From the seventeenth century Tibet had been under the rule
of a line of Dalai Lamas, priest-kings perpetuated not by family
succession but mysteriously 'discovered' as infants believed
to be reincarnations of a previous incumbent. The Dalai Lama
governed from his remote capital, Lhasa, with the assistance
of a clique of Buddhist priests and officials, and a feudal class
of nobles. Tibet, which had been virtually isolated from the

world, was extremely backward by world standards, the society consisting of poor herdsmen and farmers supporting a large class of priests and nobles, who owned most of the arable land. The monasteries gained their wealth from taxes on their tenants, money-lending and trade.

In 1951 China signed agreements with the Dalai Lama not to disturb his authority or the Tibetan way of life. For a time the Chinese maintained this conciliatory policy, but in 1956 the Khamba tribesmen of eastern Tibet rebelled. They were supported by other elements in the community, notably the monasteries, which provided them with weapons. The Khambas had had a long tradition of hostility towards the Chinese. They had harried the Communists at one stage during the Long March, and this, too, had not been forgotten by either side.

The revolt spread throughout Tibet, reaching a climax in 1958. The Dalai Lama and his government fled into exile in India. Chinese control of Tibet was now much more severely administered. The revolt was forcibly put down with a considerable loss of life, the lama (monk) class was proscribed, and the monasteries forcibly closed. The religious-feudal organisation of Tibetan society was unacceptable to the Chinese government, who have taken all possible steps to destroy it and convert Tibet into a Chinese province like any other. To this end many thousands of ethnic Chinese have been resettled in Tibet and a major programme of 're-education' of the Tibetan people undertaken. Numerous deaths, imprisonment and reports of torture are said to have been associated with this process. However, there is also evidence that Chinese reform of agriculture and the establishment of industries in Tibet has improved the material conditions of life for many people who were previously little better than slaves.

The Communist state was then, consolidated by its redistribution of land, its establishment of a pervasive chain of authority, and its demonstration that it could improve the health and living standards of the people modestly.

'Correctness' – a severe Communist orthodoxy – became the dominant political virtue in China. There is abundant evidence of Chinese use of educational and psychological means to control the thought of their people; to implant hostility in their children towards outside nations regarded as enemies; and to correct 'wrong thinking' in individuals. These techniques, called 'brain-washing' by Western critics, were known by the Chinese as thought-cleansing. They were designed to alter the opinions of those with critical or independent points of view, and justified by the assertion that Communism as dictated by the state must always be right, so that all citizens are bound to give it not only obedience but acceptance.

The peasants continued to live together in families, each in its own house with a small strip of land and livestock. It was nearly five years before the government began to change this rural society. Then, from 1954 onwards, a series of policy decisions attempted to organise the people into co-operatives and later into 26,000 'communes' – completely collective societies in which private ownership of land and real property was abolished.

This policy was in part motivated by China's rapidly increasing population due to a falling deathrate. Although heretical to Marxist theory, an intense campaign for birth control began in 1956. This 'deviation from orthodoxy' so offended many party members that it was soon discontinued, and another solution was suggested. This was to be nothing less than a rapid, sudden breakthrough to complete Communism, until then seen only as an ideal to be achieved in the indefinite future. By late 1956 the government was calling for a much quicker rate of collectivisation, and peasants who resisted it were punished.

In 1957 the government apparently decided to test the loyalty of intellectuals by inviting free discussion of its policies – to allow 'a hundred flowers' of opinion to blossom. There was a considerable volume of criticism – this was the time of the first Democracy Wall in Beijing University, containing posters critical of the Communist Party. When it was at its height the government countered with a sudden and severe wave of repression. A thorough purge of the public service followed. This was no small incident – more than 300,000 intellectuals, including most of China's brightest and most independent minds were indicted as 'rightists', imprisoned, sent to labour camps, or to unaccustomed manual labour in the countryside. This unexpected blow was very significant in China's development, confirming the iron hand and severe orthodoxy of the Communist Party.

In 1958 the central committee ordered the complete reorganisation of Chinese society into 'peoples' communes'. The commune concept ran directly counter to two longstanding traditions of Chinese life – private property and the family. In some places cottages were torn down and the materials used for communal barracks. Children were cared for in creches while both parents worked at tasks assigned to them by the commune. Production quotas were fixed and the whole system dominated by an almost military discipline. In some instances the communes seem to have prospered, but in others, probably the majority, the changes were resisted. Three successive bad seasons in many parts of China, including a serious drought in the Yellow River basin, coincided with this planned social dislocation and greatly aggravated its bad effects. Severe food rationing had to be introduced and China was forced to import huge amounts of grain.

The problems were worsened by the diversion of large amounts of labour to infrastructure development to make 'a great leap forward'. This disastrous campaign collapsed in less than two years, even though the Chinese, tough and sturdy though they are, were driven to efforts almost beyond human endurance. Twelve and 14 hour workdays were common, and press reports told of 'heroes' collapsing from fatigue. Huge results claimed were later shown to be false. Much effort was dissipated on badly-conceived projects, such as the creation of 60,000 'backyard furnaces' to make steel. The product of these was often so bad it could not even be used for simple agricultural implements.

It is impossible to estimate accurately the cost of these huge mistakes, but it is generally accepted that deaths, mainly resulting from malnutrition, ran into the millions, possibly tens of millions, with China's population actually declining in 1960 and 1961. In many places the hungry and despairing populace rioted, with some reports of armed revolts against the government. The retreats from the commune system and the 'great leap forward' were simultaneous and virtually complete by 1963, although the communes have been retained as an administrative framework, with most planning and day-to-day administration in the hands of the much smaller production teams.

Then in 1966 came renewed struggle between moderate and extreme Communists – the so-called cultural revolution, in which the ageing Mao, crippled with Parkinson's syndrome, incited thousands of youthful Red Guards into a noisy and destructive campaign against traditional Chinese culture. This largely urban campaign, extending for almost a decade, caused widespread dislocation of industry and education and the wilful destruction of large quantities of China's art, writing, and classical buildings.

In China in 1975 I saw ancient temples in which all of the Buddha images inside had been smashed, childish and ludicrous, yet still malicious, posters reviling Confucius, heard stories of eminent scholars forced to kneel on broken glass in public recantations of their 'errors', heard how the staff of whole universities were compelled to coach politically acceptable factory workers to academic standards in circumstances where competitive examinations had been abolished. Disastrous subsequent results, including attacks on the Red Guards by exasperated workers, forced the ending of these excesses, and dramatic changes in policy ensued, especially after the death of Mao and his closest associate, Chou En-lai (Zhou Enlai), in 1976.

Rigid birth control measures were introduced in 1979, penalising families with more than one child. This in itself has created an unprecedented situation in China, a generation substantially of only children who, it must be said, have been generally spoilt, cosseted and indulged by their parents – 'little emperors'. At a state dinner in China once I sat next to an aged veteran of the Long March who with every course uttered dire predictions about the risks of spoiling only children, who, he averred, could not be normal because they have not experienced the complex network of family relationships so traditional in China.

Nevertheless, even now China remains only a few steps ahead of famine, and the population has more than doubled during the 50 years of the Communist state, to 1.3 billion. That is almost a quarter of all the people on the planet. To feed these China has only six per cent of the world's arable land.

While recent decades have shown a liberalisation, especially in the economic sphere, there is little indication that the rigid hold the Communist Party, with about 50 million members, has on the country will be relaxed. While there has been a considerable shift towards regional autonomy, the Communist Party and the army remain dominant in decision-making institutions at all levels of the community, and in all places. The Central Committee of the party, with several hundred members, elects a political bureau, or Politburo of perhaps 20 people. But even this is not the ultimate leadership, this residing in a standing committee of the Politburo of around half a dozen members.

Movements towards democracy have been decisively repressed, the most publicised example being the military suppression of student demonstrations in Beijing's Tien An Men Square and the broad boulevard that runs east from it, Changan Avenue, on 4 June 1989. Tanks, armed personnel carriers and truckloads of soldiers fired into the crowds, causing deaths variously estimated at between 200 and 2000. Thousands were subsequently arrested, with some initial executions for sedition – probably not more than 50 people. By standards of early Chinese Communist history, the reaction was moderate, with 18 people reported to have been given prison terms, some hundreds more 're-educated'. Nevertheless, the message was quite clear: 'Bourgeois liberalism', 'attempts to topple the Communist Party, overthrow socialism', were not acceptable.

While there was considerable support for the students in some major cities, especially Beijing, there is little evidence that the vast majority of Chinese had much sympathy for them. To the contrary, most seem to have accepted the government's official line that the students were subversives, attempting to wreck the established social order.

Since the Tien An Men Square 'massacre' has been the most talked about and written about event in China since the birth of the Communist state, its history is of some importance. The facts, reported by reputable Western journalists in Beijing at the time, are briefly these:

Demonstrations in the square began three weeks earlier, coinciding with a state visit to China by Soviet President Gorbachev, and subsequently turned violent, with hand to hand fighting and mobs throwing bricks, bottles and firebombs at the troops and police.

On 3 June, 10,000 unarmed troops sent to the square to persuade the demonstrators to withdraw were forced to retreat. Later that day stone-throwing crowds attacked troops guarding the residences of the Chinese leaders, and seized an army bus loaded with weapons. Western reporters saw an armoured personnel carrier stopped by petrol bombs and its crew bludgeoned to death as they tried to escape. A pitched battle seemed to have occurred at Jianguomenwai, a large cloverleaf interpass, where reporters noted four burned out army vehicles and a number of dead soldiers. There are other reports of soldiers cut down, hanged, disembowelled or burned to death, and burned-out army trucks.

Casualties on both sides were miniscule when compared with earlier events in China itself, killings in East Timor by Indonesian soldiers, even regular police actions by India against tribal minorities, deaths in Afghanistan and Burma. The essential difference was that the Chinese allowed the Tien An Men events to be portrayed on world television – and they were shocking enough, including the crushing of young people under tank tracks and the shooting of young children.

However, the crackdown on June 4 plainly came after many

misgivings. For instance the 38th Army based on Beijing refused to move against the people and it was left to the 27th Army from Shanxi Province to make the assault. There are Western reports that they seemed frightened and on edge, and undoubtedly over-reacted. Rumours, promoted by the Western media, that there might be fighting between these two armies – effectively civil war with the attendant breakdown in Chinese society that must have ensued – may well have helped to push the Chinese leadership into final action.

Chi-chen Wang, emeritus professor of Chinese Literature at Columbia University commented in the *New York Times*: 'The 40 years of Communist rule is the only period of stability in China this century. It might be one of the longest periods of effective government in all Chinese history, and it has been a period of unparalleled progress and comparative prosperity . . . The students called for democracy in vague terms and then demanded the resignation of Premier Li Peng. In effect they called for the eclipse of the government. They disrupted traffic, set fire to cars and buses and refused to disperse. When troops were finally called in, they resisted with fire bombs and rocks . . . It seems very unreasonable to expect the legally-constituted government of China to yield to such lawlessness.'

The volume of criticism heaped on the Chinese government – far greater than that accompanying any other recent human rights matter in a very naughty world, and repeated with monotonous regularity for nine years – has had two consequences, which ought to have been foreseen by the world leaders concerned and their advisers. It has assisted in the eclipse of moderate elements in the Chinese leadership and continuing power of the hardliners. It has resulted in statements from Beijing that the Chinese government will now not listen to criticisms from the rest of the world, but will act only as it sees fit.

Meanwhile, the 11th Central Committee of the Chinese Communist Party meeting late in 1978 had declared Mao's policies to have been mistaken and decided to 'correct the "leftist" errors committed prior to, and during the so-called cultural revolution'. The failures of the 'class struggle' era Mao had insisted on maintaining were observed. It was decided that management of farming would revert to families, who would also be given back the right to hold private plots. The economy was now to become the most important consideration and private enterprise not only tolerated but encouraged.

The driving force behind these reforms was the exasperation of the Chinese people with nearly three decades of hardship. Their architect was a tough, diminutive veteran of the Long March, Teng Hsiao-pi'ing (Deng Xiaoping). His authority and iron willpower sufficed to turn China on to a new course – towards capitalism, but in the Chinese government's rhetoric, socialist capitalism. However, it was not enough to sustain his protege and possible successor, the youthful Hu Yaobang, who was forced to resign as general secretary of the Communist Party in 1987 because he was seen by the party's hardliners as 'soft' on student demonstrations for democracy. Hu's eclipse – he died of a heart attack two years later – and the repression of the student movement triggered by his state funeral in 1989, must be seen as a significant triumph for hardline elements of the government.

Meanwhile, economic liberalisation had again permitted private enterprise in China, allowing for employment of two adults and five apprentices in small businesses. Joint enterprises, largely financed by foreign capital, were encouraged and these now exist on a massive scale. There are once again very rich and very poor people in China, and the government, with some publicly-expressed qualms, has accepted this, since the economic results have been impressive. Chinese manufacture through a wide range of consumer goods is exported worldwide at highly-competitive prices; in 1997 China's surplus of exports over imports was a healthy $46 billion, and she was among the world's top exporters, compared with 29th position in 1980. Since 1978 there has been a steady growth in the gross national product of about ten per cent per year, with impressive increases in average wages and the virtual transition of urban China to a consumer society in modest terms. In spite of the Asian downturn, foreign investors put more than five billion dollars into China in November, 1998 – 17 per cent more than the previous November. However there has been a considerable cost – a pool of unemployed people variously estimated at between ten and 100 millions, bouts of inflation and widespread financial corruption.

The Chinese leadership is committed to huge public works programmes – around $750 billions – in Keynesian solutions to problems of unemployment and hesitancy in the economy. Due for completion in 2009, the Three Gorges Dam project on the upper Yangtse River is the world's largest engineering project, designed to control flooding on the river, produce billions of kilowatt hours of electric power and to make the river navigable as far inland as Chungking (Chongqing), more than a thousand miles from the coast. The dam includes massive shiplifts, which will raise vessels of up to ten thousand tons from the lower river to the huge lake behind it.

One of the more interesting and significant manifestations of the new economic freedom are the collectives – trading and manufacturing businesses owned and controlled by the people who work in them. These new and rapidly-expanding businesses, in such areas as transport, clothing manufacture, packaging materials, bricks and other building materials and farm machinery repair and manufacture, are turning thousands of Chinese villages into small industrial towns. The collectives are being encouraged by the government and may well represent in the future a massive industry which is neither capitalist nor state-owned and managed – indeed a socialist capitalism. In the six years to 1984 the share of retail sales by the state sector halved to 46 per cent – a figure closely approached by the collectives, rising from seven per cent to 40 per cent, while private business rose from two to 15 per cent.

Meanwhile, the state-owned enterprises still dominate much of the economy, especially heavy industry, and employ around 20 per cent of the workforce. They are inefficient and uneconomic, but the government has had difficulty phasing them out because this involves mass unemployment of workers who have become used to regarding their jobs as absolutely secure – the 'iron ricebowl', meaning one that could not be broken. Nevertheless state enterprises are being closed or sold to private enterprise, at considerable social cost. Agricultural productivity has improved since the inception of contracts with families. These mostly cover general farming, but they can be specific, allowing individual households to become specialists in such things as animal breeding and fish farming, or even the production of handcrafts. However, the Chinese countryside retains many problems, and its peasants are generally worse off in money terms than city workers. Girls who have left home to work in the urban factories might earn ten times as much as their father still on the land. There is also a massive labour surplus in agriculture. Tens of millions have deserted the land to seek work in the cities, with varied success.

In July, 1997, the British colony of Hong Kong, with its seven million people, reverted to China on expiry of the original leases. One of the world's largest trading centres and a major tourist destination, Hong Kong appears to have settled down peacably to incorporation within the mother country, although its prosperity has diminished and unemployment rates have increased.

Hopes that China's authoritarism might give place to Western-style democracy look very much like wishful thinking. In the last weeks of 1998 the authorities arrested the leaders of the fledgling China Democratic Party when it sought to register as a formal opposition to the Communist Party. The charge, the serious one of subverting the state, resulted in a sentence of 13 years in prison for the party's leader, Xu Wenli.

When in China on official delegations and the like it is possible at times to talk privately with the cadres who are always in attendance on 'foreign friends'. I asked perhaps a dozen Chinese the same somewhat dangerous question – dangerous to them, that is. Around half angrily refused to respond.

The question was: You are expected to obey the government in all things, give up your personal freedoms more than just about anyone else in the world would be prepared to do. How do you feel about that?

The answer generally was something like this: China has been poor and weak for generations. We must all agree to obey the government, if China is to catch up. Of course in many ways I don't like that, but on the whole I believe it is what we all must do, we must all pull together for China.

Impossibly idealistic? Government-dictated propaganda? Maybe. But my own impression was that many Chinese really do see it this way – a variation on 'Shut up and I'll let you get rich.' Perhaps, 'Shut up and I'll make us all great.'

20

Indonesia: Sukarno and After

Indonesia's first decades of independence were stormy and chaotic. The acute shortage of trained people caused grave inadequacies in administration and failures in the everyday necessities of a modern state. Telephones, electric power, the railways, the ports, customs – these and many other public services came close to collapse for want of expert control.

Actual bankruptcy at this point was averted partly because of Indonesia's basic prosperity and because of continued control of the bulk of her export-earning industries by foreigners. The key industry – the oilfields – paid royalties which provided the bulk of government revenue. The Chinese, as they still do, owned most of the other industries and retail outlets, including the important rice distribution system, and, by and large, contrived to keep these things going.

Apart from overcrowded problem regions in central and east Java most of the villagers were protected by a bountiful natural endowment that automatically provided self-sufficiency without too much work. Much of Java looks like a well-kept garden. The small, brown houses, often set high up on stilts, are almost lost in the lush growth of fruit trees that surrounds them, and the warm, even climate demands only simple housing and clothes.

Other than the opportunity to buy such things as a bicycle, a sewing machine, or a radio, little of the modern technical world touches most of these villages. Hence the political froth in Jakarta affects national life less than people who do not know Indonesia realise. Although there are areas of actual want, even of famine – and these increased with population growth and the 1997/8 El Nino drought – these problems do not yet compare with those, for instance, of India or Bangladesh.

Industries in Indonesia have often been basically uneconomic, state-subsidised to the benefit of the country's military leaders and their families, and financed by huge loans obtained overseas. The financial chaos that resulted from these excesses in 1997 and 1998, have had major repercussions. The fall of the *rupiah* to a fraction of its former value in a matter of months made it impossible for hundreds of businesses to meet their obligations. Widespread bankruptcy and unemployment of factory workers resulted, as well as inflated prices of basic food, which led to rioting in many areas, especially in the slum-like shanty-towns around the major urban areas to which country-dwellers shifted to find work in the city. For hundreds of thousands of such people unemployment and inflated prices of basic necessities such as rice, cooking oil and kerosene created a desperate situation.

In 1901 a son was born to an impoverished Javanese school-teacher of aristocratic *priyayi* origins and his wife, who was from a Balinese rajah's family. This child, named Sukarno, is said to have exhibited early a lively, charming and intelligent personality. An influential friend, the early nationalist leader Tjokroaminoto, made it possible for him to enter Surabaya High School, where he studied for five years. Tjokroaminoto personally trained Sukarno as an orator as soon as he realised the boy had a natural talent in this direction, and arranged for him to attend the Bandung Technical Institute, the first semi-tertiary institution founded in Indonesia. Here Sukarno trained as an architect and an engineer.

During the 1920s Sukarno was an impassioned advocate for

Indonesian independence. He was arrested in 1929 by the Dutch and gaoled. After two years in prison he was briefly released, then arrested again in 1932 and exiled to the long narrow eastern island of Flores, with its eight smoking volcanoes. He read a great deal – Abraham Lincoln, Emerson, Jefferson, Nehru, Lenin, Marx – all were absorbed during this phase of development of his political thought. As time went by he became a martyr and a legend in his own time – immensely well-known and popular among the people.

In 1949 the Indonesian government published a book called *Illustrations of the Indonesian People's Revolution*, designed to capture, in words and more than two thousand drawings and photographs, the spirit of the years of struggle. There is a fascination in the seemingly endless succession of pictures, nearly all of people.

However, perhaps the most interesting is a picture taken on 17 August 1945. It is ten o'clock in the morning and the place is outside a house in a Jakarta street – 56 Pegangsaan Timur, which was then Sukarno's home. Sukarno stands before a microphone, reading from a small slip of paper held in both hands. On the same page is a close-up of the paper, half a sheet of ordinary writing paper, somewhat dog-eared and containing some 30 words of writing in Indonesian, with some deletions and crossings-out under the heading, written in a firm hand and underlined twice *Proklamasi*. The photograph is of the actual declaration, read out by Sukarno in these words: 'We, the Indonesian people, herewith proclaim the independence of Indonesia. All matters pertaining to the transfer of power, etc, will be carried out in the shortest possible time.' Some hours later the declaration was broadcast from behind locked doors in the studios of the national radio in Jakarta.

A sporadic war with the Dutch followed, but international sympathy, notably from Australia and the United States, was with the independence movement, especially after Sukarno was arrested and deported to the island of Bangka in 1948. On 28 January 1949, the United Nations called for a transfer of sovereignty 'at the earliest possible date'. Dutch rule ended

in December of that year, finally bringing the Republic of
Indonesia into effective existence.

> We are only scattered bones
> But we are yours.
> You must now evaluate these scattered bones.
> Whether our souls have departed in the cause
>   of independence,
> Victory, or hope, or for nothing.
> It is to you that we speak now
> We who do not know, who can no longer speak,
> We talk to you in the stillness of the night.
>
> When our minds are at peace
> And the clock ticks on the wall
> Remember, remember us,
> Continue, continue our spirit.

These lines indicate as well as any other the post-independ-
ence mood of Indonesia – a sense of elation and mission,
vaguely-defined, perhaps, but glorious. They are from the pen
of a modern Indonesian poet, a Sumatran named Chairil Anwar,
who died of typhus in 1949, while still in his twenties.

One of Sukarno's first acts was to abolish 'The United States
of Indonesia' – the federal form in which independence had
been achieved – because of his mistrust of Dutch 'divide and
rule' tactics. It could be argued, and strongly, that for Indonesia, with its 3000 islands and diverse ethnic patterns, a federal
form of government would be most suitable. Nevertheless on
17 August 1950, Indonesia became 'a unitary state' based on
central rule from Jakarta. In the same year the 1945 'revolutionary constitution' which had given such wide powers to
the president was replaced by one which made Cabinet responsible to a national parliament, not to the president. So
Indonesia began a disastrous experiment with Western-style
parliamentary democracy.

There were already signs of disunity between Jakarta and

the outer regions, which were less enthusiastic about the unitary state. The Dutch-sponsored Republic of the South Moluccas proclaimed its independence, but this dissident 'government' later became one of exile in The Hague. The extremist Darul Islam movement, which wanted an Islamic state, turned terrorist and fought the government from mountain strongholds in West Java and Sumatra.

Official inexperience in administration began to tell increasingly as the months and years passed. In order to obtain revenues the government increased customs duties to a level that made smuggling really worthwhile. No resources existed to police the huge sweeps of coastline, and soon more goods were coming in over the beaches than through the ports. Also the government refused to devalue its currency, the *rupiah*, and the black market became a flourishing illegal business. By 1956 *rupiahs* could be bought on the streets of Djakarta with foreign currency at a quarter the official price and by 1960 this had fallen to a tenth.

In 1956, my first personal experience in Indonesia, it was no longer possible to get a telephone connection from one part of Jakarta to another, although one could still ring up within suburban exchange areas, at the cost of much time and patience. The capital's streets became narrow, muddy tracks full of deep potholes and ruts, partly due to the army's habit of running tanks over them to the detriment of the bitumen. Cars and spare parts, subject to duties of up to 500 per cent, were so valuable everyone removed such accessories as hubcaps and wiper blades before venturing out, because these were frequently stolen if left on the vehicle.

There were grave difficulties in achieving any coherence in the political system, divided as it was between four main influences – Sukarno, the Parliament, the growing Communist Party and the armed services. Sukarno had fallen out with the army chief-of-staff, General Nasution, dismissing him in 1952. The following year Nasution published a book, *Fundamentals of Guerilla Warfare*, which had such important implications for Indonesia's future it deserves attention.

'The Indonesian National Army,' Nasution wrote, 'has been taught many different and often contradictory things. Things such as "The army should not engage in politics" ... "The army is a tool of the country, an instrument of the government." All these expressions are merely slogans, and the person who suggested them used them for his own needs.'

Nasution argued next, at some length, that because the Indonesian Army was a guerilla, not a professional, force, its members must involve themselves in politics.

'They are different from a permanent army or a professional army whose soldiers carry a gun because they are instructed to do so by their master. The people's army is an army which defends the ideology of those people.

'The guerilla soldier and partisan ... is not merely a tool to be ordered about. He must be taught the country's ideology and policy. He must not be isolated from politics. He must have both feet firmly in the middle of politics.'

Nasution was back in charge of the army again only two years later, restored as chief-of-staff by the Parliament while Sukarno was absent on a pilgrimage to Mecca. The Communists warned that this might be the beginnings of a military dictatorship. When Indonesia's first elections were held in 1955 six million people had voted for the Communists, who had campaigned on a major 'land for the landless' theme which appealed to the poorer people. However, three other parties, Sukarno's PNI and two Moslem groups, the Masjumi and the NU, had each polled somewhat better out of a total vote of 37 million.

Sukarno spent a good deal of 1955 out of Indonesia. He visited the United States and China, and seemed oblivious to the mounting problems at home. He spent money freely on this foreign travel, refusing to listen to advice about the country's financial problems. 'Economics,' he is said to have remarked, 'make my head ache.' On his return he expressed impatience with the political parties and gave notice of a new concept he had in mind called 'guided democracy'. Early in 1957 it became a reality – a kind of national consensus based on traditional village government.

On 30 November 1957, a large, black car drove smartly up to the Tjikini School, a private establishment attended by the children of Jakarta's leading families, including Sukarno's eldest son and daughter. Even the waiting *betjak* – bicycle rickshaw – riders called out and waved to the confident-looking, smiling man in the black *kopiah* hat. It was the president going to a school prizegiving – a mundane but felicitous occasion which saw Sukarno in a relaxed and unguarded mood. As he came out the crowd drew closer, leaving only a narrow lane for Sukarno to cross the footpath to his car at the kerb.

Then came a loud explosion and a flash of light as the first bomb exploded almost at his feet. His bodyguard pushed Sukarno to the pavement as the second bomb went off. Already the air was full of the screams of injured women and children. A third bomb exploded. Sukarno appeared to be uninjured although his clothes were dirty and splashed with blood. Pale and shaken, he stood up and began to move towards the car, but his staff, taking him by the shoulder, moved him swiftly behind the car and across the street.

Just as they did so a fourth bomb exploded inside the car, wrecking the interior. The president and his group, running across the road, were about to enter a house when Sukarno, in the belief that it was owned by a Dutch woman, refused to take refuge there, even though a fifth bomb exploded just behind them. They dodged back and went into the house next door.

The Tjikini Raya affair shocked the Indonesian nation deeply. Of the ten people killed six had been children, and this had a tremendous impact in a country where children are virtually worshipped. The four men arrested turned out to be Moslem extremists of the Darul Islam movement, who reiterated their hatred of Sukarno even in the court that finally condemned them.

Sukarno and those who guarded him were fully aware of the danger of a further assassination attempt. The president moved with considerable fear along the narrow ribbon of road linking Jakarta with the presidential palace at Bogor. One morning when I was driving with an Indonesian friend to a picnic spot at Puntjak, he swung the car off the road on to the grass verge for no apparent reason.

'What is it?' I asked.

'Bung Karno.'

Then I heard the sound of motor horns in the distance and within minutes the leading motor cycles were in view, lights full on in the bright sunshine. There were four of them, followed by a white jeep, then a long, black car, which seemed to be empty but for the driver, and finally, more armed motor-cyclists.

In the front of the jeep stood an army officer, wearing dark glasses, his hand resting lightly on the windscreen. In the black car was Sukarno, crouched down low on the seat even though the doors were lined with sheet steel and the windows fitted with armoured glass.

The white jeep became something of a legend in and around Jakarta and a host of stories, persistent, if of no verifiable authenticity, grew up around it. It was said that the officer in sunglasses used a bicycle chain, with which he lunged out to smash the windscreen of any vehicles obstructing the convoy.

In 1959 Sukarno ordered a return to the 1949 constitution, thus returning executive power to himself and weakening the other areas of government. Parliament was further debilitated by the addition of more appointed members than elected ones. But behind this apparent dominance by Sukarno a bitter and intense enmity was developing between two major forces in the society – the army and the Communists.

By 1961 Sukarno felt strong enough to demand transfer of the western part of New Guinea – West Irian – which had been a Dutch colony, to Indonesia. He entrusted a tough regular soldier, General Suharto, with the task of readying a 25,000 strong invasion force. In April the first guerilla forces were dropped into the jungles of West Irian. The Indonesian military performance in this sporadic war was no better than indifferent. However, there was no stomach for the war in Holland, and this, combined with strong United States opinion that Indonesia should have West Irian, carried the day.

In 1963, as Sukarno knelt in prayer at a religious meeting,

a fanatic took out a pistol and fired a full magazine at him. Again he was untouched, but five people around him were wounded. Now even more elaborate measures were taken to guard him, including an elite palace guard all of the same blood grouping as the president. Its men tasted his food and drink before he touched it, and searched visitors for concealed weapons.

Largely isolated from his people, Sukarno became a myth in his own time and some curious stories circulated about him. His interest in women and marital problems were expanded to give him a reputation as a great user of women in the tradition of the rajahs of the past. He was said to go out at night, embrace trees, and walk barefooted during thunderstorms. He appeared at a function barefooted and explained that this was because he wanted to pick up electricity from the ground.

Such things, and the extravagance of his daily life, served only to make the common people love and revere him all the more. This adulation was not so much towards Sukarno as a person as to his position as ruler. It must be considered a continuing and significant political force in Indonesia.

When the federation of Malaysia was formed late in 1963 Sukarno opposed it – first with words and then by sending armed forces into Sarawak. In 1964 he announced 'the Year of Living Dangerously', a confrontation against what he saw as the forces of capitalism and neo-colonialism.

There was increasing speculation about his health. Already an old man by Indonesian standards, he was plagued by a liver complaint that needed surgery. This he refused because he had been told by a fortune teller that steel would cause his death. Rumours spread that he might die at any moment may well have been the cause of a confused military coup in September, 1964.

The first action seems to have been a rebellion by leftwing elements in the army supported by armed Communist activists at Halim Air Base. They claimed they had acted to prevent a planned coup by the generals to depose Sukarno. Armed bands of soldiers surprised leading members of the Council of Generals in their homes during the night. Six were murdered, at least one after being subjected to torture. A warning telephone call allowed General Nasution to escape over the back fence of his house in his pyjamas at 4 a.m. There was some shooting there, killing his six-year-old daughter.

General Suharto, the leader of the elite strategic reserve of the Indonesian army, became prominent at this stage, rallying loyal troops to break the 'revolt' by force of arms. There was fierce fighting with young Communist guerillas at Halim Air Base and in central Java. The Communist leader, Aidit, was killed.

His death was only the first of many in a massive campaign, said to be against the Communists, but actually against many others, especially the Chinese. This huge bloodletting is perhaps the greatest stain on the Indonesian nation, and was an ominous portent for the future. Research teams from Indonesian universities reported 800,000 deaths in Java, 85,000 in Bali and about 100,000 in Sumatra. Large numbers were identified as ethnic Chinese.

Independent eye-witnesses in Indonesia during December and January reported that not only men, but also women and small children, who could not possibly have ever had a political idea, were butchered by mobs of Moslem extremists. While army units stood by and watched this happen, and in some cases took part in mass executions in the villages, the carnage aroused horror and revulsion among the majority of the people, and within much of the armed services. Terrible though the death of the generals had been the scale of the retribution seemed beyond all reason.

Much of this violence involved the *marhaen*, the proletariat, landless and uneducated peasants who have drifted to the cities in the hope of improving their fortunes. Often unable to find work even for a pittance, they join one or other of large aimless bands that loiter in the streets, always ready to undertake any activity from a political demonstration to beating up a Chinese shopkeeper and looting his home. This group, one of frightening potential for irresponsible destructiveness, without aim, and without any real hope of legitimate employment, is often enough the spearhead of violence during political riots in Indonesia.

A restless, drawn-out struggle for power between Sukarno and General Suharto continued for a year. Sukarno's policies were steadily reversed. The confrontation with Malaysia ended, Indonesia rejoined the United Nations. Sukarno was placed under house arrest. In February, 1967, Suharto assumed all real powers of government, and a year later became Indonesia's second president, *bapak*, the father of the nation.

A stocky, slow-moving man who dislikes publicity, Suharto was born into a peasant family near Jogjakarta in 1921. After a primary education at a village school he enlisted in the Dutch colonial army at the age of 19, not long before the Japanese occupation. He was a regimental commander when the republic was formed, a colonel in 1957, and a brigadier-general and deputy-chief of the army staff three years later.

His 'new order' government continued to be anti-Communist and brought Indonesia into much closer orientation with the West, and in particular, the United States. The Indonesian army became a vast administrative machine with the weapons to support its demands. Many army officers did not hesitate to use this position to their own advantage. *Newsweek*, 16 June 1969, in an article about General Ibnu Sutowo, the then head of the state-run Pertimina Oil Corporation, commented: 'When he married off his daughter in March, the general threw a party that was truly sultanic in splendour. In a week-long festival of dances and ceremonies city streets were blocked for miles around to accommodate the 1000 guests who poured in each night to pay their respects. Closed-circuit television was installed so all could see and be seen and Djakarta's largest electrical generator was commandeered to provide power. Among the reported wedding gifts: 18 cars and a yacht.' In 1976 Suharto dismissed Sutowo as a result of one of the most massive defalcations in modern history, leaving Pertamina $10.5 billion in debt.

However, the huge wealth accumulated by the Suharto family – estimated as high as $40 billion – also became a major scandal.

Official enquiries in 1998 estimated that a car importing concession to Suharto's son Hutomo (Tommy) had cost the nation
$1.5 billion. Hutomo was allowed to import cars from Korea
without paying tax, and sell them in competition with all other
importers, who had to pay tax. This was only one example of
a complex pattern of dishonesty, involving major political figures
and their families and friends, which came to be known as
'cronyism'.

On the credit side for Suharto's New Order was an impressive growth in GDP in the 30 years to the early 1990s, a
doubling of the manufacturing share of GDP to 24 per cent,
increases in the rice yield, and predictable responses in international affairs. However, gains in agriculture were mainly
due to improved seed and the greater use of pesticides, and
resulted in sharp disparities in wealth in rural areas between
those controlling these new methods and the former small-
holders, many of whom have lost their land.

Advances in industry and the raised GDP did little to benefit the vast majority of the people, most of the proceeds going
to the small minority of the wealthy and influential. These
industries, almost always joint ventures with foreign capital,
included labour-intensive manufacture like clothing and shoes,
but also extended to glassware, electrical goods and motor
parts. Indonesia became the world's largest exporter of plywood,
although this industry eventually prompted a major scandal
because of its rapid depletion of the country's timber resources
and diversion of much of the proceeds to a few 'cronies'.

On 7 December 1975, Indonesia invaded East Timor, using
a large naval task force, aircraft and 10,000 troops, choosing
a time of political instability in both Portugal, the colonising
power, and in Australia, less than 400 miles to the south. Many
Australians were angered because Australian commandos in
Timor during World War Two had been protected by the local
people, at great cost to the Timorese due to brutal Japanese
retaliation.

East Timor makes up roughly half of the island of that name,
the western section, formerly a Dutch possession, having become

part of Indonesia at the time of independence. Since Indonesia had no historic, ethnic or political claim to East Timor, the invasion created widespread criticism within the United Nations and in communities and parliaments around the world. A civil war ensued following resistance to Indonesia from FRETILIN, a political party which had declared the territory's independence not long before the invasion. The Indonesian military contended they had invaded because FRETILIN was Communist, but the organisation has denied this.

In November, 1975 five Australian television journalists were killed by Indonesian troops in the small town of Balibo ten kilometers from the border of Indonesian Timor. Timorese spokesman Jose Ramoz-Horta says they were simply taken prisoner by the Indonesian army and shot, and that 'the Indonesians were determined to "teach a lesson" to the Australians, as Radio Kupang (in Indonesian Timor) boasted that evening.' The Indonesian army claimed the journalists died when they were caught in crossfire. However, subsequent eye-witness accounts in 1998 indicate that they were shot and knifed by Indonesian troops in cold blood after no more than token FRETILIN resistance in Balibo had ended. Soon after the Balibo incident another Australian journalist, Roger East, was shot in particularly brutal circumstances by Indonesian soldiers on Dili wharf. Indonesian government refusal to investigate these matters and, if justified, press charges of murder, has been a major impediment in Australian–Indonesian relations.

According to Ramoz-Horta's book, *Funu*, as many as 200,000 Timorese died between 1975 and 1981, partly due to acts of war, but substantially because of 'a deliberate strategy of starvation through destruction of food crops and continuous military operations that left the population unable to cultivate the land.' Thousands more have perished since. However, a FRETILIN guerilla army maintained the struggle against Indonesian occupation. East Timor was returned to world attention by major television coverage of 'the Dili massacre' – an attack by Indonesian troops in 1991 on an unarmed assembly in Santa Cruz cemetery in the capital of the territory that resulted in an estimated 300 deaths – and the award of the Nobel Prize for Peace to Ramoz-Horta and the Bishop of Dili, Bishop Carlos Belo.

After much negotiation the Indonesian government agreed to a vote of the East Timorese people in August, 1999 to decide their future.

Following the shooting of five students by the army at a peaceful demonstration in Jakarta in May, 1998, and major rioting in many parts of the country, Suharto resigned from the presidency. Under his former protege and successor, President B.J. Habibie, came limited signs of liberalisation and the promise of fair elections within a year. However, although it was evident the army, over 200,000 strong, remained a major area of power, continued rioting, mob murders and burning of Chinese houses and shops and Christian churches made it equally plain they were unable, or unwilling, to maintain law and order.

These events and the economic crisis from July, 1997, served to bring many problems to the surface, but not to solve them. The bare facts of that situation were alarming enough. The Indonesian rupiah plummeted wildly from July, 1997, seven months later stabilising uneasily at 9000 to the American dollar, barely a third of its pre-crash value. With the private sector foreign debt at around $70 billion, Indonesia immediately faced its worst financial crisis for 30 years. The value of shares in Indonesian companies fell in sympathy. The situation was not improved by the effects of a long drought, which had obliged Indonesia to import large amounts of food. The cost of imported rice rose more than three times, and even after government subsidies, was twice as dear in the shops and markets.

Meanwhile the collapse of hundreds of businesses had increased unemployment by millions. Rusting steel skeletons in Jakarta's business centre were only too eloquent of the sudden cessation of work on high-rise building projects whose finance, loans coming from overseas, had dried up. Loss of income combined with rising food prices created a highly volatile situation, with food riots reported from many parts of the country.

A disquieting aspect of the situation was regular violence against the Chinese. Barely 5 per cent of the population, they control well over half of Indonesia's wealth. The early weeks of the campaign to make the Chinese the scapegoats for unemployment and rising prices brought some evidence that the government and the courts were encouraging it. Western journalists on the spot reported reluctance by the police and the army to prevent the looting and burning of Chinese shops. They also reported that only a small minority of the looters were brought to court, and were then given only light sentences – a matter of months. By contrast a Chinese woman who shouted at youths for beating a drum during the early hours of the morning was reportedly gaoled for three and a half years for crimes against Islam.

More rioting, bringing thousands on to Jakarta's streets, came with a meeting of the People's Consultative Assembly in November called by President Habibie in an effort to resolve some of the nation's problems. An announcement that elections proposed for May, 1999 would be delayed until July increased the wrath of protestors. Hundreds more people were killed in these riots, often under the most brutal circumstances. That month also saw the revelation of a major killing campaign, including women and children, by the Indonesian army on the island of Biak, part of the former West Irian, and evidence of further army killing in the Atjeh (Aceh) region of west Sumatra, where government from Jakarta has never really been accepted.

The economic consequences of the social instability became considerable, virtually crippling the economy. Flight of Chinese capital from Indonesia was conservatively estimated at $10 billion by mid 1998. During the riots 5000 buildings and 2000 vehicles were damaged or destroyed, a total damage bill estimated at half a billion dollars, with a death toll of thousands.

However, the 1999 elections passed relatively peacefully. Sukarno's daughter Megawati achieved the highest vote, 34 percent, while that of the intellectual modernist Amien Rais was disappointingly small at around 12 per cent. An Indonesian comment: 'They voted for the father.'

Early 1999 saw a decision by the army to arm thousands of young men and form them into civilian militia units. In East Timor refugees camped in Dili refused to return to their homes because they were afraid of the newly formed militia, many of whom were armed with assault rifles.

When 78.5 per cent of the people of East Timor voted for independence the pro-Indonesia militia and units of the Indonesian army shocked the world by visiting a terrible revenge on them, murdering, torturing, burning down almost every town and village before they were replaced by an Australian-led peacekeeping force. However, in October the Indonesian Parliament decided reluctantly to endorse the East Timor vote, making way for the evolution of a new nation in Asia.

In Djakarta earlier major rioting resulted from an attempt by the military to assume virtual martial law powers, forcing suspension of the authorising legislation. More public anger came with a government decision in October, 1999, to drop an investigation into ex-president Suharto's corruption. IMF and World Bank economic assistance was suspended after revelations that $105 million of aid money had been misappropriated by the 'crony' circle of Suharto's Golkar Party, which also has close associations with the military.

In a surprise decision of the parliament Megawati was defeated by 373 votes to 313 for the presidency, the frail, almost blind leader of the largest Moslem party, NU, Abdurrahman Wahid, becoming Indonesia's fourth president. Severe rioting followed the decision.

Whatever happens to Indonesia is of major importance to the world. It is, after all, the fourth largest population on the planet, with almost 200 million people. With the prospect of actual shortages of basic foods, even of starvation for millions of people, becoming very real, Indonesia presents an alarming prospect for the future.

As Sukarno once said: 'The stomach will not wait.'

21

Malaya: Malaysia, Singapore and Brunei

Malaysia is a new nation in more ways than one. Her development as an organised community has taken place almost entirely within the last century and a half. Kuala Lumpur, the capital, and now the major centre of population and industry, was settled only after tin was discovered there in 1860. In the late nineteenth century the total population was perhaps a twentieth of the current 22 millions – probably well under a million people. They were mostly seafaring tribesmen who lived in wood and *attap*-thatched villages straggling along the muddy banks of river estuaries. Apart from the brief and limited traditions of Malacca and Johore there was little sense of nationhood.

Peninsular Malaya, the central state of today's Malaysia, was important to the British East India Company in the first half of the nineteenth century because of three settlements along the west coast established as staging posts on the trade route to China. These were Georgetown on the mountainous island of Penang, Malacca and the island of Singapore.

Britain was uninterested then in the jungle-clad, largely mountainous and lightly-populated interior. Here were no wealthy, fertile delta areas, no known mines of gold or precious stones, no developed societies that might provide sources of raw materials and a market for manufactures. The climate was hot, humid and enervating, most of the soil was poor. There were no roads, much less railways, and except for a few miles on either side of the river estuaries, the bulk of the snake, tiger and leech-infested country was inaccessible. It swarmed with the deadly mosquito *anopheles*, as yet not identified as the carrier of malaria. Most of this country had never been explored, and there seemed little incentive for either Malay or European to do so. There was no land traffic between the east and west coasts, which are divided by ranges of high, steep and rugged mountains, to this day largely unexplored.

The opening of the Suez Canal in 1869 brought Malaya into much greater strategic and economic prominence. In 1867 the passage from London to Singapore was 116 days. Three years later one of 42 days was recorded.

In spite of the forbidding deathrate from malaria, rural oppression and population growth in their home country drove tens of thousands of Chinese to Malaya as indentured coolies, mostly to work in tin mines in the northern states of Perak and Selangor. Up till then Malay mining had been inefficient and intermittent. Chinese labour and Chinese methods developed the industry so that by the end of the century it was the world's largest producer. The biggest migrations of Chinese were in the 1860s, when tens of thousands crowded into the shabby, lawless camps that grew up around the mines.

There was scant law in up-country Malaya other than the knife and the gun. Because of this individual miners were more than willing to swear oaths of allegiance to a number of competing Chinese secret societies. These societies soon became rich and powerful, their rivalry more bitter and violent. Pitched battles were frequent; members of one society boasted their shirts were dyed with the blood of their rivals. Initiates were bound, as they still are today, to obey orders without question and to reveal absolutely no information about the society, on pain of death. Present-day initiation rituals of these societies, so far as they are known, can be traced back many centuries in mainland Chinese history.

These circumstances laid the foundation for Malayan society

as it is now, with a wealthy and influential Chinese minority numbering a third of the population, within which the secret criminal societies, like the Triad, still prosper, exacting 'squeeze' from shopkeepers, running brothels, engaging in illegal smuggling. They beat up opponents with bicycle chains, kill with the knife. Generally speaking, there is a deep underlying mistrust between the Chinese and Malay peoples, and it is government policy to give a preference to Malays in official appointments.

During these formative decades struggles for power, plundering of neighbours and warfare were almost incessant among the Malay princelings. As new and productive tinfields came on line, so also did disputes as to who should get the royalties. Piracy off the coast became more and more impudent and common, with armed guards on merchant shipping regularly having to fight off attacking boats. General lawlessness in the end persuaded British authorities of the need to intervene in 'up-country' affairs. In 1873 the authorities in Singapore were required 'to employ such influence as they possess with the native princes to rescue these countries from the ruin that must befall them if the present disorders continue unabated'. The provision, from 1874 on, of residents to advise local rulers led to an extension of British rule throughout the country. Dynastic squabbles were skilfully exploited by British diplomats to this end. The Malay rulers were obliged to accept British 'advice' in all matters except those relating to the Moslem religion and custom.

By this time British interest was increased by two events that must be considered milestones. The first was the introduction of the rubber tree from its native Brazil and recognition that here was one export crop that would thrive on Malaya's poor soils, and for whose service there was an adequate pool of cheap labour. The second was the identification of *anopheles* as the vector of malaria, and the development of measures to control it.

For the first time it became practicable for British planters to make a life for themselves and their families in the interior.

Roads and railways were built, the coastal plain west of the mountains was cleared and cultivated and inland cities like Kuala Lumpur and Ipoh grew and prospered. Kuala Lumpur acquired a curious collection of public buildings, like the Jame Mosque, in the north Indian Mogul style, because in most cases the architects were Englishmen trained in India. The mass production of the car made all the difference to the infant rubber industry. It boomed from 1906 onwards, and by 1937 there were more than two million acres of rubber plantation, exporting nearly three-quarters of a million tons a year.

An 'agreement' with Thailand in 1909 resulted in four northern states, Perlis, Kedah, Kelantan and Trengannu being transferred to British Malaya. This event almost doubled the area of Malaya at the expense of its neighbour.

Although a Communist party was founded in 1930, largely among the Chinese, no independence movement evolved comparable to those in India or Indonesia. The multi-racial nature of the society was partly responsible for this: There was also by now a large minority of Tamil labourers from India, who had been imported to tap the latex sap from the rubber trees, and whose descendants now make up almost ten per cent of the population.

Although the world depression of the thirties caused some setbacks, life and progress continued in an orderly way – the Malaya of Somerset Maugham's novels, a placid plantation life made up of the casual social round in the Europeans' bungalows, with their wide verandahs and slow-moving ceiling fans. By 1940 the population had grown to four millions.

In 1941 the Pacific war burst on this peaceful scene without warning. The Japanese landed in Kelantan only the day after the United States fleet was destroyed in Pearl Harbor and quickly extended their bridgehead. Early in 1942 Singapore fell, its massive batteries pointing uselessly seawards. The Japanese failure to maintain preventive health services resulted in a major flare-up of malaria. The Japanese treated Malaya's people with the same brutality they exhibited elsewhere in occupied south-east Asia, but reserved their especial vindictiveness for the Chinese.

A resistance movement, largely Communist, grew up among the Chinese, and continued in jungle hideaways during British reoccupation of Malaya. In 1948 the Emergency, a bitter, protracted war between the Communist independent platoons and the colonial government, began. Soon the countryside took on a wartime aspect. The villages were surrounded by eight foot high barbed-wire perimeter fences, closely guarded and floodlit and under curfew at night.

Working in Malaya during the last years of the Emergency, I shared the stringent conditions imposed on everyone driving a car – the order to be inside a wired perimeter by nightfall or be fired on, not to stop between villages, not to carry food, money, canvas, plastic sheeting, writing paper, typewriters, arms and a host of other things that might be useful to the Communists. We were supposed to join convoys, trundling along behind a 'coffin' – an armoured personnel carrier – but this proved so likely to attract attack it was safer, and faster, to travel alone. I recall ending up just on dusk in a village in which a tent was an officers' mess of the King's Own Scottish Borderers.

'Ye'll have a whisky, lad? Soda or water?'

'Water, thanks.'

A grin.

'Just as well now. Ask for soda here, we put ye outside the wire for the night.'

The Emergency dragged on largely because it was as much a Chinese as a Communist initiative. I was once a guest at a dinner of a number of wealthy Chinese in Penang, where several of the company drank so much they literally fell off their chairs, female staff of the restaurant discreetly carrying them off to bed in specially-prepared rooms. One of these, a Chinese banker, after considerable brandy remarked to me . . .

'Ah . . . it is *our* army in the jungle.'

Political events in the end were more effective in ending

the Emergency than the very costly and attritive military ones, which included herding much of the population into concentration camps. Whole villages were forcibly depopulated, a melancholy sight as one drove through the country. The misery and poverty caused by this British army policy did much to ensure that the Communist independent platoons had so many willing recruits they were able to keep up their numbers throughout the Emergency.

All three major Asian communities formed political associations dedicated to the task of achieving independence as a Parliamentary democracy. The coming of internal self-government in 1955 was unexpected. The intention of the British government was that only limited powers be given to those chosen in Malaya's first general elections in that year. However, the Alliance Party, representing all three racial groups, won 51 of the 52 elective seats, a result so eloquent its leader, Tengku Abdul Rahman, was able to get an undertaking for full independence as soon as possible. On 31 August 1957, Malaya became an independent dominion within the British Commonwealth.

Malaya was fortunate in its first leader. A Malay prince, an educated, kindly man very aware of the risk of communal violence, one of his most eloquent acts was the adoption of Chinese children into his family.

The Communist insurrection did not long survive the achievement of independence. Only isolated trouble spots remained and the state of emergency was officially ended in 1960. Nevertheless the Communist leader Chin Peng and a small army of his most loyal and fanatical followers retreated to the jungle-clad hills at the Thai border, finally announcing the end of their armed struggle in 1989.

A major step forward was taken in 1963 with the inclusion of the British colonies of Singapore, Sarawak and Sabah with Malaya in an extended federation, called Malaysia. Oil-rich Brunei declined to become a member. Because it is mostly Chinese, the city-state of Singapore eventually, however, also elected to become an independent republic, leaving Malaysia in 1965.

Modern Singapore is an extraordinary testament to what can be achieved by what its architect, Lee Kuan Yew, calls 'Asian values'. Not only do three and a half million people live on this tiny island of only 250 square miles, they do so in economic and social standards that are among the highest in the world. In 1994 Singapore's GDP was $75 billion – more than $25 thousand per capita. That is one of the highest figures in the world, as also is life expectancy. Infant mortality is among the lowest, the literacy rate is over 90 per cent and population growth a low 1.1 per cent. All this is the more remarkable because the island lacks natural resources. The soil is mostly poor, and Singapore relies for more than half its water on neighbouring Malaysia, to which the island is connected by a causeway. Almost all food is imported.

During the 1950s the Foreign Correspondents' Association of South-east Asia had regular lunches at the Hotel de l'Europe (the Cockpit) in Singapore. Here I saw and occasionally exchanged a few words with a young smartly-dressed Chinese lawyer everyone knew as Harry Lee. You would not call him Harry now. In 1955 Lee Kuan Yew achieved the highest vote of any individual candidate in an election for an assembly in Singapore, although still with limited powers. He was one of three members of the leftwing People's Action Party (PAP) to be elected. The PAP now developed as a party in which two major factions struggled for power. One was the moderates under Lee Kuan Yew and the other a Communist 'front'. Britain gave Singapore full internal self-government in 1959. Lee Kuan Yew's remarkable charisma and political acumen were demonstrated when he attracted enormous applause by speaking to a large audience of Singaporeans in Malay after some less well-received speeches in English.

A general election later that year gave the PAP a landslide victory. The PAP however split, giving Lee's moderates a majority of only one, and for a time the new party, the Socialist Front, seemed likely to take over the government. However, Lee distinguished himself as a shrewd, pragmatic leader. A general election in 1963 gave his party 37 seats out of 51. A remarkable combination of ruthlessness and efficiency enabled Lee to continue to dominate Singapore, and to become a world figure during the next three decades. By using actions in the courts and both subtle and not-too-subtle coercion to destroy opposition in the Parliament, he came close to being a one man government of Singapore.

On this basis he transformed it from a Chinese provincial city on a south-east Asian island into a modern, wealthy and influential industrial power. Its former thatched shanty towns – so often the scene of horrific fires – and crowded terraces of Chinese shophouses were torn down and replaced by rows of modern high-rise apartments.

A virtual obsession with hygiene transformed the city from one of many smells – it must be admitted – to a clean aseptic metropolis, with the best-educated, healthiest and most prosperous population in Asia. For instance, it is an offence not to flush a public toilet in Singapore – a small detail of strict laws controlling air and water quality and public hygiene. Singapore has a severe and harsh legal system by world standards, especially for drug offences. Its government justifies this by pointing to the island's very low crime rate.

Singapore's economic miracle derives almost entirely from the intelligence, hard work and intense competitiveness of its people, three-quarters of whom are Chinese. Something of its nature can be deduced from the fact that almost three-quarters of GDP derives from services, mostly in the fields of finance, business, trade and tourism. All but a small fraction of the remainder comes from manufacturing. Much of this, especially electronics, is in the 'smart' category, with considerable attention given to information technology.

In 1841 the Sultan of Brunei gave the Borneo territory of Sarawak to an English adventurer, Captain James Brooke, in return for Brooke's help in subduing 'pirates'. The Brooke family ruled Sarawak from its *istana* – palace – in the river capital of Kuching for several generations, over the door of their home the motto 'What I have I hold.' After some hesitation the British government recognised this dynasty of 'white rajahs' in 1864 and granted British protection in 1888. After World War Two the third rajah ceded it to the British Crown. The first elections were held in 1959 to establish a degree of self-rule under a legislative assembly called the Council Negri.

Sabah, which was then called North Borneo, lies to the north of Sarawak, and like that territory, shares a wild mountain border with Indonesian Kalimantan. Most of this has never been explored. Sabah has fewer than half a million people, of whom a hundred thousand are Chinese and the rest native tribes, the Murut, Dusun and Bajai being among the most numerous. Like Sarawak, Sabah came under British protection in 1888 and, with the small island of Labuan off its coast, became a Crown colony after World War Two. Like Sarawak Sabah has an essentially agricultural economy, exporting timber, rubber, copra, pepper and some tobacco.

In this essentially rural scene Brunei stands out in vivid contrast. The total population is around 300,000, and it occupies only some 2000 square miles of the Borneo coast. But it does have rich oilfields, and is for its population size one of the wealthiest states in the world, with a per capita GDP above $15,000.

Brunei's era of glory was the sixteenth century, when the sultanate is believed to have controlled most of Borneo and many islands in the Sulu Sea which are now part of the Philippines. It became a notorious haven for piracy until the middle of the nineteenth century when the British navy destroyed the pirate fleets. Brunei's territory and influence had declined by then, and when it became a British protectorate in 1888, it was no more than a tiny, poor and obscure Moslem principality on the banks of a muddy estuary. Since oil was found near the coast at Seria in 1929 it has brought in so much money in royalties the state has difficulty spending it. A banker in Brunei told me the whole population could live comfortably into the indefinite future on the income from its overseas investments. The sultan is the third richest man in the world, with assets of about $50 billion. The town of Brunei has a huge marble mosque, completed in 1958 to look like the Taj Mahal, modern schools, hospitals, and roads.

Brunei became an independent state in 1984, and has close relations with Singapore, including training of defence forces. Brunei has spent at least $2 billion on modern defensive weapons systems, such as Exocet missiles. The sultan rules by decree. Not surprisingly, Brunei has one of the most restrictive immigration policies in the world.

Severe racial rioting in Kuala Lumpur in 1969, in which 200 people were killed, led to a suspension of the Malaysian parliament for two years and a general tightening of law and order procedures. A consequence of this has been government preoccupation with the ethnic issue, especially a continuing situation in which most business and money is controlled by Chinese and Indians, with considerable poverty among the Malays. In 1970 over half of the Malays were estimated to be below the poverty level, but as a result of government intervention to admit Malays into occupations formerly dominated by non-Malays, this has now been reduced to under 20 per cent.

Successful offshore exploration for oil and gas after 1970 greatly assisted the economy. Reserves are estimated at 4 million barrels of oil and 80 billion cubic feet of gas, and hydrocarbons make up nearly 10 per cent of Malaysia's export income. Palm oil plantations began to replace the less profitable rubber estates. Manufacturing had become the most important area of export income by the mid 1990s.

Malaysia's initial democracy had hardened into authoritarianism by the late 1980s. The fourth prime minister, Mahathir Mohamad, who took office in 1981, used Malaysia's draconic

internal security laws – a hangover from the Emergency – to
close down four newspapers and arrest 119 political opponents and independent-minded journalists in 1987. More were
to follow during the next decade. People arrested under these
laws could be and were imprisoned without trial. Since that
time Malaysia has had a sycophantic and compliant press, and
political opposition has been severely discouraged. Mahathir,
the first Malaysian leader to challenge continued British patronage, made vigorous attempts to reduce the dominance of
British companies in the rubber industry by acquiring their
shares and placing them in a state-owned corporation,
Permodalan. Malaysia's relations with Britain deteriorated from
this point on.

The collapse of the economy in 1997 and the attendant
hardships caused increasing discontent with government authoritarianism. As elsewhere in Asia people were prepared to
tolerate it as long as they were modestly prosperous – what
has been succintly described as 'Shut up and I'll let you get
rich.' In 1998 this discontent coalesced around the person of
the dismissed deputy-prime minister, Anwar Ibrahim, leading
to extensive demonstrations and pitched battles between the
'rioters' and the police.

Anwar, who had attracted worldwide respect for his moderate and enlightened attitudes, had been expected to succeed
the ageing Mahathir. Instead Mahathir dismissed Anwar. Anwar
was immediately charged with a variety of offences and imprisoned. When he appeared in court with head injuries inflicted
by the arresting police, many world leaders – even those of
some other Asian countries, spoke out in his support. Anwar
was not alone in this predicament. Hundreds of the thousands
who regularly took to the streets to support him were beaten
or arrested by police.

Early in 1999 Anwar was sentenced to six years in prison,
following a bizarre trial which raised serious doubts about the
integrity of the Malaysian system of justice. However, Mahathir
was returned to power in an election later that year, although
with a reduced majority.

22

Japan: The Iron Triangle

The opening of Japan to trade with the rest of the world after almost three centuries of isolation, and her rapid progress from a seemingly rigid feudalism to a Western-style capitalist economy, made her a major world power within a single generation. This was without doubt a revolution, although quite different from those in colonial Asia. Even so, the transformation of Japanese society after she concluded the first trade treaties with the West in 1854 was not as sudden as it seemed. Feudalism, already far into decay, was ready to collapse at a touch.

In the decade after the 'opening of Japan' the society became even more fluid. Western merchants took advantage of Japanese inexperience by exploiting the *bakufu*'s unrealistic exchange rate between gold and silver, about twice that on world markets. Foreign traders made huge profits and there was a tremendous, destabilising drain on Japan's gold reserves. This, coupled with similar manipulation of other export commodities, caused disastrous rises in the cost of living, rice increasing twelvefold, raw silk trebling, in eight years.

As a result, the decision to admit foreign traders provoked widespread hostility. In 1863 the large and powerful Choshu clan fired on American, Dutch and French ships from its shore batteries dominating the narrow and strategic Straits of

Shimonoseki. The next year a Western fleet retaliated by destroying the batteries. Choshu, a clan traditionally opposed to the *bakufu* now placed themselves firmly behind the emperor. Armed with 7000 modern rifles bought from the West, in 1866 they defeated a *bakufu* army easily. The following year the *shogun*, making a realistic assessment of the facts, abdicated voluntarily.

In 1868 the 16-year-old emperor, advised by a *samurai* clique largely consisting of Choshu men and their allies the Satsuma, announced his assumption of full authority. This was confirmed by important changes in the state ethic. Official Confucianism and Buddhism, which had been the popular religion during the Tokugawa period, were displaced, and Shinto, the animist religion of the ancient Japanese, restored to primacy. However, Shinto now became more than a religion. It was carefully modelled into a national cult, designed to promote belief in the virtual divinity, infallibility and invincibility of the emperor. In this way the new clique in power sought, as the Tokugawa had done, to stabilise the new order and ensure the obedience of the people.

The fact that the Western powers, with their modern weapons, had been able to force Japan into trade, and their own inability to resist, made a deep impression on the Japanese. Envoys sent out to study the outside world recommended that Japan adopt Western science, trade methods and industry as quickly as possible. The feudal system was officially dismantled, and the *daimyo* ceded their lands to the emperor, who moved his court to Edo in 1868. The city was renamed Tokyo, which means 'eastern capital'. The new era, called Meiji after the reign-name taken by the emperor, led to the transformation and modernisation of Japan at a breakneck pace.

In 1871 the *samurai* lost their notorious right to 'kill and go away' and in 1877, in spite of a rebellion in which 30,000 of their number died, were replaced by a conscript army. Torture as a routine legal practice was abolished in 1876. Farmers were permitted to ride horses on public roads. Japan was linked to the outside world by cable telegraph. Gas lighted the streets of Yokohama in 1872. Railways spread across the country and urban complexes, complete with steel mills, power plants and other appurtenances of the modern industrial state, grew rapidly. Western styles of dress, Western methods and designs and Western manners were carefully studied and imitated. The Japanese word for a Western style business suit, *sevilo*, derives from Savile Row.

But to attribute all this to a mere passion for copying is to miss the point. The motive was astute appreciation that only by change could Japan survive as an independent nation. The Japanese did not copy the West so much because they admired it as from a desire to put themselves in a position to compete with it in material terms. The carefully-restored Shinto cult was a conscious rejection of Western, indeed all foreign cultural ideas.

Japan's new leaders were determined she should be strong. A powerful modern navy was built in British shipyards and trained by British officers, and an army was developed on the German model. A major difficulty was the position of the two million *samurai*. Eventually the class was dispersed as such, although much of the tradition was carried over into new occupations – as police and military officers, teachers and bureaucrats. This term, rather than public servant is used, because the Japanese bureaucracy did not see itself as servants of the people. There is a saying, *kansom minpi*, which means 'official exalted, people despised'.

Decisive land and sea victories over China and Russia established Japan as a world power – moreover as an imperialist power. Although the forms of parliamentary democracy had been established in 1890, they had little effect until in 1925 universal male suffrage was introduced. However, by then two major catastrophes were affecting Japan. One was the world economic depression, the other Japan's worst natural disaster – the 1923 earthquake and fire that destroyed most of Tokyo and Yokohama and killed more than 150 thousand people.

By the middle of the decade militarism, which had seemed

to be in decline after World War One, was again on the ascendant. From May 1925 every school of middle grade or upward had a military officer on the active list attached to it. To the new generation educated to a fanatical nationalism, moderate policies appeared only as weakness. During the 1930s the army acted as a force above and beyond the law. The year 1932 was marked by a series of brutal assassinations of senior Japanese statesmen by young army officers. There was a similar series of murders in 1936. From then on the army, led by General Tojo, took over control.

Open war and invasion of China in 1937 involved atrocities that brought protests from around the world. The sacking of the Nationalist capital, Nanking (Nanjing), was especially brutal. Japanese soldiers killed 150,000 civilians, including women and children, mostly by the sword, and the Yangtse (Yangzi) River, which passes through the city, was said to have literally run red with blood. The Chinese claim there were 300,000 dead. Eye-witnesses told of groups of up to 20 young people being tied together and thrown into the river to drown, people buried to the waist in the ground then torn to pieces by Alsatians, bizarre biological research, including injections of plague, anthrax and cholera. The refusal of Japanese Prime Minister Keizo Obuchi to apologise for these atrocities during a visit to Japan of Chinese President Jiang Zemin in 1998 led to a breakdown in talks designed to improve relations between the two nations.

In 1940 Japan placed herself on a complete war footing. The political parties were disbanded, making Japan totally subordinate to the military. The loss at Hawaii's Pearl Harbor of eight American battleships, three cruisers and at least half the effective air power of the Pacific Fleet, brought Japan into four years of war that would ultimately prove disastrous. In spite of fanatical resistance, the Japanese were forced back from their initial Pacific conquests, which had brought them to New Guinea, the very doorstep of Australia. Damage to Tokyo was so great from aerial bombing that its population fell from seven to three million due to casualties and evacuation. In July 1945 the Western Allies called on Japan to surrender unconditionally.

On 6 August 1945 an atomic bomb that would ultimately cause 200,000 deaths was dropped on the Japanese city of Hiroshima. Three days later a similar weapon destroyed Nagasaki. Five more days brought Japan's surrender. In the words of Emperor Hirohito '. . . we have resolved to pave the way for peace for all future generations by enduring the unavoidable; by suffering what is insufferable'. Many people, including prominent national leaders and their wives, killed themselves. Thousands kneeled outside the Imperial palace to beg forgiveness for their insufficient efforts. Yet as a result of the war almost two million people alive in 1940 were now dead, almost nine million homeless.

Japan was ruled for seven years from 1945 by a military occupation force – virtually personal rule by the Supreme Commander for the Allied Powers, General Douglas MacArthur. Japan seemed amenable to changes in direction and its military clique became hated and despised, not so much because of the misery and damage of the war, but because Japan had been defeated.

Basically occupation policy was to guide Japan into new and democratic ways of government, and to reshape the education system and the economy. The big industrial conglomerates, the *zaibatsu*, were dissolved because of their close association with the military. The emperor became a constitutional monarch, but his popularity grew rather than declined because of efforts to 'democratise' his position. The Japanese saw these as attempts to humiliate him, and this increased their feelings of loyalty. When the occupation ended in 1952 he visited the shrine of the Imperial Ancestors at Ise and reported to them that Japan was again free.

The permanent effects of the MacArthur 'shogunate' were few indeed, since most of its reforms have been reversed. In fact the reconstitution of the *zaibatsu* and the limited restoration of the armed forces began before the Americans left, and with their concurrence. Land reform was perhaps the most valuable and lasting result of the occupation. Peasant ownership of land doubled to almost four millions, the beneficiaries being former tenant farmers.

However, there was nothing temporary or illusory about the regeneration of Japan's economy, which was no less impressive than that of the Meiji restoration. Japan rapidly became the world's biggest shipbuilder, a major car manufacturer, and evolved through heavy industry to become a world leader in information technology. This 'great leap forward' began in the 1960s, and was based substantially on a policy of ploughing profits back into development, rather than dividends. Typical of this was the Sony Corporation, which had humble beginnings in a small Tokyo shed and an initial capital of $500. Riding on the floodtide of demand for transistor radios, it was selling over a billion dollars worth of its products annually by the 1960s. Japan built the world's largest ship, a tanker of 276 thousand tons and the world's fastest train, the Tokaido bullet train. In 1960 Japan had only 3.5 million cars and most people used an adequate public transport system. Thirty years later there were 65 million cars choking the roads, creating an urban nightmare of pollution and delays. This motor explosion quickly demanded more and better roads – thousands of kilometers of freeways were built, a major element in what has become known as the concretisation of Japan.

An early symptom of this was the destruction in 1967 of Frank Lloyd Wright's Imperial Hotel in Tokyo, internationally regarded as an architectural masterpiece, and so well designed it was one of only a few buildings to survive the 1923 earthquake. A characterless 17-floor hotel replaced it. The pressure on land became enormous, leading to massive reclamation projects from the sea, such as the new Osaka airport built on a wholly artificial island. Tokyo has no natural coastline left at all, and the areas adjacent to it only a few kilometers. There are also staggering plans to go upwards – buildings as much as a mile high are on the drawing-boards.

During the 1970s heavy industry began to run into trouble

due to pollution and the sheer lack of suitable sites. The Tokyo–Kobe–Osaka region, the Kansai, in the words of one Japanese environmentalist, was rapidly becoming uninhabitable. Japan commenced a switch to post-industrial, high tech industries. Strenuous efforts to decentralise these to regional technopolises – entirely new cities – have had varied success.

The massive infrastructure growth in Japan has not been driven by demand so much as by corrupt links between the government, the construction industry and the bureaucracy. This collusion, *yuchaku*, became so blatant it was finally investigated in 1994 and a number of politicians and high level businessmen were gaoled. The investigations revealed that as much as three billion dollars a year were being stolen from the frugal and long-suffering Japanese people – much of it going back to the Liberal-Democratic Party government which had authorised the expenditure in the first place and channelled it to 'suitable' contractors. These would then kick back funds to 'feed the troops', that is, to the vote-buying system of Japanese politics.

This remarkable people, the modern Japanese, have billions stashed away in the one financial institution they trust – and the world's largest of its kind – the Post Office Savings Bank. By the 1980s, their hard work, obedience and skills had produced an enormous river of money that spilled over from Japan into all parts of the world, but especially into Asia and Australia. Land values in Tokyo escalated crazily, until at one time it was estimated that the 284 acre grounds of the Imperial Palace were worth more than all the land in Australia.

Billions of dollars were used to buy real estate and golf courses; new resorts, ski-slopes, burgeoned in Japan itself. Huge sums went into overseas investments, mostly in Korea and south-east Asia. When this bubble burst at the end of the decade real estate values in Japan fell heavily. One recent statistic: Forty per cent of Japanese householders have mortgages exceeding what their properties would realise on today's market.

The corruption scandals in the construction and finance industries contributed to a defeat of the LDP in 1993, after 38

years continuously in office. Hopes that this might presage
genuine reform of Japanese politics dwindled as four uneasy
coalition governments became necessary over as many years,
during which Japan's financial situation caused increasing
concern. Elections in 1996 brought the LDP back to government, although not this time with an absolute majority, since
it won only 239 of the 500 lower house seats. However, the
tetsu no sankakukei, the 'iron triangle' of politician, bureau-
crat and big business, appeared to have survived intact, as
able as ever to resist change, especially if this would threaten
its common interest.

In 1995 an earthquake struck the Kobe area, killing six thousand people and destroying 20 per cent of the houses in the
city. It also revealed elements of the construction industry as
being more than financially corrupt. Some of the collapses of
freeways and bridges were found to be due to bad building
and skimping on specified material such as reinforcing steel.
Assistance to the stricken city was much less than adequate,
especially since offers of assistance from the outside world
were refused. Kobe's experience, tragic enough in itself, also
caused a further anxiety: What would happen to the Tokyo
area if a similar earthquake occurred?

Contrast is the essence of Japan. In the great, brightly-lighted
shopping centre of Tokyo, the Ginza, Westernisation seems
complete. People wear Western clothes, the music systems in
the big stores play Beethoven, Bach, Mozart. Yet just around
a corner in a quiet street, behind an unobtrusive entrance, a
traditional inn provides an environment and service largely
unchanged from the Tokugawa.

In the industrial city of Osaka, under its pall of smoke, a
whole region is given up to concrete, tall chimneys, noisy
machines, construction cranes and the urgent clattering through
a vast railway junction of the wheels of a score of over-crowded
electric trains. Yet as one looks out of the carriage windows,
there between the points of two converging lines is a little
plot of rice growing, brushed by the bogies of every passing
train.

On the quiet shore of Lake Hacome, in the mountains not far from Tokyo, one may watch hundreds of Japanese reverentially looking out over the water at the cone of the sacred mountain, Fujiyama. An hour later one struggles to keep one's feet in the dense crowding of a railway carriage, rowdy with a hundred shouted conversations, the floor strewn with the unconsidered debris of the picnic crowds.

In 1988 the Takeshita government gave a million dollars to each of Japan's three thousand local government areas to spend as they saw fit to invigorate their communities. The results showed a remarkable diversity, in many cases going back to traditional crafts and industries – making charcoal, straw sandals, growing mushrooms, nurturing older varieties of plum trees, attracting fireflies, eliminating bright lights in a place traditionally noted as being the best for looking at the stars. This regional diversity contrasts with a depressing uniformity of lifestyle in the Kansai cities. Those who live there nevertheless seem to tolerate the ever-present throng of people and cars, the smog, the unnatural heat generated by so much concrete, with remarkable stoicism. Families live in tiny apartments, the breadwinners travel, usually standing, up to four hours a day in commuter trains. Many get home only at weekends, sleeping weeknights in tube hotels where the 'rooms' are not much larger than coffins – just big enough for a human to lie down in.

In spite of this severe restriction of the natural advantages of life, such as space, fresh air, peace and quiet and untroubled leisure, the Japanese people are affluent in material things, with every imaginable form of technical gimmickry available to them. Efficient, fast cars clog the roads, regularly able to average little more than a walking pace, restlessly redirected by huge signs over the freeways warning of traffic lockups ahead.

Numerous restaurants offering a wide range of foods are

usually crowded, because most Japanese homes are too small to entertain in. Men buy the best in golf clubs and accessories, but mostly use them alongside hundreds of others inside driving ranges. Access to real golf courses is so expensive it can only be afforded occasionally. There is a lavish range of 'theme parks' available to the public but little natural countryside or seaside.

Food is also very often artificial and most of it has to be imported – indeed Japan imports more of its food than any other country. More and more the older, frugal and healthy diet is being abandoned, often for expensive and wasteful items such as grain-fed beef. The Japanese like seafood and the world's oceans are scoured for it.

Will Japan revert to the worst aspects of the 'emperor system', with its overtones of military aggression, absolute obedience of the mass of the people to an oligarchy and insistence on the myths of Shinto? Certainly the physical means are there – Japan is one of the world's biggest spenders on weapons for its 'self-defence force', a large and modern army, navy and air force using mostly American matériel.

There is evidence of some revival of the Japanese attitudes of the 1930s, also an insistence at high levels in the society and the academic community of the purity and uniqueness of Japanese society. A major Japanese motion picture – *Pride, The Fatal Moment*, was produced in 1998 which presented a picture of World War Two idealising the wartime prime minister, General Tojo, who was executed for war crimes in 1946. This film, which showed to capacity audiences in Japan, rewrote history in several important ways – justifying Japan's actions and derogating those of the United States, ignoring atrocities like the carnage in Nanking, and presenting a kind of pan-Asianism in which Japan's neighbours admired and supported her. When the Mayor of Nagasaki publicly acknowledged in 1990 that Emperor Hirohito must bear some responsibility for the war he was shot in the back in an assassination attempt.

It is worth noting without overstressing the point that pre-war militarism developed in conditions of economic stress, a situation again emerging in Japan at the time of writing – ironically enough, mostly because her people prefer to save their money rather than spend it. This hesitancy of the home market, together with dwindling exports due to world over-production of commodities, caused a stubborn recession in Japan, with few signs of recovery by 1999.

The Japanese society remains hierarchic – the most important element is the group – the *dantai* – the least important the individual person. Almost all decision-making is collective – innumerable meetings and conferences are characteristic of Japanese business. Social relationships are rigid and complex, with set forms of language, especially for greetings, to be used between people of different social levels. This is the basis for the generally-observed politeness and formality of Japanese people – also the absolute necessity for a *meishi*, a business or calling card, so the social position of a new acquaintance can be established on first meeting.

This permits a proper operation of *nakama*, the cement that holds together the groups to which all Japanese are attracted, be it a workplace, a club, a school, an office. *Nakama* means 'insider' and in its broadest sense, involving the whole country, includes Japanese and only Japanese. Foreigners, even though they will be treated with formal politeness, are *yosomono*, a mildly derisory term meaning 'outsider', and will remain so no matter how long they live in Japan.

Discrimination does not apply only to foreigners, of whom Koreans are the most substantial group. There is a minority of three million Japanese which is the equivalent of India's untouchables. These, the *burakumin*, are the descendants of hereditary low caste groups who butchered animals, worked with leather, or dealt with the dead. They live in segregated communities in most larger Japanese cities, and suffer severe educational, social and economic disadvantages.

23

Thailand: Land of the Free

Thailand, as Siam came to be renamed, is in many respects the most advanced state in mainland south-east Asia, in spite of the fact that the succeeding authority to its absolute monarchy has been the army. Repeated attempts to establish parliamentary democracy there have regularly been upset by military coups. The Thai armed forces, numbering more than 200,000, remain the most significant force in the community, and their authority is increased by an obligation for all male citizens between 21 and 30 to serve for two years in the military as conscripts.

Nevertheless, Thailand provides free and compulsory education for all its children, and the literacy rate is a high 93 per cent. Around 300,000 students are enrolled in tertiary institutions, with as many again in open universities.

The position of women in Thailand is favourable by Asian standards, with equal access to men for education and work opportunities. Women are heavily represented in the professions and in business management. More than half the workforce is employed on the land, mostly growing rice, but there is a growing manufacturing industry which has absorbed about 15 per cent. Food processing, textiles and clothing, and electronics are the main industries, which are mostly centred on the capital and only large city, Bangkok. HIV/AIDS has emerged as a major health problem, affecting close on a million people.

King Mongkut's son, Chulalongkorn, continued his father's policies of change and reform with enthusiasm when he inherited the Siamese throne in 1868. At that time there was no proper code of law, no public education system, no organisation of state revenue, and few communications. During his reign until 1910 Siam acquired all these things and more.

Chulalongkorn sent his own children abroad to be educated and, with the help of his numerous brothers and sisters, energetically imposed on the nation a veneer, at least, of modernity. He used British advisers in almost every field of administration, and encouraged British investment. Two reforms were typical of him. He ended the custom that obliged subjects to crawl into the royal presence on hands and knees, and abolished slavery.

His reign is otherwise notable for the adroitness with which he kept his country out of the hands of any one of the great powers. Even so, French gunboats steamed up the river to blockade Bangkok, forcing Siam to return all territory east of the Mekong River to the French colonies of Laos and Cambodia. Britain and France agreed in 1904 to uphold an independent Siam as a buffer between their colonial empires. However, five years later it was obliged to surrender what are now the four northern provinces of Malaysia.

The country was being transformed by a steady flow of British capital, which by the 1930s amounted to 70 per cent of all foreign investment. However, Chulalongkorn refused overtures from a group of eleven Siamese, including four princes, who had been abroad, to introduce Cabinet government. By the 1930s the absolute monarchy was the last in the world in any country of consequence, and increasingly appeared an absurd and repressive anachronism.

In 1931 the king, Prajadhipok, had to go overseas to be

treated for failing eyesight and, when he returned, retired to his seaside palace at Hua Hin to convalesce. Prince Paripatra acted as regent. It was a time of considerable interest in the dynasty, because Rama I had predicted it would last only 150 years. That anniversary, however, passed without incident on 6 April 1932. Then early in the morning of June 24 tanks rumbled into the grounds of the royal palace in Bangkok and Prince Paripatra, still in his pyjamas, was taken away to join other members of the royal family being held hostage by the leaders of a coup d'état – the first of many in the nation's modern history.

Probably only 60 or 70 people were involved in the 1932 coup, which was almost bloodless. Severe economic problems were a major reason for the coup. Siam insisted on staying on the gold standard when the rest of the world had abandoned it, and as a result was pricing herself out of the world export market for rice and timber. The civilian leader of the coup was the professor of law at Chulalongkorn University, Pridi Pananyong, who had drafted a constitution providing for an elected assembly whose advice the monarch must take. The army leader was a young captain called Pibul Songgram. These two major figures, at first allies, later became rivals for power. While the country was introduced to representative government with apparent ease, it proved difficult to make it work. It became necessary to invent words hitherto unknown in the language for such concepts as revolution, politics, constitution.

Only a year later Pridi disappeared from the scene, accused of Communist leanings. The political pattern from that time was now set – a military oligarchy in which virtually every public position of consequence was occupied by an army officer 'wearing another hat'. Pibul, who was the architect of this system, was an admirer of European Fascism and Japanese militarism. It was he who changed the name of the country from Siam to Muang Thai, which means the land of the free people.

Thailand granted the Japanese free movement over her territory to invade Malaya during World War Two, although later

the Thais found the Japanese unpleasant guests. Pibul, briefly
ousted after the war, was back in charge by 1947. Elections
were held ten years later on the insistence of the United States,
but were so unashamedly rigged they led to a major public
outcry, and another coup, the declaration of martial law and
another phase of military rule from 1958.

I was in Bangkok at that time. Near the airport and at street
junctions soldiers had dug into foxholes from which machineguns
peered, belts of ammunition in the breeches. In the main streets
tanks and armoured cars dominated major intersections. The
unwritten rules for coups in Thailand were again observed,
however, and this one was bloodless. Soldiers manning the
tanks sat out on top of them, regarding the passing crowds in
good natured idleness, or reading papers. As for the public,
so used was it to this kind of demonstration they took no
notice at all. There have been 17 such military coups over the
last 60 years.

General Sarit Thanarat, who thus came to power, did do
some useful things. A native of the grossly under-developed
north-east, he diverted public funds to what had been a forgotten region, and made an attempt to curb the opium trade.
He liked to walk around the streets handing out fines to people
he found throwing fruit peelings on the pavement. However,
like those of other Thai strongmen, Sarit's reputation did not
long survive his death in 1963. It was disclosed he had acquired
a huge personal fortune, and in 1964 his estate was required
to repay most of this to the national treasury.

Military rule has continued more or less continuously. Elections in 1996 involving the usual vote-buying and intimidation,
brought to the office of prime minister Chavalit Yungchaiyudh,
a former army commander, who was, predictably, supported
by the armed forces, the security police and the bureaucracy.
However, public disquiet at the corruption and cronyism which
contributed so much to Thailand's economic difficulties of 1997
brought a popular civilian leader, Chuan Leekpai, to the prime
ministership in November of that year with a mandate for reform.
However, that year saw Thailand overwhelmed by the Asian

financial crisis. In mid 1998 the government announced the cost of the economic crisis in a single year – a recession of the economy by nine per cent, heavy losses in the value of real property and stocks, and a million unemployed.

Outside its one large city, Thailand consists mostly of thousands of small villages. Almost half of these are on the immensely productive river plain of central Thailand. This fertility ceases abruptly at the sharply-defined line where the lush, green ricefields, like a calm sea, meet a range of rugged, dramatic hills, full of peaks and cliffs of weathered limestone. Beyond these ranges is the north-east, comprising about a third of the nation's area.

Until the successes of Vietnamese Communism made it 'strategic', this region was allowed to remain neglected, virtually medieval, approached by only a single horrific road with tottering wooden bridges. When the first medical surveys were made, it was estimated to have almost a quarter of a million lepers. Other diseases, like malaria and liver fluke, were widespread. Even as late as 1966 liver fluke, a debilitating and life-shortening parasite, affected more than 80 per cent of the adult population. Considerable efforts were made to improve conditions there, especially in the north-east capital, Khon Kaen, but, as elsewhere in Thailand, have since been considerably eroded by a massive growth in the national population.

My work in the north-east took me to hundreds of villages, many of them so remote they had never before been visited by Europeans. Here – other than from savage dogs, many of whom might be rabid – one meets an unfailing courtesy, a placid calmness of demeanour, and a social pattern than seems successful in spite of the absolute lack of the facilities westerners take for granted. Life in this arid region is especially difficult during the six months of the dry season. Even Khon Kaen's water supply became spasmodic then, and it became necessary to leave taps on and place three foot high *klong* jars under them to obtain water when and if it started to flow. We came home one evening to find water flowing out the front door. A short drive along the road following the pipeline revealed why the supply was so variable – scores of punctures engineered by villagers, with dozens of laughing, shrieking children playing under these fountains.

But one finds a bleaker picture at the fringes – the poorest most remote land to which young people have been forced because of overcrowding in their home villages. In these hamlets of the crudest shanties one finds a very evident lack of hope, humanity forced back on to the ropes, existing in a narrow margin only just on the living side of death. In spite of an appalling rate of infant mortality here there are plenty of children, all with the bulging bellies that tell of acute malnutrition. There are millions living like this throughout village Asia. Their tragedy – and the world's – is that they don't make news, nobody does anything for most of them, there is little enough indication that many even care.

Early in the mornings a file of barefoot, yellow-clad, shaven-headed monks passed through the town. The mistress of every household waited smiling at the gate to put a spoonful of rice into the begging-bowl each of these men carried. But as with much else in Thailand this appearance of humble, impoverished mendicants was deceptive. The apparent poverty, the need to beg for food – these things are chosen voluntarily by the Buddhist monkhood, many of whom are highly-educated men and who willingly shoulder the burden of being the social cement, and often the means of education, even in small villages. Almost all Thai men enter the monkhood for a period of weeks or months. There are estimated to be 140,000 Buddhist monks, occupying nearly 20,000 *wats* – monasteries – which will be a feature of even small villages.

From time to time when I got home from work two or three would be sitting patiently on the floor of my house waiting for me. They spoke excellent English, they were versed in the European humanities. They would have some questions for me, and after a discussion – it might be about anything from

nuclear weapons to birth control – they would rise quietly
and leave without a farewell.

Thailand has a population of 60 millions, growing at around
1.4 per cent a year. This has resulted in considerable social
and economic problems. Pressure on rural land, as elsewhere
in Asia, has encouraged an organised industry selling young
girls into prostitution, both within Thailand and overseas. There
has been some growth in Thailand's industry, provided with
cheap labour by peasants flocking to the capital in search of
work. However, working conditions are often dangerous,with
hundreds of deaths in recent years from factory fires. Bangkok has become heavily polluted, its narrow streets unable to
accommodate some of the heaviest and most congested motor
traffic in the world, even though most of the city's characteristic canals – *klongs* – have been filled in to make room for
cars.

The Thais are pleasant, charming people on the whole,
maintaining a sophisticated, highly individual way of life which
has seemed to be able to accommodate and readily absorb
Western influences and technology, and to cope with the military
dictatorship. But as elsewhere in south-east Asia, all this has
been threatened by population growth and the intrusion of
'globalising' economics. The nation seemed early in 1999 at
a crisis-point – a divide, with economic indicators showing
that financial recovery must still be some way off. Among
them, an estimate that bad debts constituted 46 per cent of all
loans in the banking sector.

24

The Philippines: Trouble in Paradise

Like Indonesia, the Philippines is a chain of islands, of which Mindanao in the south, and Luzon in the north, are the largest, between them making up rather more than half the total land area of the republic. The central part consists of eight larger and thousands of smaller islands, collectively known as the Visayas. Most of the others are tiny islets – some four thousand of them so small they are not even named. Off to the east is the long, narrow Palawan, grouped around which are 200 more islets, many no more than barely visible coral reefs.

Most people live near the sea. The interiors of the larger islands are lonely, mysterious regions of smoking volcanic cones and forest-clad mountains, in which cinnamon, cloves and pepper still grow wild. The coastlines are idyllic. Atolls and islands, strands of dazzling white sand, brilliant corals, clear lagoons of placid green water, are all exactly like the standard dream of a tropical paradise of people living in colder, less-favoured regions. There is a rich natural endowment – gold, copper, nickel, coal, uranium, and offshore natural gas fields.

Regrettably this paradise is flawed. Population pressures are now becoming extreme, impelled by one of the highest rates of increase in the world – 2.2 per cent, more than a million additional people every year. Over the last decade the population has grown by almost one-third to 80 millions. There is also one of the world's largest gaps between the minority of the very rich and the great mass of the very poor. This has led to a high crime rate, and heavily-guarded new suburbs like Forbes Park in Manila for the affluent. They are typically surrounded by walls as high as 12 feet, topped with barbed wire and broken glass. Night and day armed guards watch the barricades at the only entry and exit points. These are fortresses built against the surrounding sea of poverty and lawlessness.

During the ice age glacials land bridges connected the Philippines with Borneo and the Asian mainland. The first Filipinos whose origins can be assessed with any accuracy moved in at that time. They were small-built people of the type anthropologists call *negrito* and were closely related to the pygmies of Africa. A few thousand of them can still be found in the Visayas, where their presence gave one of its islands – Negros – its name. However, the majority of Filipinos are of Malay type, closely resembling Indonesians and Malaysians. They were seafarers who settled on the islands and established *barangays* – loosely organised autonomous states which fought one another whenever they came in contact. They had a feudal type of social organisation based on family and clan ties which can properly be regarded as the origin of the strong family loyalties of present-day Filipinos.

Barangay-type communities continue to exist today, especially among the Moslem *moros* of the south, which have a social organisation comparable with the ancient form. They are ruled by a chief, the *datu*, supported by a small class of nobles. Below these is a 'middle-class' of freemen, and in pre-colonial times each *barangay* had slaves, usually prisoners-of-war and their descendants.

One of the more common misconceptions about the Philippines – indeed, about many parts of Asia – is that Europeans 'discovered' it, and that trade and development began with their coming. In fact the major cities of the Philippines were thriving trading centres long before then. The cotton textiles for which the Ilocano people of north-west Luzon are still famed were prized by the Chinese, whose big trading junks plied regularly to Luzon with the monsoons to buy cotton. During the fourteenth and fifteenth centuries the southern part of this varied, busy world was also reached by the trader-missionaries of Islam.

It was 40 years before Magellan's landings in the Philippines were followed up by Spain, with the establishment in 1564 of trading posts, which were eventually consolidated on Manila in 1571. The main initial importance of the Philippines to the Spanish Crown was the Manila entrepot, for it was here that the important trading of silver from the Spanish Mexican colony for Chinese goods took place. Chinese ships brought silk and a wide range of artifacts – carpets, ornaments of jade, pearl and ivory – which became fashionable and hence valuable in Europe. Spain controlled the galleon trade between Acapulco and Manila.

Meanwhile the missionary friars were operating in their own interests in the rest of the country. Village chiefs who agreed to become Christian became exempt from tax and their authority was deemed hereditary provided they saw to it that the rest of their village paid tribute and provided corvée labour. Large areas of what had been communal land were taken over into vast estates, the *encomienda*, owned by the church and later by individual families.

In most cases the people of Luzon and the Visayas were receptive to Christianity, partly because they had no formal religion with which the new faith must compete. They were animists, believing in nature spirits, but there was no definite body of doctrine and no organised church with a vested interest in their religious devotion. By the middle of the seventeenth century there were half a million Filipino Christians, almost all Catholic. The Dominican friars established what is now Asia's oldest university, Santo Tomas, in Manila in 1611.

European trade with the Philippines increased considerably after the opening of the Suez Canal in 1869, bringing greater influence and wealth to a new and growing class of merchants. In many cases these families had Spanish blood. Possession

of landed estates was such an important mark of social distinction in Spain that the Spaniards in the Philippines, both
traders and priests, were made feudal grants of huge tracts of
land and given the right to administer and use the labour of
the 'Indians' living on that land.

Spanish rule was cruel and oppressive. Laymen and priests
alike regarded it as natural and proper that the Filipino peasants
should labour for their support, and give them implicit obedience.
The friars of the Franciscan order were particularly grasping
in their ambitions to acquire more and more land, on which
they lived in idleness. The people had no part in the government of the islands, although a form of democracy was kept
alive in the villages – the *barrios*, which retained the village
councils as they had traditionally always done. However, rapid
population growth was causing increasing poverty and rest-
lessness. Discontent centred on the repressive policies of the
government and the continued alienation of agricultural land
to the religious orders.

In 1872 about 200 soldiers and workmen mutinied at the
arsenal at Cavite, near Manila. They killed three Spanish soldiers and seized the port. The rebellion was planned to coincide
with another uprising inside the walls of Manila itself, but its
timing was premature and the revolt was easily subdued. The
Spanish authorities, alarmed by the growth of nationalist feeling, executed 13 of the rebels. It is likely that most Filipinos
would have accepted this, but they did not tolerate so readily
the further execution, by strangling on the garrotte, of three
Filipino priests charged with instigating the revolt – one of
them a man of 85.

Among those deeply impressed by this incident was a ten
year old boy named Jose Rizal, who was to become the most
honoured Filipino patriot. He became a man of remarkable
achievement and personality. A product of the growing middle-
class and educated in Europe, Rizal was a competent author,
musician and painter as well as a teacher, linguist and surgeon. He was also the first serious advocate of Filipino
nationalism.

When he formed the Liga Filipina in 1892 he was arrested and deported to a remote part of Mindanao, even though this nationalist association was, like Rizal himself, moderate and in the final analysis opposed to violent methods. However, there were other nationalists who were more extreme and, after Rizal was exiled, the cause fell into the hands of the militant Katipunan, an organisation founded by Andres Bonifacio and some associates, also in 1892.

An emissary of the Katipunan visited Rizal in exile to seek his support for an armed uprising against Spain. Rizal, however, declined. He had given his word not to try to escape from exile, and believed the people were not yet ready for independence. Without his moderating influence the nationalist movement quickly developed from an organisation of talk and pamphlets into an underground resistance dedicated to violent terrorism.

Rizal, who felt he was wasting his life in exile, asked to be sent to Cuba as a surgeon to the Spanish garrison there. The authorities agreed, and he was actually on his way when he was arrested, brought back to Manila and executed by a firing squad in 1896. Spain had provided the nationalist cause with its martyr. Rizal's books were read as never before and his name became a rallying-cry.

Rioting and terrorism flared up in many parts of the Philippines and within a year of Rizal's death Spain was forced to commit 50,000 soldiers to the task of pacifying the colony. The Spanish eventually came to terms with the rebels, paying their leader, General Aguinaldo, to go into exile in Hong Kong. Aguinaldo complied, but used his time in Hong Kong to negotiate arms purchases for a further rebellion.

Fourteen months after Rizal's death an event far from the Philippines broke the stalemate. Relations between the United States and Spain over the then Spanish colony of Cuba reached breaking point. When Spain refused an American ultimatum to leave Cuba, war broke out. Spain was easily defeated. One of the few major battles of the war took place in Manila Bay, where a squadron of American ships attacked a Spanish fleet, mostly of old and decrepit ships. One of the two bigger ships, *Castilla* was a wooden steamer that had to be towed into action. *Castilla* and her smaller consort *Reina Cristina* were soon in flames and the smaller ships and shore batteries at Cavite were knocked out within hours.

General Aguinaldo, in Singapore when he heard of the war, hurried to Hong Kong to discuss co-operation with the Americans. Shortly afterwards a United States ship returned him to the Philippines. He was quickly able to raise a large revolutionary army, which mounted a siege on Manila and extended the rebellion into other parts of Luzon. The Filipinos seemed to have no doubt the Americans were helping them to gain complete independence, since the United States was then regarded as the champion of oppressed colonial peoples.

The nationalists established a revolutionary civil government, with a constitution modelled on that of the United States. Although there were 13,000 Spanish troops inside Manila, the city capitulated after a two month siege in which there had been little more than sporadic fighting. With this came the first nationalist doubts about American intentions. Manila was occupied by United States forces, whose commander unexpectedly refused to allow the Filipinos to enter the city, threatening to fire on them if they attempted to do so.

Nevertheless, most of the nationalist army remained outside the city while Aguinaldo and other leaders withdrew to the north to establish their seat of government in the Luzon provincial city of Malolos. There they declared an independent Republic of the Philippines on 15 September 1898, the first such declaration anywhere in the colonial regions of Asia.

However, unknown to the nationalists, President McKinley of the United States had privately told his envoys to the Paris talks ending the war with Spain that they must press for the cession of Luzon at least to the United States. These secret instructions were given the day after the establishment of the Malolos Republic. A representative was sent by the republic to Paris to plead its cause, but the other parties refused to recognise it. So matters were finalised without reference to the nationalists. Spain agreed to renounce control of the whole of the Philippines which, with Guam and Puerto Rico, became a colony of the United States. The acceptance of responsibility for the Philippines as a colony was unwelcome to many Americans and Filipinos. The fact that the United States, an ex-colony that had had to fight for freedom, was now becoming imperial master of another people was widely opposed in America. The Filipinos found it a cause for war. In a pitched battle outside Manila in 1899 the Filipino irregulars were defeated. Two months later, Malolos was occupied by the Americans. Aguinaldo and his men retreated northward. The bitter ensuing guerilla war cannot be under-estimated, although some books dismiss it with a phrase. The civilian population, looted and oppressed by lawless elements of Aguinaldo's army, suffered most. Deaths probably exceeded 100,000. The war ended with Aguinaldo's capture in 1901 and later acceptance of United States rule. It cost the lives of 4200 Americans.

Thereafter matters improved rapidly. The United States granted the first elements of limited self-government with an elected lower house of parliament in 1907 and more extensive powers in 1934, although complete independence did not come until 1946. This transfer of American-style political institutions was not without its problems. Election of officials such as police chiefs became politicised and corrupt in the Philippines. Freedom to carry arms has contributed to a high crime rate – especially a high murder rate. It became quite usual to see notices at the entrance door outside Manila nightspots – 'deposit your firearms here'.

However, the United States redirected many of its soldiers in the Philippines into peaceful projects. They acted as teachers in *barrio* schools, started road-building programmes, and organised such small but collectively important tasks as digging deep wells to provide the villagers with disease-free water. The importance of this work was emphasised by epidemics of cholera so severe they resulted in an actual decrease in the population.

The Americans worked enthusiastically and effectively and conditions soon improved. The United States recruited and sent almost a thousand American schoolteachers to the Philippines, many of them Quakers. As none could speak the local language, Tagalog, they first had to make their pupils literate in English. A direct result is the present widespread knowledge of English, especially on Luzon. By 1921 there were a million children at school.

The United States paid the then considerable sum of seven million dollars to reclaim the huge estates held by the Franciscan order. The Filipinos had bitterly resented the alienation of land to the friars, and this action did much to reconcile them to United States rule. Nevertheless, American land reform programmes failed to meet all the problems. Many big church estates were left untouched, and the land bought from the Franciscans was not distributed to the farmers who worked it but was sold to wealthy Filipino families, often of Spanish blood. Most of these proved to be harder taskmasters than the friars had been.

American policies also resulted in the alienation of huge areas of riceland to export crops like sugar, pineapple, tobacco and coconut, to the advantage of big American corporations, but at the cost of ending Filipino self-sufficiency for food. They did little to improve the serious under-privilege of the bulk of the people, indeed the first president of the Philippines, Manuel Quezon, commented in 1939 that 'the men and women who till the soil or work in the factories are hardly better off than they were under the Spanish regime'.

World War Two caused terrible hardship in the Philippines. The islands' dependence on exports caused almost universal unemployment when these were cut off. In spite of the relatively small population there were not enough food crops to feed the people, and widespread starvation resulted, especially during the years of Japanese occupation.

In 1942 the Communist leader, Luis Taruc, launched in Central Luzon a resistance movement called 'The People's Army against the Japanese'. The first word of the Tagalog translation of this is *hukbalahap*, hence the resistance fighters became known as the Huks. By 1945 the Huks had a well-organised Soviet operating in Central Luzon. It redistributed the holdings of absentee landlords, levied taxes, dispensed justice and even ran schools.

Post-war politics were bedevilled by the fact that three-quarters of the pre-war Congress had collaborated with the Japanese. One such, Manuel Roxas, became president as a result of a highly-corrupt election in 1946. Among other things Roxas refused to allowed Huk congressmen elected from Central Luzon to take their seats. He forced through Congress legislation pardoning all collaborators, and acts which confirmed United States economic dominance of the Philippines. Under these unfortunate circumstances the Philippines became an independent republic.

The Huks returned to their strongholds to wage war on the government. After some initial successes they were controlled by a more efficient government army trained and equipped by the United States. The young Filipino Defence Secretary overseeing this campaign, Ramon Magsaysay, became president in 1953 in what were said to be the first honest elections ever held in the republic. Magsaysay introduced liberal policies, including the first genuine attempt at land reform. Then, one night in March, 1957, an airliner crashed on the island of Cebu. Among the dead was President Magsaysay. His liberal policies were largely abandoned after his death. There was widespread rumour – although no proof – that the air crash may have been deliberate sabotage. Whatever the truth of that, the political scene again became one of barely-concealed corruption and self-seeking. The economy sagged, and the national rate of growth fell far behind in its race with an explosive population increase. By the end of 1966 more than a million Filipinos were unemployed.

Some hope for reform came with the election of a charismatic former resistance fighter, Ferdinand Marcos, in 1966, as sixth president. However, this was shortlived. During his 18 year presidency Marcos used his position to amass a huge personal fortune, exploiting and abusing the Filipino people mercilessly. Claiming that the nation was threatened again by Communism, Marcos declared martial law in 1972, and ruled thereafter as a dictator. In 1983 Marcos' military murdered his principal political rival, Benigno Aquino, publicly, shooting the popular Aquino in the head as they were escorting him from the aircraft returning him to Manila after medical treatment in the United States. More than a million people marched through Manila's streets in his funeral procession.

The government imprisoned people without trial, and there was increasing evidence of torture and murder by elements of the army to discourage opposition. Marcos' wasteful use of public money and the diversion of funds to himself and his cronies resulted in a huge foreign debt. Public unrest grew to an unprecedented extent. Two million people joined protest marches in Manila, more than a million petitioned the murdered Aquino's widow to run for president in elections in 1986. This led to the election of Corazon Aquino, the Philippines' first woman president. In spite of a 60 per cent vote in her favour, Marcos attempted to keep power. A revolt by military elements led by the army deputy chief of staff, Fidel Ramos, massively supported by the people, proved necessary to dislodge him.

Again there were high hopes for significant reforms in the government and the economy. Sixteen military officers were brought to trial and convicted of the Aquino murder. However, Mrs Aquino, like most Filipino leaders since independence, came from the wealthy land-owning class directly responsible for the nation's problems, and her influence proved disappointingly slight.

There was little significant improvement during the administration of President Fidel Ramos, who replaced Mrs Aquino in 1992. The rapidly-growing population and the disinclination of governments to face the nation's basic and urgent problems made these beautiful islands a place of nightmare, with one of the highest crime rates in the world, major inadequacies of public services and utilities, massive unemployment, and a huge disparity of income between the rich and the poor. Some progress was made, however, in 1996 in settling the longstanding rebellion against the Manila government by the Moro National Liberation Front. This revolt was conducted by Moslem dissidents in the traditionally Islamic areas of Mindanao. The peace agreement, which provided for a special development zone in the Moslem areas, did not however bring peace, other rebel groups outside the liberation front continuing an armed struggle.

Widespread discontent in the Philippines resulted in the election as president in 1998 of 61-year-old former movie star Joseph Estrada, on declared, if vague, policies to help the poor and disadvantaged.

25

Korea: Divided Nation

Korea is divided into two states – Communist North Korea and the southern Republic of Korea, which confront each other across one of the most heavily-militarised frontiers in the world. This situation is to an extent a consequence of Korea's geography and her history. The north has long had ethnic and cultural associations with China and Manchuria, while the south, although also influenced by China, has tended to look outwards across the sea, especially to Japan. Sometimes this relationship has been amicable, but more often hostile.

Korea consists of a coastal strip of Manchuria bordering China, a peninsula extending south about 600 miles, and more than 3000 islands. The north particularly is mountainous, with high plateaux and mountains up to 9000 feet. This mountain chain continues almost the whole length of eastern Korea, dropping into the sea in sheer pine-clad cliffs interspersed with coves at the mouths of short east-running rivers. Westward are larger rivers, with fertile plains, and formidable mountain spurs which divide the country into definite regions. These set the boundaries of independent states early in Korea's history.

According to the mythology, in the year 2333BC a bear was miraculously transformed into a young woman. Hwanung, son of the Creator, came to earth and breathed on her. As a result she gave birth to Tangun, Korea's first king. A more credible legend is the displacement of this royal line by Chinese invaders in 1122BC.

However, there is no substantial evidence for either these events or their dates, although North Korea, in particular, makes much of the Tangun myth in her modern ideology, asserting a continuous culture and nationalism going back more than four thousand years. The actual archeological evidence indicates primitive neolithic societies, hunters and shell fishermen, during the fourth millennium BC, with the evolution of agriculture coming perhaps two thousand years later. At about this time a distinctive style of pottery ornamentation spread to Korea from China, the probable beginning of a profound and enduring Chinese cultural influence on Korea. However, it was not until 109BC that Chinese annals record a successful invasion, after which four Han Dynasty garrison cities were established in Korea. During this time many elements of Chinese culture were transferred to Korea.

Wars against the Mongolian tribes during the first centuries of the Christian era forged a large and highly-professional military class in the mountainous, largely infertile north of Korea. Their new state, Koguryo, slowly became the dominant force in the north, and by the fifth century controlled not only north Korea, but also much of Manchuria.

The Sui Dynasty in China could not accept such a large and aggressive neighbour. Four huge armies – one said to have numbered over a million men – were despatched to bring Koguryo under Chinese control. The first three were defeated at great cost – it was probably the enormous drain of these Korean campaigns that weakened and brought down the Sui Dynasty. The fourth fared little better, but a peaceful relationship between China and Korea was finally achieved. Thousands of captured Chinese soldiers were returned home and officials of the succeeding T'ang Dynasty came to Pyongyang for the rites associated with the burial of the bones of the Chinese dead.

T'ang influence soon came to dominate most of Korea, especially the southern state of Silla, which looked across the narrow sea to Japan. Silla became a maritime trader of consequence, dominating the sea trade between Korea, China and Japan. An intensive period of sinification commenced with a combined Silla-Chinese defeat of Koguryo in 668. Pyongyang, the capital of a state of perhaps three million people, was almost totally destroyed.

Koguyro is significant because it unified much of Korea for the first time, and because of the resolve and toughness of its people, who after all had withstood repeated invasions from their vast neighbour for 70 years. From the fourth century on it became an important centre for *mahayana* Buddhism, which was taken on to Japan by Koguryo monks. There is evidence of a considerable Koguryo literature, written in Chinese, most of which was destroyed at the fall of Pyongyang.

Its heir to at least partial unification of Korea was Silla, which now expanded rapidly in a close association with T'ang China. Subordination to China was guaranteed by the despatch of Silla princes to the great Chinese capital, Ch'ang-an, as hostages. Thousands of Koreans studied there. Chinese medicine, astronomy, music, literature, administration and laws of land ownership, were all transferred more or less intact to Silla.

Silla's capital, Kyongju, with almost a million people, was one of the world's largest and richest cities at that time, and was known and admired as far away as Arabia and India. The opulence of the Silla aristocracy was based on unlimited power over the peasantry as absentee landlords, and their possession of large numbers of slaves. The numerous Buddhist monasteries were also large land-owners. As the T'ang Dynasty in China declined, so did Silla in Korea. Weakened by regular and bloody disputes over the throne, it fell in 936 to a revived northern state, Koryo. The name Korea derives from Koryo.

The pattern then is one of client states of China, rising and falling in parallel with the fortunes of Chinese dynasties, nevertheless fiercely independent and following the Chinese example because they admired it rather than as a result of conquest; of a northern region of warriors and a more prosperous southern region of traders; and of efficient and ruthless oligarchies battening on a sturdy and resilient peasantry who were, however, far from compliant, rebelling regularly against their masters. It is tempting to see an echo of this in the hostility between late twentieth century Korean workers and their employers, the huge family-based industrial conglomerates. Koryo was controlled by such an oligarchy, who nevertheless so admired the achievements of the Chinese Sung Dynasty that they emulated them, and even improved on them. Koryo celadon pottery, with its restrained ornamentation, sophistication and transparent blue-green glaze, was regarded as the finest in the world.

The twelfth century saw unrest and banditry on a major scale, including warlordism similar to that in China in times of chaos. Into this social maelstrom came a succession of Mongol invasions, a small part of the huge military campaign of Kublai Khan that subjugated China. Mongol savagery was no less extreme in Korea than elsewhere. The walled cities resisted bravely, attracting praise even from Mongol generals, but in the end fell to the relentless professional assaults, which included elaborate siege machinery and firecarts fueled with human fat made from boiling down prisoners. Nearly a thousand Korean ships were used in Kublai's massive but unsuccessful attacks on Japan, sharing the disaster of the *kamikaze* – the divine windstorm that saved the day for Japan.

Mongol rule of Korea was firmly established by 1270. It was predatory to a disastrous extent, bringing fresh horrors of starvation and disruption to a society already on its knees. This occupation lasted for 130 years. By 1368 the new Chinese Ming Dynasty had driven the Mongols out of China, However, seven years before that a young Korean soldier, Yi Songgye, had been active in campaigning against the Mongols. He rose to be a general, and, after some bloody infighting among the Korean elite, became the founder of a dynasty that would endure into modern times. Its capital was Hanyang, the city now called Seoul, and the state was called Chosen, the land of Morning Calm.

Hanyang became virtually a new city. A conscript labour force of over 100 thousand built palaces and quarters for the ever-present bureaucracy – the tentacles of which now embraced the nation as never before. Every Korean was obliged to provide an identity tag bearing name and place and date of birth for verification with an official seal. The material for these virtual identity cards ranged from ivory down to plain wood according to rank. Movement outside a person's home province was forbidden, and this was closely policed. Within the counties the maintenance of the law and collection of tax was led by officials called *yangban*, a hereditary ruling class whose performance was guaranteed by the despatch of their sons to the capital as hostages. Less fortunate were the next level down, basically policemen and tax collecting clerks. They were conscripted into their duties, for which they received no payment other than what they could 'squeeze' from the peasantry.

The people actually working the land were closely supervised and controlled, five households being lumped together into a group jointly held responsible for the good behaviour and corvée responsibilities of all its individuals. Peasants paid 50 per cent of their production to the landowner, and both were liable to a ten per cent tax to the state. Other payments were exacted by regional government offices and a tax could be paid in lieu of compulsory military service. The state itself owned hundreds of thousands of slaves, who were often so much better off than the peasants that many free men actually sought to become slaves.

Agriculture, mainly *padi* rice, which was the occupation of the great majority of the people, was carefully studied and improved wherever possible. Thousands of water storage dams were built, and raingauges were issued to the provinces in 1442. The land was carefully surveyed and mapped, allowing the imposition of tax to become an exact science.

Movable iron type, using Chinese characters, was used in Korea early in the fifteenth century. Books were produced in thousands, often beautifully illustrated in colour with woodblocks. Many of these books were designed to promote the neo-Confucian ethic then current in China – family values, the authority of fathers, the obedience and humility of children

– all these 'virtues' became deeply inculcated at all levels of Korean society. An alphabet of 28 letters was evolved, far better suited to the Korean language than Chinese ideographs, but scholars considered it vulgar, and it languished for many centuries. When the Japanese Shogun Hideyoshi conceived the unrealistic ambition of conquering China the obvious stepping stone appeared to be Korea. Angered by Korea's natural reluctance to co-operate he invaded the country with an army of 160,000 *samurai* in 1592, and pressed on to Seoul in spite of heavy losses. In the capital the invaders were helped by a revolt among the slaves, who set fire to buildings housing the slave records. A Korean appeal to Ming China brought a less than adequate response, but did involve China in the wars, which dragged on until Hideyoshi's death in 1598.

One of the curiosities of this war was the turtle ship of Admiral Yi Sunsin, an armoured barge propelled by a square sail and 20 oars, considered to be the world's first ironclad. These small armoured vessels caused such destruction to Japanese supply ships the Japanese ruler Hideyoshi demanded some proof of his army's valour. The bizarre response was the despatch to Kyoto of the ears cut from almost 40,000 Chinese and Korean heads, pickled in salt. The war caused enormous destruction in Korea, including the burning of many monasteries. But the chief victim was the old social order. Much of the opposition to the Japanese had come from peasant guerillas, and in some cases bands of slaves. The leaders of these irregulars became powerful enough to enter the ruling classes, fighting their way into positions of influence.

In the seventeenth century Korea was again invaded as a consequence of a power change in China. In 1637 Korea became a tributary state of the Manchus, who, although deadly enough in battle, were indolent in administration. They left Korea much to itself to recover from half a century of war. Gold, silver, cloth and especially the small Korean cavalry horses were required as tribute, but the Manchus had little permanent influence on Korean society.

Even so restoration of the old social order was next to impossible. The slave and taxation records had been destroyed, and the government found itself largely impotent from sheer lack of money. Recovery was slow and gradual, and involved important social and commercial changes. There was more private, rather than state, enterprise, and a wealthy commercial class developed. The number of slaves was greatly reduced. Their use in state enterprises ended in 1801, although private families and businesses continued to own slaves until 1894.

The centuries of Yi rule set an enduring pattern for Korean society, much of which remains today. A hereditary caste system which placed the scholar-official at the highest level made necessary accurate genealogical records spanning many generations, and quite complex rules determining who should marry whom. Of current importance too is the concept that only the 'first son' – the eldest – has *chong-che*, the mystic capacity and right to succeed his father. This, often perceived by Westerners as nepotism, extends from the control of family property and businesses through to politics. The succession in North Korea from Kim Il Sung to his eldest son Kim Jong Il is typical.

The Korean caste system, by no means as pervasive as the Indian one, nevertheless had its equivalent of untouchables, among them those who butchered animals and dealt with the dead. There remain today different ways of addressing people in different social categories. The Confucian concept of respect for elders involves the use of special honorifics whenever they are addressed, and is basic to an elaborate system of family hierarchy with a distinct ranking position for every member, the father at the top, wife obeying him, daughters (and daughters-in-law) subordinate to the mother, younger children below older ones.

However, the superficial appearance that such a system must be tyrannical, even cruel, is mistaken. Korean parents tend to indulge their children, and will extend themselves financially to an extraordinary extent to educate them. Obedience and loyalty to the family structure come not so much from discipline as from the deep respect children have for their parents. Children too, take their education very seriously from infancy and make every effort to learn up to the limit of their capacity, to do their best in whatever they undertake. This lay behind the remarkable economic growth Korea achieved in the late twentieth century.

By the late eighteenth century government was again destabilised by almost constant warring between factions of the ruling classes, typified by the murderous and lecherous conduct of a crazy prince, Sado. Since it would be a crime to kill royalty, Sado was persuaded to be shut in a wooden box which was left out in the hot sun. Thirteen days later he was dead.

The ordinary people suffered appallingly from flood, famine and especially plagues. A cholera epidemic in 1821 dragged on for two years, killing a million people. The impotence of central administration led the people to resort to mutual aid societies, and villages worked together in specialist co-operative enterprises. Banditry was widespread, as also were regional revolts against the central authority. One of these, in 1811, developed almost into civil war.

During a famine resulting from two years of drought in 1812 and 1813 an estimated 4.5 million people starved to death. As the countryside sank into deeper and deeper despair crime and rebellion became even more prevalent. Merchants and officials were slaughtered in 18 southern cities by bands of peasants, and in 1894 followers of a religious and mystic cult, Tonghak, began a revolt so serious that China and Japan once again intervened in Korean affairs.

As in China, the nineteenth century had brought increasing contacts with European ships. These were attacked and looted whenever possible. In 1866 an American ship, the *General Sherman*, was boarded and burned when she grounded in the Taedong River, following an incident in which American sailors fired into a crowd on the river-bank. Reprisals were inevitable. In 1871 American warships fired on the batteries at Kanghwa Island, which guards the entrance to the river. When the marines landed to attack the forts the Korean defenders fought back ferociously, but ineffectively, since they lacked modern weapons.

Four years later a similar incident involved a Japanese naval vessel. These incidents prompted an official Korean policy of strict isolation from the outside world. However, gunboat diplomacy would not be denied. Following the arrival of a formidable Japanese fleet in 1876 a treaty was signed with Japan, opening three ports to international trade. Subsequent trade treaties were signed with Britain, several European states and the United States. The number of these treaties does not indicate any desire on the part of Koreans to 'open up' the country. Rather it was hoped that by dealing with many contending interests outside influences would be kept at bay.

Such was the situation when the Tonghak rebellion brought both Chinese and Japanese expeditions to Korea. At that time Japan was modernising itself rapidly. One of the last acts of the *shogunate* had been the establishment in 1865 of the Institution for the Study of Barbarian Literature, which two decades later became the Tokyo Imperial University. Those selected to study the ways of the outside world recommended that Japan adopt Western science, trade methods and industry.

In Korea a 'progressive' faction, sponsored by Japan, felt Korea should take this same course. The conservatives, centred around the monarchy, maintained their allegiance to China. Two successful Japanese wars – with China in 1894/5 and Russia in 1904/5 decided the outcome. In 1905 Korea was placed under Japanese 'protection', and in 1910 it was formally annexed to Japan. Ironically, ideas of nationalism and freedom had reached young Koreans mainly from Japanese intellectuals, only to be crushed by Japanese military imperialism. The Koreans resisted strenuously. During this rebellion hundreds of villages were burned and perhaps 20,000 people killed.

Japan's colonial control of Korea, which lasted until the end of World War Two in 1945, was equally harsh – even brutal. Resistance movements persisted throughout the occupation, during which thousands of people were killed or imprisoned. In 1919, Korean protestors were burned alive in a church in with they had taken refuge at Sunron, near Seoul.

As with the other colonisers, Japan did improve the infrastructure, creating an extensive rail network, chemical fertiliser
plants, and major irrigation and land clearing works to maximise
the rice crop. However, these were primarily motivated by
the constant need to provide rice to meet food crop shortages
in the Japanese homeland, where the population was growing
rapidly. Half the Korean rice crop went to fill Japanese stomachs.
Korean rice consumption dropped by almost as much, causing
mass malnutrition and poverty.

During the 1930s brutal Japanese militarism increased the
extent of repression. Koreans were ordered to take Japanese
surnames, and even the use of the Korean language was banned.
Shinto shrines were built, at which Koreans were forced to
worship. During World War Two almost two million Koreans
were conscripted as slave labour in Japan, much of it 12 hour
days under appalling conditions in mines. Among these conscripts were well over 100,000 'comfort women' – young girls
forced into prostitution to serve Japanese soldiers. Seven thousand Koreans were set to work in 1944 to build a retreat bunker
near Mount Fuji for the Japanese Emperor, under conditions
so harsh over a thousand died. At least 10,000 Korean conscript workers died in the atomic bombing of Hiroshima and
Nagasaki.

As the war ended the Russians occupied the north of Korea,
United States forces the south. Two states, Communist north
and American-supported South Korea resulted. Both were harshly
authoritarian and corrupt. By June, 1950 they were at war – a
war that was really an expression of the zonal rivalry between
the United States and the Soviet Union and China.

This war caused enormous suffering and loss to the Korean
people. A major American aerial bombing campaign began with
General MacArthur, in command, ordering the destruction of
every aspect of infrastructure and human society, even villages, in North Korea. The capital, Pyongyang, was virtually
destroyed. The war solved nothing, achieved little except destruction, the two rival states at the end still facing each other
across a border at the 38th parallel of latitude.

South Korea subsequently passed through a phase of re-markable industrial development, making it a major exporter of many commodities until this expansion was checked by the Asian economic crisis. By then it had become the world's twelfth largest economy. Most families had television sets, refrigerators and washing machines. South Korea became a major ship builder and exporter of motor vehicles. Education was actively encouraged, so that now almost the whole population is literate.

Nevertheless these decades of growing prosperity were marred by virtually a state of war between the workers and the big industrial conglomerates, backed by a rigidly authoritarian government and a large and frequently brutal military, who did not hesitate to use mass killing, torture and imprisonment to put down opposition. The massively-increased industry and urbanisation also resulted in major changes in Korean society, including a drop in the rural population to only 18 per cent, compared with 55 per cent in 1965. Exports increased sixfold from 1980 to 1995, in which year they had reach $125 billions.

A military coup in 1961 brought Park Chung Hee to power as virtual dictator. Although some of the trappings of democracy appeared in 1963, Park, by now president, continued as an autocrat. In 1972 he imposed martial law, with rigid suppression of any opposition, a situation which continued until his assassination in 1979. Little changed during the rule of several dictators who succeeded him. However, the Korean people had become increasingly unhappy with the corruption and authoritarianism of the government, and took to the streets in millions in 1987 in protest. This pressure and others forced slow progress towards greater freedom. In 1992 President Kim Young Sam made vigorous attempts to control corruption and redress some of the wrongs of the past. Two former dictators were indicted and sentenced to gaol terms.

Relations with North Korea, however, deteriorated, Pyongyang announcing in 1996 that it would no longer honour the agreements which had ended the Korean War in 1953.

In 1997 much-persecuted democracy activist Kim Dae Jung

was elected president of South Korea. During the previous two decades several attempts were made to murder him, a sentence of death on him for sedition was commuted only after American intervention in 1980, he was exiled in 1982, and on his return to Korea two years later, was placed under house arrest. However, his accession came in difficult times – the severe recession caused by the Asian financial crisis. It left Korea with debts estimated at more than $150 billions. It is typical of the Korean people that they made a gift to their government of gold jewellery and other family treasures which, when melted down, amounted to a staggering 220 tons of bullion. It is also typical that as unemployment mounted suicides of laid-off workers became numerous – so numerous that the government had to grease the framework of a bridge in Seoul to prevent people climbing it and jumping off.

Meanwhile one of the world's few remaining Communist states persists in North Korea, its nature and policies readily identifiable with its past. For its population – 25 millions – North Korea is intensely militaristic, with armed forces numbering over a million, among the largest in the world. This figure is maintained by compulsory conscription of adult males for three to as long as ten years.

The regime has presided over a shattered economy, with poverty so extreme it had resulted in deaths from starvation in rural areas during the late 1990s estimated by some observers in the millions. United States Congressman Tony Hall, who visited North Korea in November, 1998, put deaths at between one and three million, and quoted UN statistics indicating that 30 per cent of North Korean children under two were acutely malnourished.

He brought out with him a bag of 'substitute food' being distributed at a government food station: 'Dried leaves and straw, so coarse even cattle would turn away from it.' Mr Hall said. 'They grind it into powder and make it into noodles.

The noodles have no nutrition and are indigestible, leaving people holding their aching stomachs.'

North Korea is reclusive and secret, shunning contact with the outside world as much as possible. Because foreign observers are discouraged and allowed little freedom of movement if they do get into the country, there is little accurate information about contemporary North Korea. However, North Korea appears to be persisting with nuclear facilities capable of producing weapons grade plutonium, and in 1998 test-fired a long range ballistic missile into the Pacific. The government's propaganda, which typically depicts laughing, singing crowds organised into colourful processions and festivals, contrasts so sharply with the known background of famine it can scarcely be taken seriously. Hence the true state of North Korean society remains enigmatic.

26

Vietnam, Laos, and Cambodia

As the world depression of the 1930s deepened French exploitation of the Vietnamese people became extreme. Tens of thousands were herded into palm-thatched sheds in the rubber plantations and forced to work 12 hours a day or more tapping the trees. Plantation owners in France insisted on higher and higher work quotas until people dropped with exhaustion or even died. The punishment for those who failed to meet the quotas was beating on the soles of the feet, after which they were forced to run.

In 1930, 8000 people set off on a march of protest to the provincial capital of Vinh. The march was peaceful – not so much as a bamboo spear or a knife was carried – and to emphasise its pacific nature the front ranks were all women and children. It has been said that the first use of military aircraft against civilians was at Guernica, during the Spanish civil war. But six years before that Potez biplanes from the French Armee de l'Air massacred 700 of the Vinh marchers. The attack was made on a narrow section of the road, hemmed in on both sides by paddy-fields and trees. The first 22 lb bombs were dropped on the front of the march, among the women and children. After dropping their full load of bombs the three aircraft strafed the marchers with Lewis machine-gun fire.

As early as 1916 there were plans for a rebellion against the French which involved the young emperor Duy Tan. They were discovered almost on the eve of the revolt. It collapsed and the emperor deposed and exiled. Nationalist feeling was then effectively subdued by police measures for two decades. A hundred thousand Vietnamese conscripts fought for France during World War One. Many came back with nationalist and some with Communist ideas. These last looked for leadership to a man then known as Nguyen Ai Quoc, which means Nguyen the patriot. This man, later to be known as Ho Chi Minh, formed the Indo-Chinese Communist Party in 1930.

In that year there was widespread unrest in Indo-China, partly due to unemployment and poverty caused by the depression. The Communists led uprisings and proclaimed two Soviets – self-contained rebel states – in the north. French repression of these uprisings was severe to the point of brutality and again included the strafing of villages from the air and systematic torture. There was some liberalisation in the second part of the decade – due mainly to Leon Blum's Popular Front government in France – but the political scene remained substantially unchanged at the coming of war again in 1939. France, quickly overwhelmed by the German blitzkreig, was subsequently governed by the puppet Vichy regime, which permitted Japan to occupy Indo-China from late 1940 onwards.

At this stage there was already a group of North Vietnamese patriots, partly Communist, known as the Vietminh, or League of Independence. They had fled across the border into China following an attack on them by the Vichy authorities in 1941. One of the Communists among them was a 30-year-old man, Vo Nguyen Giap, who, in spite of humble origins, had achieved a doctorate at Hanoi University. He was later a teacher. When Giap fled to China his wife and her sister were both arrested by the French and died in captivity.

In 1942 the Americans saw the value of the Vietminh as a resistance movement against the Japanese, but it was thought that the name of Nguyen Ai Quoc should not be used because of its pre-war associations. It was at this time he assumed the name of Ho Chi Minh, which means 'he who enlightens'. When the Japanese surrendered in August, 1945, the Vietminh took over control of Hanoi. By the end of the month there was a Vietminh government claiming control of the whole of Vietnam. It was backed by a toughened partisan army of about 12,000.

The returning French at first offered independence within a French Union but ultimately negotiations failed because the French refused to accept a government that included what was then a minority of Communists. Instead a Dominion government was set up that was virtually devoid of popular support. The result, quite the opposite of that sought by the French, was a significant increase in Communist influence within the nationalist movement which, by 1949, had become Communist-dominated. Alarmed, the United States government began to provide military equipment to France for use in Vietnam.

This did not happen without some misgivings. In the *New York Herald Tribune* of 4 April 1950, respected commentator Walter Lippman seriously questioned French motives and wrote the following prophetic words: 'The French army can be counted to go on defending south-east Asia only if the Congress of the United States will pledge itself to subsidise heavily – in terms of several hundred million dollars a year and for many years to come – a French colonial war to subdue not only the Communists but the nationalists as well.' This identifies accurately the beginning of the great tragedy of Vietnam, commencing with the elimination of non-Communist elements of nationalism or their compulsion to join forces with the Communists.

The Vietminh quickly infiltrated the Red River delta around Hanoi, and proved more than a match for 180,000 French troops guarding almost a thousand concrete forts. Unrealistic direction of the war from Paris and a fear that the Vietminh would invade Laos led the French to attempt the defence of a mountain hollow called Dien Bien Phu, more than 200 miles from Hanoi in wild upland country, in 1954.

A ferocious Vietminh assault destroyed the steel matting aircraft runways, cutting off Dien Bien Phu for good. In an attempt to reinforce it, day after day transport aircraft dropped paratroopers over the doomed forts. The Communists killed most of them before they reached the ground. The siege lasted 56 days. Such was the bitterness of the struggle the survivors who returned to France were described as 'like Christ off the Cross'. When Dien Bien Phu surrendered it represented the first defeat of a major European power by an Asian Communist army. It cost the French 16,000 dead or captured and ended their will to go on fighting. They had lost a battle, a war and an empire.

The United States accepted only with disquiet the Geneva agreements that ended the war, for they had created a new Communist state, North Vietnam, above the 17th parallel of latitude. Close on a million people, mostly Catholics, fled to the south. For several years, the northern and southern halves of the country devoted themselves to consolidation and recovery.

The first prime minister of South Vietnam, Ngo Dinh Diem, was firmly supported by the United States. The Geneva agreements had stipulated that an election should be held in 1956 to determine who would govern the whole of Vietnam. When Diem had refused to hold the elections four years after the agreed date, the Hanoi government decided on a military infiltration of the south. This coincided with a decline in the popularity of Ngo Dinh Diem's administration because of his autocracy and nepotism.

In November 1960 Diem narrowly missed being deposed in a coup organised by paratroops of his own army. In 1963 his government drew major opposition from the Buddhist organisation. Around three-quarters of the people of south Vietnam are Buddhist. The world was shocked by the campaign Diem – a Catholic Christian – launched against the Buddhists, especially by the protest suicides of seven monks, who soaked their robes in petrol and set fire to themselves in protest.

Another army coup in 1963 brought a point of crisis. Diem was arrested and murdered, with other members of his family. A phase of political instability followed, with ten prime ministers taking office in 20 months. Associated with this was the steady increase in United States military involvement in the war with the north. American military advisers were assigned to Vietnam in 1962, and by 1968 half a million American troops were involved in a destructive and controversial war that seemed to have no ending and increasingly no point.

The deathrate on both sides and the refusal of many young Americans and Australians to accept conscription to fight in Vietnam brought massive public opposition to the war, especially after the massacre by American soldiers of 400 unarmed civilians, mostly women and children, in the village of My Lai in 1968. That incident and a worldwide outcry at the devastation of huge tracts of forest from aerial spraying of a dangerous herbicide, Agent Orange, hastened the ending of the war and the re-unification of Vietnam as a Communist state.

So deep was the trauma of the war that Vietnam was not assisted by the Western world to recover from the damage caused by the most intensive aerial bombing in history. Only in the 1990s was Vietnam able to approach normalcy, with moves away from doctrinaire Communism towards a free market economy and enhanced relationships with the outside world. A trade embargo imposed by the United States was not lifted until 1992.

Development of oil and gas fields assisted the economy, with exports of 30 million barrels of oil a year providing about a third of the country's export income. Timber exports were banned in 1992, in order to preserve forests which cover about 40 per cent of Vietnam. However, by 1997 Vietnam still had a trade deficit of US$2.6 billion, in spite of a considerable recovery in the rice industry which has made her the world's third largest exporter. A population of 27 millions in 1957 had grown to 80 millions 40 years later, with an disquieting annual increase rate of more than two per cent.

Among the great buildings of Angkor, early in the fourteenth century, a marriage took place between a princess of the Khmer royal line and the 16-year-old son of an exiled chief from the region now called Laos. This youth, Fa Ngum, was educated at the court of Angkor by Buddhist monks and scholars, and subsequently led a Khmer army back to recapture his father's lands. The kingdom thus established was called Lan Xang, the Land of the Million Elephants and One White Parasol. The transference of Khmer methods and culture to this remote hill country allowed the new kingdom to develop rapidly. There was considerable territorial expansion. What is now north-east Thailand became part of Lan Xang, hence the strong Laotian influence still evident there in the language and culture. After almost four centuries of continuous existence Lan Xang was replaced by three principalities based on the main towns, Luang Prabang, Vientiane and Champassak in the south. Vientiane, the most vulnerable, was conquered by Siam (Thailand) in 1778. It was not until 1896 that French pressure forced the return of these Vientiane lands to Laos.

Most of Laos consists of high rugged mountains that march across the country, range after range, to form an almost complete barrier to easy communication. These are clothed in dense forest, and all but the larger towns can only be approached by footpaths. There is no industry of consequence other than the illegal export of opium, which is grown by the Meo (Hmong) hilltribes. However, like many south-east Asian countries, Laos has begun to market its considerable timber resources to feed the increasing world hunger for wood.

French colonial dominion over Laos was unprogressive, but not onerous. A few French scholars became interested in the region's past and resurrected and rationalised the history of Lan Xang, by that time almost lost in obscurity. This permitted Laos to acquire at least the basis of a national identity. Nevertheless, nationalist feeling scarcely existed until the 1930s, when a Marxist group was established in northern Laos. This, the Pathet Lao, was probably the mildest and most eclectic Communism in the world until in 1954 it was stiffened by cadres from the Vietminh, at that time locked in their final struggle with the French. A shadowy, slow-moving war ensued

until, at the end of the Vietnam War, the Communists controlled most of Laos, subsequently forming the government.
In 1975 the Lao monarchy was dissolved, and replaced by the
Communist People's Democratic Republic. With this the long-
drawn-out war also ended. Among its less attractive aspects
were heavy American B52 bombing of many parts of Laos,
including a remote and beautiful upland, the Plain of the Jars,
and recruitment by both the Americans and the Communists
of Meo hilltribesmen, who were thus compelled to fight against
each other.

Although the French maintained the monarchy in Cambodia
throughout the colonial period, they did little else for the country.
Education and health services were minimal. Between the world
wars roads and railways were built to service rubber plantations and to facilitate rice exports, to the benefit of French
planters and an increasing number of Chinese businessmen.
The Cambodian peasant was however heavily taxed – around
a third of his income in direct tax and indirect taxes on rice,
salt, opium and alcohol.

In 1941 the French selected, from among some 400 possible contenders for the throne, the 18-year-old Prince Norodom
Sihanouk. He led the traditional life of leisure and luxury over
the next decade, but even in this he displayed the restless
energy that was to become characteristic. He interested himself in jazz music, wrote his own songs, learned to play the
saxophone, and conducted his own band. He travelled widely,
married four times and had 13 children.

France granted Cambodia a measure of self-government in
1949, but real independence did not come until after Dien
Bien Phu in 1954. Sihanouk abdicated in favour of his parents,
became leader of a political party that won a landslide victory
in a general election and made a widely-publicised transition
from king to prime minister. He held this position until his
father's death in 1960, when he again became head of state.

Cambodia under Sihanouk became something of a model for south-east Asia. A large rice export surplus kept the economy in a healthy state and provided funds for development. A descendant of the Khmer kings, he took a particular interest in the restoration of Angkor, which became a major tourist destination. Driving through Thailand to Angkor at about that time, I can recall being impressed at the succession of tidy, prosperous and placid villages in Cambodia. After living in north-east Thailand, with its sad-eyed children showing the telltale pot-bellies that betray malnutrition, it was a pleasure and a relief to see well-dressed and well-fed children and contented-looking communities.

Unfortunately this arcadian situation was not to last. Sihanouk disagreed with American policies in Vietnam. He predicted that China would come to dominate the region, and based Cambodian policies on what he saw as an inevitable need for an accommodation with her. In 1960 the two countries signed a treaty of non-aggression and friendship. Sihanouk broke off diplomatic relations with Thailand and South Vietnam, and in 1963 demanded an end to all United States aid programmes, under which $65 million had been given to Cambodia during the previous eight years. He asserted that his reason was evidence of a United States Central Intelligence Agency plot to overthrow his government, in the same way, he claimed, as the CIA had engineered the downfall and murder of Ngo Dinh Diem in South Vietnam. Cambodia turned, not to the Communist world, but to France to replace the American projects.

In spite of Cambodia's neutralism, she eventually became involved in the Vietnam War. The Vietnamese Communists used the wild eastern section of Cambodia, near the border, to move supplies and men, and this attracted heavy American bombing within Cambodia along what came to be known as the Ho Chi Minh Trail. A coup in 1970 by the Prime Minister, an anti-Communist general, Lon Nol, resulted in a disastrous direct Cambodian involvement in the war. Lon Nol's offensives against the Vietnamese in that and the following year were failures, in which the Cambodian army suffered severe losses.

The ending of the Vietnam War did nothing to improve the growing internal rivalry between the government and a Communist group called the Khmer Rouge. This degenerated into civil war in 1970, then four nightmare years of Khmer Rouge government from 1975 under the leadership of Pol Pot. Mass killings justified as 'class struggle' destroyed 20 per cent of the Cambodian people, including nearly all of the educated and professional classes and the Vietnamese minority of about half a million, in brutal mass executions that shocked the world. Estimates of the dead are as high as 1.7 million. In an echo of China's 'great leap forward' Cambodians were driven to twelve-hour workdays in the interests of a Four Year Plan for the economy that had little hope of realisation. Many more people died of overwork and malnutrition. Meanwhile relations with Vietnam became increasingly strained.

In 1979 a Vietnamese invasion was on the whole welcomed by most Cambodians. Nevertheless it brought more social disintegration and death, since the Khmer Rouge continued an armed struggle. By 1989 the Vietnamese had withdrawn from Cambodia. However, factional fighting continued and it was not until 1991 that an uneasy peace was signed. Hun Sen, a leading figure in the government imposed by the Vietnamese, emerged as the major focus of power, winning internationally-supervised elections in 1998. The last Khmer Rouge gave themselves up later that year. But even now there was no peace, with regular reports of killings by the Hun Sen government of political opponents, and savage police attacks on demonstrators.

The events of the past three decades have virtually destroyed what was previously a prosperous and peaceful country, now oppressed by a major cluster of endemic diseases, continuing malnutrition and one of the highest rates of infant mortality in the world. A United Nations food programme statement early in 1999 estimated that 20 per cent of Cambodia's children were in a state of acute malnutrition, due to shortfalls in food production from subsistence farms. Families borrowing to feed their children were being charged interest rates of up to 100 per cent. Per capita GNP is about $225 a year, among the lowest in the world. Due to the murder of so many teachers by the Khmer Rouge, few schools can now operate effectively, and the literacy rate is under 50 per cent. Cambodia has been especially cursed with landmines, estimated at between two and six million, which will take at least a century to clear up. So much of the agricultural land is seeded with these deadly devices they regularly kill at least 50 innocent civilians – often children – every month and injure several times that number. Landmine contamination has also severely affected food production, making large areas too dangerous to work.

27

Burma: Rule by the Gun

Of the countries of south-east Asia Burma (Myanmar) is perhaps the most varied and beautiful – ranging as it does from placid beaches in the south through broad and fertile river plains to snowclad uplands in the wild border regions with China and Laos. Cherry trees, rhododendrons, magnolia and juniper grow wild in these mountains, in which bears, tigers, leopards and elephants can still be found. A romantic and timeless river life continues on and alongside the huge Irrawaddy, over a thousand miles long, that divides the country as it flows to a fertile delta, once the most prolific rice growing region in the world. Bamboo and teak from the virgin forest that still covers much of the country are rafted down the river. It is the main highway of Burma, used by ancient river steamers, fishing boats, barges on which whole families live out their lives.

The people are equally varied. As in so much of Asia, Burma's boundaries were determined by the colonial power, and they include at least seven racial groups in a country that can be divided into four distinct regions. The majority are the Burmese. making up about 70 per cent of the population. Almost all of the inhabitants of Burma are Buddhist. They are friendly, tolerant and cultured people, conservative and bred from early childhood to a deep respect for established authority, politeness in social relationships, and education. They have a particular dislike of violence, both by virtue of a longstanding Buddhist influence but also due to an older animist belief which has it that those who die a violent death become evil though influential spirits called *nats*.

Burma's paradox is that it is ruled, absolutely against the declared intention of its people, by a violent, cruel and self-seeking military government, which imprisons, kills or tortures its own people as a matter of routine if they offer even token opposition, or refuse to be driven into slave labour to the financial benefit of army officers. This sinister organisation, which has brought Burma to its knees economically, and into world disrepute, is the State Law and Order Restoration Council, better known by the appropriately unpleasant acronym of SLORC. It appears not to have changed as a result of its cosmetic re-naming the State Peace and Development Council in 1997. One of its actions was to rename the country Myanmar, but such is the disrepute in which SLORC is held this name has been extensively disregarded.

Burma was governed as a province of India until 1937 – virtually the whole of the colonial period. The delta of the Irrawaddy, some 200 by 100 miles of flat plain, was largely jungle and tall grass when the British came. When they left it was a cultivated region of ten million acres, growing two-fifths of the world's rice – rice said to have been the best in the world. Largely because of this rapid expansion of agriculture Burma's population of four million in 1825 increased fourfold over the next 100 years. But this increase in productivity did not benefit the average Burmese, and the British only indirectly. Although the larger trading ventures were British, the rice-growing industry that was so large a factor in the country's sudden social and economic revolution was substantially controlled by Indian businessmen.

The diversion of such large areas of land to a rice mono-culture virtually destroyed a placid self-sufficient village life previously typical of Burma. The agrarian problems which had reduced so many Burmese peasants to destitution by the 1930s were exacerbated by the rapacious self-interest of the money-lending class, the Chettiars, who lent the Burmese peasants money on the security of their ricefields, then foreclosed on the mortgages. Interest at 18 per cent was common, and rates up to 100 per cent not unusual. The situation was aggravated by the volume of indentured labour brought in annually from India to help plant and harvest the rice crop – almost half a million in 1927 alone. While many of these Indians returned home, probably a million stayed.

Britain, which after all governed Burma, could have imposed controls on immigration and the alienation of land. But she did not do so until it was too late. Hence she must be considered basically responsible for the almost universal poverty and unrest that afflicted the Burmese in the final decades before World War Two. Violent anti-Indian rioting in the capital, Rangoon (Yangon) in 1930 was symptomatic. A hundred and twenty Indians were killed and more than 1000 injured. Rioting continued on and off throughout the ensuing years. Often these disturbances seemed to have religious origins, but their intensity and duration were really due to increasing rural poverty as the world depression deepened. As yet the rebellions were regional and lacked specific direction. The factor common to most of them was a demand to separate Burma from the Indian administration.

During the stormy years of the 1930s a group of students at the university, founded in Rangoon in 1920, banded together under the name of *thakins*, and it is in the activities of this group that a revolutionary nationalism can first be seen. The word *thakin* means master, and was customarily required of Burmese when addressing a European. The Burmese *thakins* adopted it as an assertion of their racial equality. They were to become very important to Burma, for among them were most of the leaders who would bring the country to independence.

As in India, internal self-government was granted in 1937, although Britain retained control of foreign policy, defence and finance, and the power to overrule the legislature in an emergency. However, this new constitution did separate Burma from India. In the light of later events, it is important to note that the new government had jurisdiction over little more than half the country. Important areas in the northern, eastern and western border regions, occupied by non-Burman racial groups, were outside its authority. The most important minority were the Shans, who are akin to the Thai and Lao peoples, and the warlike hilltribes called Karens, from among whom the British recruited most of the colonial police and militia. The first years of internal self-government were stormy, as the communal problems worsened. In 1938, 200 Indians were killed and hundreds of their houses and shops looted and burned. Civil disobedience campaigns became common, with persistent strikes and demonstrations. At times the transport system of Rangoon was disrupted by scores of women lying down across the tram lines. British goods, and the shops that sold them, were picketted and boycotted.

Matters did not improve with the coming of World War Two. An opportunist lawyer named U Saw who became prime minister arrested most of the *thakin* nationalists on the grounds of subversion. However, one of the more important, Aung San, escaped to Japan. U Saw was arrested and exiled when the British discovered that he too was negotiating with the Japanese.

However, when the Japanese occupied Burma in 1942 they brought with them the *thakin* exile Aung San, at the head of a nucleus anti-British Burmese army called the Thirty, which he had organised in Bangkok. While the Japanese were at first welcomed as liberators, their arrogance and brutality during the war years soon reversed public opinion. In August 1944 Aung San turned against them, operating a secret underground that was to become Burma's leading political party.

After the war the Labour government in Britain was willing enough to grant Burmese independence. Aung San did not live to see it. On a July morning in 1947 six hired gunmen assassinated him and six of his colleagues. The former prime minister, U Saw, who had been released from internment, was convicted of instigating this political massacre, and hanged early in 1948.

The astrologers, always consulted in Buddhist countries on the timing of events, decided that 4.20 a.m. on 4 January 1948, was the most auspicious moment for Burma's freedom. Accordingly, from that time she became an independent republic, outside the British Commonwealth, under the prime ministership of one of the surviving *thakins*, a gentle, devout Buddhist named U Nu. U Nu adhered so strictly to the Buddhist principle of taking no life it is said he made his Cabinet use a side entrance rather than step over a stream of ants crossing a corridor, and so risk killing one of them.

The country was immediately beset with problems – Communist, Shan and Karen insurrections among them. Within weeks U Nu had lost control of all of Burma outside Rangoon. The rebels had no difficulty arming themselves, for both Japanese and Allied arms dumps remained open to any comer. The army was white-anted with Communist cells and deserted practically en masse, leaving the Rangoon government with only a few loyal battalions and provincial units. Forty-four members of the Constituent Assembly left it to become insurgents.

For eight years Burma was the scene of an almost incredibly confused pattern of intrigue and violence. The main sufferers were the civilian population. The rebels blew up bridges, railtrack and roads, and ambushed trains and river ferries. Passengers were held until their relatives paid ransoms.

The Rangoon government moved closer to the Communist world in 1953, when it refused any further United States' economic aid. At the end of 1954 Burma concluded barter agreements with China and Russia that committed a million tons of rice a year – rather more than half her export surplus – until 1960. Considerable disillusionment resulted from this, due to the slow delivery and poor quality of the Communist goods.

Matters reached crisis point in 1958, when the army commander, General Ne Win, took over the government. A complex ideology, known as the Burmese Way to Socialism, was evolved, owing much to traditional customary law. Patterns for the present – and probably the future – were set by Ne Win's inception of a cadre system within the army, a special corps of army cadets trained at a centre near Rangoon. Recruitment was competitive and very selective – Ne Win plainly regarded them as a class of future leaders.

Burma was almost completely sealed off from the world. Ne Win's regime was reluctant to allow any foreigners into the country, and had a passion for keeping foreign influences to a minimum. Much of this was directed at Indians. Their businesses were steadily nationalised and the owners deported during the 1960s. This has not resulted in improvements. Many factories and shops have been grossly mismanaged since they became government-owned.

While the origins of these policies should be obvious in the light of Burma's late colonial history, this is no way implies that they were desirable or useful. In spite of attempts to revive and reform agricultural practice, rice production continued to decline. As late as 1968 community health remained among the worst in the world, with high rates of infant mortality and almost a million registered lepers. Military rule took a turn for the worse in 1988 with the inception of SLORC and a declaration that the country was no longer on the socialist path. Repression of unrest and student riots now became brutal, the army using its weapons, torture and imprisonment to repress any opposition. At least 4000 people were killed by the army at this time, including hundreds of students cut down by machine-gunning. SLORC committees were set up at local government levels to ensure its tight control over the community. The local LORCS also took over the judicial function under thinly-disguised martial law. The Burmese media are heavily censored, and public assemblies of more than five people are illegal.

Following continued unrest SLORC permitted elections in 1990. These the National League for Democracy, led by Aung San's daughter, Aung San Suu Kyi, won with a landslide victory, taking 392 seats of 485 contested. Parties supported by the army won only two per cent of the seats. Suu Kyi, after living and being educated abroad, had returned to Burma in 1988 to care for her ailing mother. She became a rallying point for democratic forces almost at once, and was placed under house arrest in 1989. SLORC refused to hand over power to the democratically elected party – it still has not done so – and kept Suu Kyi under house arrest. She was awarded the Nobel Prize for Peace in 1991, and has shown outstanding courage in maintaining an international profile while coming under persistent attack from SLORC. Her followers have suffered sustained and vicious persecution.

Meanwhile social and economic conditions in Burma continue to deteriorate. Burma's export of more than three million tons of rice a year before World War Two had fallen below a million tons in 1967, and is now about 200,000 tons. Production has not been assisted by the fact that growers are forced to sell any surplus rice to the government at very low prices. Exports of teak and other hardwoods make up around half her small export income. Burma is now one of the world's poorest countries.

Probably Burma's most valuable export is a theoretically illegal one. Growing and sale of opium has virtually doubled in volume over the past decade to around 3000 tons a year. It is estimated that between 60 and 80 per cent of the heroin traded in the United States is produced from opium grown in the mountains of northern Burma. Formerly exported through Thailand, this opium now trades through Yunnan Province of China.

The United States and a number of other countries have applied trade sanctions in protest at the human rights record of the Burmese military. The American sanctions were strengthened in 1997, restricting private investment in Burma. Burma's population is growing only very slowly, not because of effective birth control measures, but because of the almost universal poverty and ill-health. HIV/AIDS is becoming a major problem, partly due to the number of Burmese women who are driven by poverty into prostitution in neighbouring Thailand.

The sheer size of the military has become a millstone around Burma's neck. By 1997 SLORC had doubled the size of the army to almost half a million in order to continue its oppression of the nation's 48 million population. Nearly 40 per cent of all government spending is devoted to it. A recent development has been the conscription of thousands of ordinary citizens, at gunpoint, as slave labourers on railways, pipelines and business ventures, such as tourist hotels, often owned by army officers and their families. SLORC has orientated Burma towards China, with whom she has considerable trade and cultural contacts. China also provides much of the weaponry of the Burmese army.

28

Asia Today – and Tomorrow

Any predictions about the future in Asia must necessarily be set against a world overview, since the Asian nations make up rather more than half the planet's population. That proportion will increase rather than otherwise. There is considerable disagreement on the overall rate of increase over the next few decades, with the figures for world population ranging between seven and twelve billion. One respectable view is that it will not double again from the present 6.1 billion because of the severe effects of falling health standards, especially the high incidence of tuberculosis and HIV and the massive re-emergence of malaria.

But even assuming world population stabilises at ten billion, there can be little doubt that virtually all resources – food, water, arable soil, minerals, fisheries – will become scarcer, and that ocean and air pollution will increase. Hundreds of millions of people are already on the verge of starvation or worse, lakes, rivers everywhere are becoming polluted and depleted and almost half of all humans do not have access to safe and satisfactory drinking water. Per capita grain production in the world, after increasing steadily after World War Two, actually began to decline in the early 1980s.

These points are made not so much because of their intrinsic importance but because they signal eloquently that the billions of Asia will not be able to evolve into consumerist societies like those of the West, because the planet's finite resources and its limited tolerance for pollution will not permit it. Consequently, the drive to emulate the material profligacy of the West evident in so many Asian countries, and its encouragement by elements in the West, are terrible and potentially disastrous mistakes. One simple statistic makes this clear. The wealthiest 20 per cent of the world's people consume over 80 per cent of its resources, the poorest fifth less than two per cent. Even large surrenders of Western affluence could not permit significantly larger consumerism in the Third World.

It was fashionable until quite recently to speak of the 'Asian tigers' and 'Asia's economic miracle.' Both these terms were inappropriate, as the financial catastrophes of 1997 and 1998 have shown. The reality is that the so-called 'tiger' economies' brought substantial wealth to a tiny minority in Korea and south-east Asia, low wages to a somewhat larger but still small fraction of industrial workers, and did little to ease the massive problems of the majority of the people, who still live in villages and work on the land. The reality behind the 'miracle' was the existence of a low-priced compliant workforce ready for exploitation by Western capital.

Hence much of this industrial infrastructure was based on money borrowed from abroad, government subsidies provided by officials who were themselves the main beneficiaries of that industry, low wages and bad, often dangerous and unhealthy, work conditions. Too often, also, borrowed money has been spent on infrastructure of no real value to the bulk of the people, such as urban office buildings and golf-courses. The illusory prosperity created, for a time, work for peasants who left the villages and the fields to become labourers and factory workers, and who have now become unemployed. In most places pressure on rural resources will make it difficult for these displaced workers to go back to where they came from. Discontented, desperately poor, with no hope for the future, they must become a dangerous idle class, forced into crime, driven to become social and political malcontents.

None of this is to say that development in Asia over the last three decades has been uniformly bad. There have been innumerable innovative and useful projects – many examples in Japan and China and the advanced position of India in information technology are earnests of this. It becomes a question of what form development should take. Plainly, if the more than two billion people in China and India followed the consumerist models of the West, as Japan has already done, the consequences for the world would be disastrous. However, forms of industry that conserved the planet's finite resources and used renewable energy could achieve the desired result, which should be a happy, fulfilling and healthy lifestyle for the people of those countries. This objective is altogether consistent with the traditions of team effort, the almost universal respect for higher education and the ambition, the frugality and will to work typical of much of Asia, and it could be built on the sort of co-operative effort at village level now evident in China. That would be very much in accord with the tradition.

The 1997 financial crash, with its destructive effects of eroded currency and stock market values, left many productive and basically sound enterprises facing bankruptcy because depreciated local currencies made it impossible for them to meet their loan obligations. Achievement of an innovative and conservational industry may well require a considerable diversity of ownership and direction, and a versatile workforce. Unfortunately the tendencies in many parts of Asia are in the opposite direction. The obstacles to free enterprise initiative are therefore worth considering.

The cartel or monopoly system, during the 1930s characterised by the Japanese *zaibatsu*, is again prominent in several Asian countries. The modern name in Japan is *keiretsu*, but the system is much the same, and is dominated by much the same interests. *Keiretsu* are agglomerates which control whole areas of commerce from manufacturing through wholesaling to retail shops. Among other things they provide an effective method of eliminating competing products, especially foreign ones. The *keiretsu* are intimately associated with politics, providing funds of about $100 million a year to Japanese political parties, notably the governing Liberal Democratic Party, where the ability to raise these funds is a key qualification for becoming a faction leader, and eventually prime minister.

In South Korea the equivalent is the *chaebol*, large conglomerates like Samsung, Hyundai and Daewoo, which generally were fostered by government patronage during the Korean War from the billions of dollars poured in by the United States. Almost without exception they are owned or controlled by families from the country's traditional aristocracy. Significantly, especially in Korea, where marriage alliances are very important, most of the *chaebol*-owning families are closely connected by marriage, with links extending to government and the bureaucracy at high levels.

Severe measures have been taken in Korea to prevent the growth of trade unionism, perhaps the most extreme being the use of paratroopers to attack marching workers with bayonets and flamethrowers in the city of Kwangju in May 1980. Five hundred people were reported killed, although the number could have been much larger.

In India, most of the capital and industry is controlled by a few families. An Indian government commission in 1961 found that 1.6 per cent of businesses owned 53 per cent of private capital, with four companies, Birla, Tata, Dalmia-Sahu and Martin Burn, controlling 25 per cent of share capital. In Pakistan Bhutto campaigned against the 22 families he said dominated the national economy. Big business, the army and politics have been closely associated in Indonesia, where most large business was controlled by the generals and their immediate families. Huge fortunes were accumulated by Filipino President Ferdinand Marcos and his wife Imelda from funds that should have been used for public welfare in the Philippines. This money, deviously transferred to foreign banks, is still being pursued by the present government. Military dictatorship has been maintained in Burma in spite of elections in 1990 in which the National League for Democracy, led by Aung San Suu Kyi, won decisively. The generals who have run Burma have a deplorable record, putting down frequent and massive public dissent with murder, torture and imprisonment, running up a formidable foreign debt, mainly to support and provide weapons for the armed forces, and presiding over a ruined economy. There is widespread poverty, several regional revolts are a running sore, and even the formerly moderately-wealthy middle class largely live in penury.

Perhaps these are some of the reasons why large world money deserted the south-east Asian economies, perceiving two things: There is little point in sending money in directions which are unlikely to show a profit, and which cannot therefore be repaid; and that global markets cannot expand in conditions in which huge numbers of people are oppressed and impoverished.

The question might well be asked as to why the Asian peoples concerned tolerate their oppressors. Sometimes, of course, they do not, but where the usurping authority happens to be the armed forces, dissent becomes debatable when you are likely to be shot for it. Much of the blame for this situation must attach to the Western nations who make and supply arms, not for the purposes of defence, but to equip minorities to murder, oppress and terrorise their own people. Perhaps the most despicable are those who have made the 110 million landmines which now litter the earth, regularly killing or maiming thousands of the innocent, in many cases small children, and likely to go on doing so for centuries to come. There is little chance of significant advances in much of the Third World until such matters are effectively addressed and controlled by Western governments.

Part of the reason for acceptance of tyranny also lies in the way children are educated and brought up, taught from their earliest years to be respectful to their elders and to established authority. There is an almost universal tradition of conservatism, a learned reluctance to question or interfere with established institutions. As a Cambodian proverb has it: 'Choose the path your ancestors have trod.'

The growth of industry in Asia has been associated with rapid and large rises in population, and the advent of megacities. Shanghai is the biggest with over 14 millions, but Tokyo, Bombay (Mumbai), Beijing, Seoul are all over ten millions, with Bangkok, Dacca (Dhaka), Djakarta, Manila and Delhi all closely approaching that figure. Such large concentrations of humanity are a problem in themselves, but they are all the worse because of the nature of these cities. Most include over-populated fringe areas of slums and shanty-towns, in which people lead seriously deprived and difficult lives. Disease and shortened lifespans are the norm. They, and their environs, are also heavily polluting. A World Health Organisation report of November, 1997, warned of greatly-increased premature deaths in China due to air pollution – an increase from the present estimated 200 thousand to close on a million by 2020 – unless urgent steps were taken to provide a less polluting fuel for heating than coal. The independent Tata Energy Research Institute in India, quoted in *New Scientist* (23 August 1997), described as a 'quiet crisis' soil erosion and depletion now affecting 57 per cent of India's productive land. The report predicted drops in the yields of 11 major food crops in India by as much as 26 per cent. The researchers said the area of critically-eroded land had doubled over the past 18 years, partly due to deforestation for fuel or to create new farmlands. Intensive farming was also resulting in rapid depletion of nutrients in Indian soils.

But perhaps the most telling example of the pollutant effects of largely uncontrolled development were the huge forest fires of 1997, 1998, and 1999 in Sumatra and Kalimantan which spread a pall of smoke over much of south-east Asia, inflicted respiratory illnesses on tens of thousands, and disrupted air and sea transport.

This seems a gloomy enough picture. Is then the future inevitably one of an increasingly urbanised and impoverished mass of oppressed people in Asia, limited only by the ancient scourges of hunger and disease, visiting increasingly large volumes of pollution on the world?

Not necessarily so. The modern revolution in news and information exchange has made it next to impossible for tyrant regimes to persecute their own people without some exposure. One example is the use of the Internet to expose the excesses of the Burmese military and to encourage trade boycotts against them, and to react against the heavy censorship of news in Malaysia. Another was the massive world news coverage of the suppression of the democracy movement in China's Tien An Men Square in 1989. In many parts of Asia at least a minority are better educated and less likely to accept ideas and constraints imposed on them, and this growth of a more independent-minded middle class must continue.

The problem of pollution in the megacities of Asia may also provide its own solutions. Already motor traffic has induced air pollution at dangerous levels, a situation which must become even worse if the number of internal combustion engines is allowed to increase. However, examples of a better way are evolving, such as the decision to replace all of Mexico City's 84,000 taxis with vehicles powered by a revolutionary compressed air motor.

Chinese history at the important local level since the inception of the Communist state can be seen as one of constant experiment and adaptation, often not easy, frequently mistaken, but always attempted. In one village I visited in the Yangtse Valley, peasants were experimenting with fish farming in artificial ponds. They had established that not only could several layers of different kinds of fish be raised together because of their swimming habits, but that different types of trees and shrubs could be grown on the raised banks of the pond whose leaves, falling in, would provide food for the different fish species.

The rapidly-growing motor industry in China and India has tended to maintain vehicle models for long periods, avoiding the manic preoccupation with change, planned obsolescence, increasingly-complicated and unnecessary technology and the attendant spare parts and maintenance problems so evident in the West. This ought to give opportunity for the development of economical and low-polluting alternate fuel and hybrid vehicles in Asia, which could well compete effectively in Western markets. It is not without significance that the first two mass-produced petrol-electric hybrids are coming from Japan.

Such promising but often fragile twigs of progress need encouragement and assistance from the Western world to grow. However, foreign aid budgets are dwindling and many Asian countries are crippled by vast mountains of debt, usually incurred by unscrupulous dictators and military regimes. This third world debt will need to be honestly and fully paid out by the World Bank, with funds contributed by the world's affluent nations.

There needs to be understanding that progress in the Asian nations can come most easily and naturally upwards from the village structure, and that such developments, like the proliferation of solar cookers in India, are the most likely to be sustainable. The simplest solutions, such as higher-bearing fruit trees, efficient fish-farms, safe water supplies made possible by impervious roofing on houses and rainwater tanks, local industries at least initially labour-intensive, simple farm and irrigation machinery, reliable grain seed, are necessary to encourage a modest overall growth in prosperity. Appropriate and immediately useful small industry would grow naturally from that. Instead, too frequently in the past aid funds given directly to Asian governments have either been wasted on inappropriate infrastructure or have simply been stolen by the governing class. There is plenty of evidence to suggest that aid funds would be better channelled by Western governments to non-government agencies, which are more experienced and have a far better track record in the field.

None of the above is suggested on purely charitable or altruistic grounds. The world economy can expect huge opportunities if and when the average income and security of the billions of Asian people can be steadily improved, if only slowly. Conversely, with the Asian peoples becoming the greater part of world population, sheer lack of markets must increasingly cripple the world economy if a practical and major effort to remedy poverty is not made. Imagination and innovation are needed in this cause.

For instance, there is potential for a vast industry in the countries with desert or semi-desert and abundant sunlight to provide the metropolitan powers with hydrogen made from dissociating water or ammonia through the use of solar power, or through the use of catalysts. Research into this techology is well advanced in Israel and elsewhere. This example is quoted because it is of a nature that would provide the Asian countries with a permanently-renewable, non-polluting source of industrial income. Liquid hydrogen could be carried by existing tanker fleets or pipelines to the metropolitan powers, which will need alternative fuels quite soon.

World assistance to Asia will need to be based on a proper understanding of Asian traditions. Unpalatable though this conclusion may be, control of whole peoples by militarist regimes is likely to continue since, as we have seen, that failing some potent new influence the tradition favours them. World indifference to such regimes – even more so support for them for muddled political or unscrupulous economic reasons – hence ought not to continue. Considerable political and economic pressure, including trade boycotts and sanctions, ought to be used routinely to support such just causes as those of Burma's Aung San Suu Kyi and her followers, and Cambodia's courageous Sam Rainsy.

On the other hand, the West, having taken the trouble to understand the Asian traditions, must also accept that it would be dangerous and inappropriate to promote Asian governments and economies which are copies of Western models. The sheer numbers of people involved, the availability of resources and potential danger-levels of pollution must prevent any such things. New solutions, based on existing Asian social patterns, minimal pollution, the best possible use of resources and permanently-renewable energy, are, then, not only desirable but essential. Given encouragement and support in the right direction, these solutions may well be devised by the Asian peoples themselves, with the potential to offer new models to the world. This presents a remarkable opportunity, a third millennium challenge well worth meeting. To do so successfully would transform the planet. To fail to do so may well result, quite soon, in its worst catastrophes since the Black Death.

The West ought also to recognise the rejection in Asia of Western political style in favour of new forms consciously based on past traditions. This is evident in the eclipse of the Congress Party in India to the benefit of Hindu nationalism, the recent adaptations of Chinese Communism, the resurgence of Shinto in Japanese political rhetoric, the persistence of autocratic governments in south-east Asia, and a turning towards traditional Islam in Pakistan, Bangladesh and Afghanistan. Why are these things happening? Where will they lead? Can an informed Western interest influence these institutions for good or ill?

This gives further, and not the least, importance to an intelligent general knowledge of the Asian traditions. If this book has assisted the reader towards a beginning of that process it will have served its purpose.

Suggested Further Reading

The following are books the reader or student might look at if they wish to go a little further into areas this book has touched on.

The Cambridge Histories and Encyclopedias of South-east Asia, South Asia, China and Japan, all issued over the last decade or so, offer useful and reliable sources, and should be available in most public libraries. However, they are organised to approach the subject from many differing angles and by many authors, and so are suggested as references rather than reading *in toto* by all but the most enthusiast.

EAST ASIA

China

The Search for Modern China, Jonathan D. Spence (1990), gives an excellent background from the beginning of the Ming Dynasty on, and a thorough and detailed account of the growth of Chinese nationalism and the modern Communist state.

The Pacific Century, Frank Gibney (1992), is a readable background to east Asia, especially its relations with the United States.

China, a Short Cultural History, by C.P. Fitzgerald (1986) provides a readable summary covering the whole span of Chinese history.

Several books written by J.K. Fairbank specialise in East Asia. *East Asia: The Great Tradition* (1978), written in collaboration with E.O. Reischauer, covers the subject broadly.

China Without Deng, Goodman and Segal (1995) offers some interesting insights into recent Chinese history, as also does *Return to a Chinese Village*, J. Myrdal (1984).

Tremble and Obey, T. Watson (1990) – an eyewitness account of the clashes between students and the government in Beijing in 1989.

Treasures of China, Michael Ridley (1973) is a manageable, well-illustrated paperback which deals mainly with Chinese art of all periods, but also has some good historical sections which help to bring the two fields into focus.

The Opium War Through Chinese Eyes, Arthur Waley (1958). *The Boxer Rebellion,* C. Martin (1968).

The Rape of Nanking: The Forgotten Holocaust of World War Two, Iris Chang (1998), gives a graphic and horrifying account of Japanese atrocities in Nanking (Nanjing), although some Japanese claim it is over-stated.

East and West, Chris Patten (1998), comments broadly on modern China, and has interesting chapters on Asian values and the 'tiger' economies.

Everyday Life in Early Imperial China, M. Loewe (1973).
The City in Late Imperial China, G.W. Skinner (1977).
The Chinese in South-east Asia, V. Purcell (1951).
Tibet, P. Levy (1996).
The Penguin Book of Chinese Verse, ed A.R. Davis (1962).

Japan

There are numerous short histories of Japan: *Japan,* Reischauer and Craig (1989), *A History of Japan,* M. Kennedy (1963), *A History of Modern Japan,* R. Storry (1960), *Japan, A Short Cultural History,* G.B Sansom (1931) among them. Rather broader but illuminating, and concerned with trends in modern Japan are *The Undefeated,* R. Harvey (1994), *The Emptiness of Japanese Affluence,* G. McCormack (1996), *The Japan We Never Knew,* David Suzuki and Keibo Oiwa (1998). *Introduction to Japanese Politics,* L.D. Hayes (1992), *An Introduction to Zen Buddhism,* D.T. Suzuki (1949), *The Japanese Seizure of Korea,* H. Conroy (1960), *The Meiji Restoration,* W.G. Beasley (1972), *The Christian Century in Japan,* C.R. Boxer (1967). *The Tale of Genji,* S. Murasaki should be read for its own merits – I found the 1933 translation by Arthur Waley very readable.

The Japanese Challenge, The Success and Failure of Economic Success, H. Kahn and T. Pepper (1979), deals mainly with post-war economic matters but relates these well with other aspects of Japanese society. An interesting harbinger of later Japanese economic problems.

Anthology of Japanese Literature, ed. D. Keene (1955). This early anthology, a Unesco production and claiming to be the first such anthology in English, is still a good start to the area.

Meeting with Japan, Fosco Maraini (1959), by a respected observer and beautifully written and illustrated is still worth a look.

The Lady and the Monk: Four Seasons in Kyoto, Pico Iyer (1992), is a sensitive and illuminating picture of contact with modern Japanese on a one-to-one basis. Not a history, more a wide-ranging personal view, which nevertheless makes points not to be found elsewhere.
Hiroshima, John Hersey (1946). This account, first published in the *New Yorker*, is still the outstanding report of the atomic bombing.
Korea's Place in the Sun, B. Cumings (1997) is penetrating and interesting by an observer who knows the country well. More formal works are *A History of Korea*, W.E. Henthorn (1971), *The Koreans and Their Culture*, C. Osgood (1951) and *The Arts of Korea*, E. McCune (1961).

South Asia

There are two short histories covering the whole area – *South Asia, A Short History*, H. Tinker (1989), *An Introduction to South Asia*, B.H. Farmer (1993).
General introductory histories of India include *India*, S. Wolpert (1991), *A Concise History of India*, F. Watson (1974), *India: A Modern History*, T.G.P. Spear (1961), *A History of the Indian People*, D.P. Singhal (1983).
India: Labyrinths in the Lotus Land, S. Brata (1985) gives a personal insight by an expatriate Indian into the complexities and problems of the modern society.
Autobiography of an Unknown Indian, N.C Chaudhuri (1951) does much the same for the independence struggle.
The Great Mutiny, C. Hibbert (1978) gives a readable account of the 'Indian Mutiny', researched from contemporary documents.
The Ravi Lancers, John Masters (1981). A novel, gives a vivid picture of the effects on World War One on Indian society.
Akbar, The Great Mogul, V.A. Smith (1928).
Muslim Civilisation in India, S.M. Ikram (1964).
The Wonder that was India, A.L. Basham (1954).
Daily Life in Ancient India, J. Auboyer (1965).
Modern India; The Origins of an Asian Democracy, J.M. Brown (1994).
Bangladesh, V. McClure (1989), *Bangladesh*, C. Baxter (1984), *Bangladesh: A Legacy of Blood*, A. Mascarenhas (1986).
Sri Lanka, R. Zimmerman (1992), *Ceylon*, S. Arasaratnam (1964).
Pakistan, J. Yusufali (1990).

South-east Asia

Introductory formal histories of South-east Asia include: *A History of South-east Asia*, D.G.E. Hall, (1981), *South-east Asia*, B. Harrison (1963), *The Making of South-east Asia*, G. Coedes (1966), *A Concise History of South-east Asia*, N.A. Tarling (1966), *South-east Asia: Past and Present*, D.R. SarDesai (1990). Wideranging, interesting and not too massive is the *Cambridge History of South-east Asia* (1992). *Indonesia*, B. Grant (1964) and *Indonesia*, J.D. Legge (1964) are good general histories up to that date. *Nusantara, A History of Indonesia*, B.H.M. Vlekke (1959) gives a detailed account from the earliest times and considerable treatment to the colonial phase. *Max Havelaar*, E. Douwes Dekker, was the first expose and protest at the excesses of Dutch colonialism. My edition, the first in English, is dated 1868.

The Story of Indonesia, Louis Fischer (1959).
The Birth of Indonesia, D. Wehl (1948).
Dutch Administration in the Netherlands Indies, W. Preger (1944).
Social Status and Power in Java, L.H Palmier (1960).
Funu: The Unfinished Saga of East Timor, J. Ramos-Horta (1987).
Challenge to Terror, T. Westerling (1952).
The Fall of Sukarno, T. Vittachi (1967).
Burma, D.G.E. Hall (1960).
The Making of Burma, D. Woodman (1962).
Burma, S.M. Yin (1990).
Thailand, A Short History, D.K. Wyatt (1984).
Thailand, W. Blanchard ed. (1958).
The Hill Tribes of Northern Thailand, G. Young (1962).
A Short History of Cambodia, M.F Herz (1968).
A History of Cambodia, D.P. Chandler (1992).
Angkor: An Introduction, G. Coedes (1963).
Angkor, Malcolm MacDonald (1960), ill. Loke Wan Tho.
The Customs of Cambodia, Chou Ta Kuan, ed. J.G. Paul (1997).
Kingdom of Laos, Rene de Berval (1956), written with the collaboration of the Laotian Royal family.
The Little World of Laos, O. Meeker (1995).
A History of Malaya, J. Kennedy (1962).
The Philippines, Colin Mason (1968).
Dragon Army: The Pattern of Communist Expansion through Asia, Colin Mason (1965).

Index

Abdul Rahman, Tengku, 230
Aceh (Atjeh), 223
adat, 147
Aguinaldo, General, 258–60
Agung, Sultan, 143
Akbar, 152–3
Alaungpaya, 126
Alexander the Great, 22
Amangkurat, Sultan, 146–7
Ambon, 142
amuk, 145
Angkor Thom, 37
Angkor Wat, 38–9
animism, 34
Annam, 40
Anuradhapura, 25
Anwar, Ibrahim, 235
Anyang, 45
appropriate technology, 303
Aquino, Benigno, 263
Aquino, Corazon, 263
'Arabic' numbers, 25
Arakan, 127
Arjuna, 20
Aryans, 14–16
Ashoka, 23–4
Asian economic downturn, 2
Asian values, 2–3, 43, 231
Assam, 127
Attlee, Clement, 179
Aung San, 291
Aung San Suu Kyi, 293–4
Aurangzeb, 154
Ayub Khan, 181
Ayudhya, 126

Babur, 151
Bangkok, 247
Bangladesh, 181
   arsenic poisoning, 183
Bali, 121

Banda, 142
Bandula, General, 127
barangays, 255
Batavia
   Chinese population, 124
   establishment, 142
batik, 30
Bayon, 38
Beijing (Peking), 122
Belo, Carlos, Bishop, 222
Bengal famine, 1943, 177–8
Bhutto, Benazir, 183–4
Bhutto, Zulfikar Ali, 183
Biak, 223
Black Death, 72
Black Hole of Calcutta, 158–9
Blum, Leon, 279
Borobadur, 31, 36, 119
British Empire, extent, 113
Brooke, James, 233
Brunei, 233–4
Buddhism
   in China, 56–7
   in India, 151
   in Thailand, 252
   origins, 21
   Zen, 68
Bugis, 31
Burma (Myanmar), 288–95
Burmese Wars, 127–9

Cambodia, 133, 284–7
Caste systems
   Indian, 17, 20, 156
   Japanese, 246
   Korean, 271
chaebol, 299
Champa, 40–1
chandals, 18
Chandragupta, 22
Ch'ang-an, 63–4

Chang Heng, 56
Chan Tsung-chang, 190
Chavalit, Yungchaiyudh, 250
Chettiars, 290
Chiang Kai-shek, 189–94
Chi-chen Wang, 204
Ch'ien Lung, 89
China
  afforestation, 196
  alchemy, 51
  ancestor worship, 43
  astronomy, 78
  Boxer revolt, 97
  Ch'in Dynasty, 48–51
  Chou Dynasty, 46
  communes, 199–200
  Communist Party, 189, 191–3
  Confucianism, 55
  contacts with Rome, 53
  cultural revolution, 201
  Entombed Warriors, 51
  eunuchs, 86
  great leap forward, 83, 200–1
  Han Dynasty, 52–6
  Harbin, bubonic plague, 194
  Hsia Dynasty, 44
  hundred flowers, 199–200
  invention of paper, 55
  invention of printing, 64
  Kuomintang (Nationalist) Party,
    188–9, 193–4
  legalist school, 48
  Long March, 191–2
  Manchu (Ch'ing) Dynasty, 87
  mandarinate, 54, 62, 79, 90
  mandate of Heaven, 47
  maritime expeditions, 84–5
  Ming Dynasty, 83–6
  Mongol Dynasty, 76–7, 81–3
  Nanking, Treaty of, 93
  Northern Expedition, 189
  opium wars, 92–4
  prehistory, 44
  Shang Dynasty, 44–6
  shipping, 79–80
  Sui Dynasty, 61–2
  Sung Dynasty, 77–80

T'ai P'ing rebellion, 95–6
T'ang Dynasty, 61–4
Three Gorges Dam, 206
Tien An Men Square incident, 203
Tientsin, Treaty of, 94
Wuchang revolt, 188
Yellow emperor, 44
Yellow River, 196
Yellow Turbans revolt, 56
Yenan commune, 191–2
Chin Peng, 230
Chuan Leekpai, 250
Churchill, Sir Winston, 178–9
clipper ships, 92
Clive, Robert, 158–9
Chola empire, 26, 28, 36
Choshu clan, 236–7
Chou En-lai, 195
Chou Ta-kuan, 37–8
Chulalongkorn, 248
Coen, Jan, 141
comfort women, 274
Confucius, 46–7
consensus politics, 34
Cripps, Sir Stafford, 177
Curzon, Lord, 166–7

Dalhousie, Lord, 128
Darius the Third, 22
Deng Xiaoping, 205
Deshima, 106
Diaz, Bartholomew, 73
Dien Bien Phu, 280–1
Diponegoro, 148
'dog' shogun, 107
Du Fu, 63
Dutch East India Company, 148
Duy Tan, 279
Dyer, Reginald, 168

East India Company, British, 74
  in China, 92
  in India, 154, 157–60
East Timor, 220–1, 224
Edo, 103
Emergency, the Malaya, 229–30
Estrada, Joseph, 264

Fa Hsien, 24
Fa Ngum, 283
Feng Yu-hsiang, 190
fish farming, 302
Franciscan Order, 257, 261
Fretilin, 221
Funan, 35

Gandhi, Indira, 185–6
Gandhi, Mohandas, 19, 167–70,
    176, 184
Gandhi, Rajiv, 185–6
Gatling, Richard, 113
Gautama (Buddha), 21
geography, 6–8
Gladstone, William, 93
Gordon, Charles, 95
Grand Canal, 64
Great Wall, 43, 50
Green Revolution, 185
Guangzhou, 63

Habibie B.J., 222
Hall, Tony, Congressman, 276
Hanyang, 268–9
Harappa, 12–14
Harris, Townsend, 110
Hart, Sir Robert, 95
Hastings, Warren, 160
Hawkins, Will, 153
Henry the Navigator, 72
Hidetada, 105
Hideyoshi, 101
Hinduism, origins, 16
Ho Chi Minh, 119, 279
Ho Chi Minh Trail, 285
hominid development, 12
homo sapiens, 12
Hong Kong, 93–4, 207
Ho-shen, 90
Hsun Tzu, 48
Humayun, 152
Hung Wu, 83
Hun Sen, 286
Hu Yaobang, 205
hybrid cars, 303
hydrogen power, 304

ice ages, 11, 34
I-ching, 36
Ieyasu, 102
Ifugao, 32–3
Ilocano people, 255
imperialism, effect on national
    boundaries, 114–5
India
    Amritsar incident, 168
    Arya Samaj, 164
    Bengal famine, 1769–70, 159
    Bengal famine, 1943, 177–8
    Bharatiya Janata Party (BJP),
        186–7
    Chauri Chaura incident, 169
    communal violence, 177–8, 185
    Congress, 166–7, 177, 184–7
    Indian 'mutiny', 161–2
    influenza epidemic, 1918, 167
    Mogul Dynasty, 151–7
    nuclear weapons, 186
    princely states, 171
    regionalism, 21
    Rowlatt Acts, 168
    salt tax, 170
    Sikhs, 186
    state of emergency, Indira
        Gandhi, 185
    suttee, 163
    Tagore, Rabindranath, 168
    universities established, 163
Indo-China
    Nguyen Dynasty, 132
    Tayson revolt, 132
    Trinh Dynasty, 132
Indonesia
    'cronyism', 220
    cultivation system, 148
    Darul Islam movement, 213, 215
    declaration of independence, 212
    Dili massacre, 221
    Dutch education policy, 118
    1965 killings, 218
    Pertimina Oil Corporation, 219
    Republic of South Moluccas, 213
    Tjikini Raya affair, 215
    West Irian transfer, 216

Iqbal, Mohammed, 176
Irrawaddy River, 288–9
Islam
  origins, 71–2
  in Pakistan, 180–1
  sharia, 180
  Sufism, 136
Ivan the Fourth, 85

Japan
  Ainu, 58
  Ashikaga shoguns, 69, 99
  burakumin, 246
  corruption trials, 1994, 242
  daimyo, 99, 103
  Fujiwara clan, 66
  geisha, 104
  Hara Castle, siege of, 106
  'iron triangle', 243
  Ise shrine, 59
  kabuki theatre, 104
  Kamakura period, 68
  Meiji restoration, 237
  migrations from Korea, 59, 65
  nuclear bombings, 240
  Onin wars, 99
  opening to trade, 236–7
  persecution of Christians, 10
  'Pride, the Fatal Moment, '245
  samurai, 68, 101, 108, 237–8
  Sekigahara, battle of, 102
  Shinto, 60–1, 237
  Taika reforms, 65
  Tale of Genji, 67
  Tokugawa, 102, 106
  Tokugawa literature, 108
  ukiyo, the 'floating world', 104
  Yamato culture, 59
Java War, 148
Jayavarman II, 38
Jehengir, 153
Jesuits
  in China, 88
  in Japan, 100
Jinnah, Mohammed Ali, 176, 179,
  181
jukongs, 31

Kalidasa, 24
Kalinga, 23
Kama Sutra, 24
Kandy, 26–7
K'ang Hsi, 88
K'ang Yu-wei, 97
Karve, D.K. 164
Kashmir, 182
Katipunan, 258
keiretsu, 298
Khmer empire, 33, 38
Khmer Rouge, 286
Khon Kaen, 251
Khyber Pass, 7
Kim Dae Jung, 275
Kim Il Sung, 271
Kim Jong Il, 271
Kim Young Sam, 275
Kings of the Mountain, 36, 38
Kipling, Rudyard, 160
Koguryo, 266–7
Kohinoor diamond, 151, 155
Korea, 265–77
Korea, North, 276–7
Korean War, 197
Koryo, 267–8
Kuala Lumpur, 225, 228
Kublai Khan, 81
Kwangju incident, 299
Kyongju, 267
Kyoto, 66, 100

Lambert, Commodore, 128
landmines, 287, 300
Lan Xang, 283
Laos, 282–4
Lee Kuan Yew, 119, 231–2
Leonowens, Anna, 131
Liaquat Ali Khan, 181
Liga Filipina, 258
Light, Francis, 139
Linnaeus, Carolus, 75
Lin Tse-hsu, 92
Li Peng, 2, 204
Li Po, 63
Lippman, Walter, 280
Li Ssu, 49

Li Zicheng, 87
loess, 44
Lon Nol, 285

MacArthur, Douglas, 240, 274
Macaulay, Thomas, 161
Magellan, Ferdinand, 73
Magsaysay, Ramon, 262
Mahabharata, 19
Mahasabha, 184
Mahathir, Mohammad, 235
Mahinda, Prince, 25
Majapahit, 134–5
Malacca, 136–9
malaria
  in Cambodia, 39
  in Luzon, 32
  in Malaya, 226–7
  in Sri Lanka, 27
Malaya, 139, 225–30
Malaysia, 217, 230–5
Malolos Republic, 259
Manchukuo, 192
Manila, 256
Mao Tse-tung (Mao Zedong), 62,
  190–2, 201
Marcos, Ferdinand, 262–3
Marx, Karl, 19
Mataram, 143–6
Mauryan Empire, 22
megacities, 301
Megasthenes, 22
Megawati, Sukarno, 223
Mehrgarh site, 14
Mekong River, 125
Menander, 24
Mencius, 47
Meo tribes, 283–4
mercantilism, 74–5
Minamoto Yoritomo, 67
Minangkabauer, 72
Mindanao, 264
Ming tombs, 42
Mongolian racial type, 12
monsoons, 29
Moslem League, 176

motor traffic pollution, 302
My Lai massacre, 282

Nagasaki, 105
Nalanda University, 24
Nanchao, 125
Nanking massacre, 239
Nara, 65
Nasution, General, 213–4
negritos, 31
Neil, James, Colonel, 162
Nehru, Jawaharlal, 119, 169, 177
Nehru, Motilal, 169
neo-Confucianism, 80
Ne Win, 292–3
Ngo Dinh Diem, 281
Nizam of Hyderabad, 154
Nobunaga, Oda, 100
Nurhachi, 87

opium
  in Burma, 294
  monopolies, 115, 124
opium wars in China, 109
oracle bones, 44
Ottoman Turks, 72
overseas Chinese, 123–4

Pagan, 126
Pakistan, 176, 179, 180–4
Palmerston, Lord, 93
Pamirs, 7
Paripatra, Prince, 249
Pathet Lao, 283
Pearl Harbor, 239
Penang, 139
Perahera tooth ceremony, 26
Perry, Commodore, 109–110
Phat Ma, 121
Philippines, The, 254–64
Phnom Penh, 39
Pibul Songgram, 249
Pignane de Behaine, 132
Plain of the Jars, 284
Polo, Marco, 76
Pol Pot, 286

Portuguese
 establishment of Goa, 73
 in China, 85
 in Sri Lanka, 27
Prambanan, 36
Prester John, 70
Pridi Pananyong, 249
printing
 in China, 5, 64
 in Korea, 269
P'u Yi, 98, 192
Pyongyang, 266, 274–5

Quezon, Manuel, 261

Raffles, Thomas S., 139
railways, 117–18
Rais, Amien, 224
Rajputs, 150, 152–4
Ramayana, 19–20, 35
Ramos, Fidel, 263
Ramoz-Horta, Jose, 221
Rashtriya Swayamsevak Sangh
 (RSS), 186
renewable energy, 298
rice culture, 32–3
Rigveda, 15
Rizal, Jose, 257
Roe, Sir Thomas, 153
Roxas, Manuel, 262
Roy, Rammohun, 163

Sabah, 230, 233
Sado, Prince, 272
Sakuntala, 24
Sam Rainsy, 304
Sarawak, 230, 232–3
Sarit Thanarat, 250
Seleucus Nicator, 22
Seoul, 268
Seyed Ahmad Khan, 165
Shah Jahan, 153
Shan states, 125, 291
Sheik Mujid Rahman, 182
Shih Huang Ti (first emperor), 49
Shimonoseki, Treaty of, 96

Shivaji, 158
Shomu, Emperor, 65
Shotoku, Prince, 65
Shrivijaya, 36
Sihanouk, Norodom, 37, 284–5
silk road, 63
Silla, 266–7
Singapore, 8, 139–40, 228, 230–2
Sinhalese, 25
slave trade, 75
SLORC, 289
Snow, Edgar, 195
soil erosion, 301
South-east Asia
 autocratic governments, 305
 economic crash, 1997, 300
 forest fires, 301
 Indian influence, 29–30
 prehistory, 31
 seventeenth-century urbanisation,
  122–3
 shipping, 30
 village societies, 31–4
Spanish-American War, 258–9
Spanish galleon trade, 256
spices, 71, 142–3
Sri Lanka, 25–8
Ssu-ma Ch'ien, 55
Suez Canal, 74, 226
Suharto, 216, 219–20
Sukarno, 134–5, 144, 210–18
Sukhothai, 126
Sunda, 34
Sun Yat-sen, 88, 188–9
Sutowo, Ibnu, 219
Su Tung-p'o, 79

Taiwan, 194
Taj Mahal, 153
Tamils
 Jaffna state, 26–7
 migrations to Sri Lanka, 25
 rebellion, 28
Tangun myth, 266
Taoism, 55
Taruc, Luis, 261–2
Tavernier, J.B., 154

Thailand, 247–253
  Bangkok, foundation of, 129
  north-east Thailand, 251–2
  Rama III, 130
  Rama IV (King Mongkut),
    131–2
thakins, 290
Thebaw, King, 128
Third World debt, 303
thuggee, 155
Tibet, 88, 197–8
'Tiger' economies, 297
Tjokroaminoto, 210
Tokyo, 237
Tonghak cult, 272
turtle ship, 270
Tz'u-hsi (Cixi), Empress, 95

untouchables, 18, 20
U Nu, 292
Urdu, 180
U Saw, 291

Vajpayee, Atal Behari, 186
Van Diemen, Anthony, 146
Vedda, 25
Venice, 70, 72, 74

Vietminh, 279–80, 283
Vietnam, 278–82
Vietnam War, 281–2
  Le Dynasty, 41
  Nguyen Dynasty, 41
  Tran Dynasty, 41
  Trinh Dynasty, 41
  Vinh massacre, 278

White Lotus Society, 91
world population, 296
Wu Pei-fu, 190

Xavier, St Francis, 138

yangban, 269
Yen Hsi-shan, 190
Yi Dynasty, 271
Yi Songgye, 268
Yi Sunsin, Admiral, 270
Yuan Shih-kai, 189
Yung Lo, 84
Yunnan, 96

zaibatsu, 240
zero, 25
Zia, ul-Haq, 183